Community Justice in Australia

This new edition of *Community Justice in Australia* expands on the discussion of how people who have committed offences can be engaged in the community. It considers how the concept of community justice can be successfully applied within Australia by social workers, criminologists, parole officers and anyone working in the community with both adults and young people.

The book defines community justice and applies the concept to the Australian context. It then explains theories of offending behaviour, considers relevant Australian legislation, policy and intervention strategies and examines the implications for both young people and adults. Restorative justice is also discussed. The latter part of the book focuses on practical issues including working in community justice organisations, technology, public protection and desistance approaches. Each chapter contains an engagement with the implications of community justice approaches for Indigenous groups and features reflective questions, practical tasks and guidance for further reading.

This accessible and practical book will be indispensable for instructors, students and practitioners working in the community with people who have committed offences.

Brian Stout is Pro Vice Chancellor of Humanities, Arts and Social Sciences, Dean of the School of Social Sciences and Professor of Social Work at Western Sydney University, Australia. He has practiced, taught and researched community justice in Northern Ireland, England, South Africa and Australia. He is author of *Equality and Diversity in Policing* (2010) and numerous chapters and journal articles. He is also editor of *Applied Criminology* (2008).

Community Justice in Australia

Knowledge, Skills and Values

SECOND EDITION

Brian Stout

LONDON AND NEW YORK

Designed cover image: © Getty Images

Second edition published 2023
by Routledge
4 Park Square, Milton Park, Abingdon, Oxon, OX14 4RN

and by Routledge
605 Third Avenue, New York, NY 10158

Routledge is an imprint of the Taylor & Francis Group, an informa business

© 2023 Brian Stout

The right of Brian Stout to be identified as author of this work has been asserted in accordance with sections 77 and 78 of the Copyright, Designs and Patents Act 1988.

All rights reserved. No part of this book may be reprinted or reproduced or utilised in any form or by any electronic, mechanical, or other means, now known or hereafter invented, including photocopying and recording, or in any information storage or retrieval system, without permission in writing from the publishers.

Trademark notice: Product or corporate names may be trademarks or registered trademarks, and are used only for identification and explanation without intent to infringe.

First edition published by Routledge 2016

British Library Cataloguing-in-Publication Data
A catalogue record for this book is available from the British Library

Library of Congress Cataloging-in-Publication Data
Names: Stout, Brian, author.
Title: Community justice in Australia : knowledge, skills and values / Brian Stout.
Description: Second edition. | Milton Park, Abingdon, Oxon ; New York, NY : Routledge, 2023. | "First edition published by Routledge 2016"--Title page verso. | Includes bibliographical references and index. |
Identifiers: LCCN 2022043924 (print) | LCCN 2022043925 (ebook) | ISBN 9781032045665 (hardback) | ISBN 9781032045672 (paperback) | ISBN 9781003193814 (ebook)
Subjects: LCSH: Criminals--Rehabilitation--Australia. | Social work with criminals--Australia. | Restorative justice--Australia.
Classification: LCC HV9430.A5 S76 2023 (print) | LCC HV9430.A5 (ebook) | DDC 364.80994--dc23/eng/20220922
LC record available at https://lccn.loc.gov/2022043924
LC ebook record available at https://lccn.loc.gov/2022043925

ISBN: 978-1-032-04566-5 (hbk)
ISBN: 978-1-032-04567-2 (pbk)
ISBN: 978-1-003-19381-4 (ebk)

DOI: 10.4324/9781003193814

Typeset in Bembo
by KnowledgeWorks Global Ltd.

Contents

List of boxes	vi
List of abbreviations	viii
A note on language	x
Acknowledgements	xi
Introduction	1
1 Community justice	5
2 Adults who have committed offences	27
3 Juvenile justice	43
4 Theories of offending and evidence-based practice	63
5 Restorative justice	80
6 Risk-management and protection of the public	97
7 Diversity	113
8 Organisation and management	131
9 Technology and community justice	147
10 Facilitating desistance and building good lives	160
11 Values, ethics, human rights and children's rights	176
12 Practitioner skills	194
References	210
Index	243

List of boxes

1.1	Justice reinvestment	7
1.2	Representation of Indigenous people in the criminal justice system	23
1.3	'Harvard Kennedy: Community corrections consensus'	25
2.1	Community service orders	31
2.2	Repay SA	33
2.3	Royal commission into Aboriginal deaths in custody	36
2.4	Collingwood Neighbourhood Justice Centre	39
3.1	The stolen generations	44
3.2	Young people in detention	47
3.3	Boot camps in Queensland	58
3.4	Multi-Systemic Therapy and the intensive supervision program	59
3.5	Royal commission into juvenile detention in the Northern Territory	61
4.1	Cognitive behavioural therapy (CBT) and cognitive behavioural theory	66
4.2	The reformatron	74
4.3	Responsivity	77
5.1	Is restorative justice effective in promoting rehabilitation?	86
6.1	The metaphors for risk-assessment	101
6.2	The community sex offender notifications scheme in the UK (Sarah's Law)	103
6.3	Probation on trial	107
7.1	Marlon Noble	115
7.2	Responding to the needs of drug users	119
7.3	Parramatta Female Factory and Girls' Home	122
7.4	Cost–benefit analysis	126
8.1	Protecting the safety of workers	139
8.2	Typologies of probation workers	145
9.1	What is GPS tracking technology?	149
9.2	3M and G4S	151

9.3	Community justice and social media	154
10.1	Desistance and life events	162
10.2	Multi-Systemic Therapy (MST) and the good lives model	166
10.3	Changing the narrative and making good	170
11.1	AASW code of ethics	183
11.2	Change the record campaign	187
11.3	Don Dale Youth Detention Centre	189
11.4	Maranguka Justice Reinvestment Project, Bourke, NSW	190
12.1	The Jersey Study	204

List of abbreviations

AASW	Australian Association of Social Workers
ACT	Australian Capital Territory
AFP	Australian Federal Police
AHRC	Australian Human Rights Commission
AI	Appreciative Inquiry
AIHW	Australian Institute of Health and Welfare
ALRC	Australian Law Reform Commission
ASU	Additional Support Unit
BJCJ	*British Journal of Community Justice*
BOCSAR	Bureau of Crime Statistics and Research (NSW)
CALD	culturally and linguistically diverse
CALM	Controlling Anger and Learning to Manage [It]
CBT	cognitive behavioural therapy
CCO	Community Correction Order
CCP	core correctional practice
CEP	Community and Environment Project
CISP	Court Integrated Services Program
CSO	community service order
DBIF	Detainee Behaviour Implementation Framework
DHHS	Department of Health and Human Services (Tas)
DPP	Department of Public Prosecutions
EIYBC	Early Intervention Youth Boot Camp
EM	electronic monitoring
GFC	Global Financial Crisis
GPS	Global Positioning System
HDO	Home Detention Order
HREOC	Human Rights and Equal Opportunity Commission
HRLC	Human Rights Law Centre
ICO	Intensive Correction Order
IDATP	Intensive Drug and Alcohol Program (NSW)
IDP	Indigenous Diversion Program
IFSW	International Federation of Social Workers
IPPC	Inter-Agency Public Protection Committee (WA)

IPPS	Inter-Agency Public Protection Strategy (WA)
ISP	Intensive Supervision Program
JJT	Juvenile Justice Team
JR	justice reinvestment
KGRADS	Koori Graduate Recruitment and Development Scheme
MAPPA	Multi-Agency Public Protection Arrangements
MST	Multi-Systemic Therapy
NAAJA	North Australian Aboriginal Justice Agency
NGO	non-government organisation
NISATSIC	National Inquiry into the Separation of Aboriginal and Torres Strait Islander Children and their Families
NJC	Neighbourhood Justice Centre
NMHC	National Mental Health Commission
NPM	New Public Management
OCSAR	South Australian Office of Crime Statistics and Research
OMP	Offender Management Plan (SA)
PACCOA	Probation and Community Corrections Officers Association
POISE	Personal Ownership, Identity and Self-Empowerment
PTSD	Post-Traumatic Stress Disorder
RCIADIC	Royal Commission into Aboriginal Deaths in Custody
RCIRCSA	Royal Commission into Institutionalised Responses to Child Sexual Abuse
RISE	Canberra Reintegrative Shaming Experiments
RNR	Risk Needs Responsivity
SAJJ	South Australia Juvenile Justice
SEEDS	Skills for Effective, Engagement, Development and Supervision
STO	supervised treatment order
SYBC	Sentenced Youth Boot Camp
TAC	Tasmanian Aboriginal Corporation
UNCRC	United Nations Convention on the Rights of the Child
UTS	University of Technology Sydney
UWS	University of Western Sydney
WSU	Western Sydney University
YCO	Youth Conduct Order

A note on language

The language used to describe people involved in the criminal justice system has always been a matter for discussion and although it has received increasing attention in recent years, it is not a new discussion. In my experience as a probation officer in Northern Ireland in the 1990s, I was working within a social work framework and those who we worked with were called 'clients'. 'Client' was considered to be a non-judgmental, supportive wording, reflecting a professional relationship. This approach was criticised by the then Conservative government as an indicator of a soft approach taken to offending behaviour, and subsequent generations of probation officers in England and Wales have been instructed to refer to those with whom they work as offenders.

Alongside the political imperatives, some of the other arguments against person-centred language include that describing someone's current status is simply a matter of fact, rather than judgment; an individual might, variously, and at different times, be described, for example, as an 'offender', a 'student', a 'musician' or a 'mother' without implying that any of these terms encompass the entirety of their identity. It is also argued that humane language can obscure inhumane approaches and conditions as well as that people can reclaim and own language about themselves that was initially stigmatising (see Cox, 2020, for a discussion of reasons both for and against the use of more humane language). More pragmatically, all the proposed alternatives for 'inmate', 'prisoner' or 'offender' tend to be phrases, rather than words, making communication slower and more cumbersome without necessarily removing the potential for labelling (Ugwudike et al., 2017a, 2017b).

In the first edition of this book, this practical reason was the dominant one and the word 'offender' was used throughout. As issues are discussed in the abstract, and the label is not applied to any real individual, the possibility of applying a stigmatising label was not too great a concern. However, as more and more organisations and publications are seeking to promote the importance of non-stigmatising language, this second edition will follow that approach and, wherever possible, use language that focuses on the individual, such as 'a person who has committed an offence'.

The guidance of Western Sydney University is that 'Indigenous', 'Aboriginal and Torres Strait Islander' and 'First Nations' are all acceptable terms. This book follows the approach of the university in preferencing the term 'Indigenous'.

Acknowledgements

In addition to those I acknowledged for the first edition, I also acknowledge the helpful work of the anonymous reviewers and all in the editorial team at Routledge. The practical task at the end of chapter two was provided by one of the reviewers. I repeat my thanks to Bec Moran for her outstanding work as a research assistant for the first edition. I'm also grateful for the research assistance work of Dr Teddy Nagaddya for this edition, particularly in her meticulous review of legislative changes since the book's first publication. All errors and omissions, of course, remain my own.

I remain thankful for the support of Cathy, Callum and Ethan in the writing of the book and so much else.

Introduction

The second edition of *Community Justice in Australia* sets out an understanding of the concept of community justice and how it might apply to Australia. It is primarily aimed at those who are interested in practice in the criminal justice system—whether that interest arises from social work, criminology or another discipline. The Australian social work literature pays limited attention to criminal justice and the criminology literature rarely focuses on practice concerns, so this book is an attempt to fill that gap. The second edition updates some of the literature, legislation, context and policy from the first edition.

My own interest in community justice arises from my personal and professional background in various community justice roles. I qualified as a social worker and started my professional career as a probation officer in Northern Ireland in the late 1990s, in the years before and immediately following the paramilitary ceasefires and the start of the peace process. I then spent three years in rural South Africa developing specific university training programs for those social workers who wanted to work in the community with those who had offences. I returned to the United Kingdom to take up a post teaching and managing degree-level training of trainee probation officers. All those roles have given me an understanding of the knowledge, skills and values required for those who work with in the community with those who have committed offences in any of these differing contexts.

Community justice has a contested and sometimes pejorative meaning in both Northern Ireland and South Africa, often being used euphemistically to refer to vigilantism or paramilitary beatings. A more positive use of the language of community justice took shape in England and Wales in the 2000s as university departments were formed around the Home Office-led requirement to provide training to qualifying probation officers. This program delivery was explicitly prohibited from being located within social work departments, so new academic groups were formed, often with community justice as a title. The advent of restorative justice at that time also brought a new focus on the involvement of communities in criminal justice processes and the language of community justice became part of the international debate on criminal justice interventions.

DOI: 10.4324/9781003193814-1

In Australia, there has been no widespread public debate on the training of workers who work in the community with those who have committed offences, and there is no real consensus about what qualifications they should hold. There has thus been insufficient opportunity for a discipline of community justice to develop or for the often-excellent scholarship that might be considered to be in that area to reach a critical mass. Juvenile justice workers and community corrections workers are recruited from a variety of backgrounds and are trained in a variety of disciplines (in some roles, in some states, degree-level qualifications are not required). Should there be an emphasis on skills training and engagement with other professionals, suggesting the need for a social work qualification? Social workers are well equipped to respond to concerns about mental health and the impact of trauma, and are trained to consider the crucial issues of oppression and diversity. However, social work degrees do not always include significant material on offending, nor do they engage in any depth with the difficulties caused by seeking to offer support to clients who may have caused considerable harm to others. Should there be an emphasis on the research into crime, deviance and offending behaviour, suggesting that professionals who work in the community with those who have committed offences be trained in criminology? Criminological research puts offending behaviour in a social and historical context, and has an increasingly sophisticated understanding of the reasons for offending. However, criminology degrees neither aspire to offer practical skills nor to cover the key ethical and values debates associated with working with those who have committed offences. Research and literature that directly relate to work with offending adults and young people will not always be covered in either degree program. In a higher education funding environment where research resources are often connected to teaching programs and student revenue, the issue of training carries an even greater importance. The high volume and quality of community justice related research in the UK is closely related to the university location of probation and youth justice training. England and Wales, Scotland and Northern Ireland all have different training contexts, but a version of community justice is taught in universities in all three jurisdictions.

Community justice draws on ideas from both criminology and social work, so it is hoped that this book will be of interest to readers from both disciplines. The criminal justice material will contribute specific subject knowledge to social work, while criminologists will be interested in the book because it draws extensively on criminological material, and at the same time focuses on practice and direct work with individuals.

Australia needs to focus on community justice. The most urgent priority is the continuing over-representation of Indigenous people in the criminal justice system, both in youth justice and in adult corrections. The response to that over-representation cannot simply be more management or better organisation. A punitive approach will be ineffective, and it will not address any of the wider social issues that contribute both to the offending behaviour itself and to the criminal justice response to it. Community justice focuses on the wider social justice context, so shifts the debate away from a focus on responding to the offending behaviour of small groups of individuals to a concern about wider conceptions of building a just society. However, it is important to draw a distinction between community justice and community sanctions and measures. Experiences elsewhere have shown that simply expanding the use of community measures is not enough to reduce the use of incarceration, such approaches can sometimes simply expand the reach of criminal justice.

The 12 chapters of this book cover the different topics that together could be said to comprise community justice. Chapter 1 considers how the term 'community justice' has been understood internationally, and how it can be applied to an Australian context. It provides an understanding of community justice that then informs the rest of the book. Chapter 2 covers the context of working with adults who have committed offences in Australia, including legislation, policy and some of the interventions available. Similarly, Chapter 3 deals with working in the community with young people who have offended in Australia. Such work can offer the greatest hope for reform because it is easier to accept the influence of wider social factors on the behaviour of young people, and it is perceived that there is more hope of rehabilitation. Chapter 4 reviews some of the theories of offending and evidence-based practice used to explain offending behaviour, with a focus on those theories that are of most use in direct practice and those associated both with the effective practice discourse and the response to it. Community justice is often associated with restorative justice, and this is dealt with in Chapter 5. Community justice has a similar value base to restorative justice and makes similar criticisms of the mainstream criminal justice system, but there are also important differences, including the contrast between the focus of on the individual case and the attention paid by community justice to wider issues of social justice.

The second half of the book starts with a discussion of risk-management and protection of the public in Chapter 6. Community justice advocates and others who seek reform of the criminal justice system can often seem to focus on minor offences and those who have committed offences for the first time. A credible community justice approach must accept that many convicted offenders pose an ongoing danger in the community and must also engage with debates about how they should be treated and how risk must be managed. Consideration of diversity issues is threaded through every chapter of the book, but the issue of diversity and Australian community justice is given additional attention in Chapter 7. The treatment of Indigenous people in the criminal justice system is the most important issue in Australian community justice, and this is discussed in every chapter. Chapter 7 gives consideration to other aspects of diversity, including mental health and the treatment of other communities in Australia. Community justice takes place within an organisation and management context, and in Chapter 8 there is a discussion of the nature of such organisations and the working practices commonly adopted within community justice. Chapter 9 looks at technology in community justice, examining whether community justice philosophical approaches can be reconciled with a greater use of technology, or whether the risk of dehumanisation is too great. Chapters 10 and 11 deal with subjects that are absolutely central to the understanding of community justice. In Chapter 10, approaches to facilitating desistance and building good lives are explored, including the need for community justice workers to co-create long-term change with the clients with whom they work. Desistance approaches are entirely consistent with community justice values, in light of their emphasis on co-working and on wider conceptions of justice. The values of community justice, including values, ethics, human rights and children's rights, are considered in Chapter 11. A particular emphasis is placed on human rights and the suggestion that human rights discourses and approaches might be appropriate ways to build an alternative voice for community justice and to find an alternative discourse beyond the competing and limited approaches of punitiveness and managerialism. The final chapter, Chapter 12, brings the ideas discussed together into a discussion of practice skills, particularly how to assess and engage with involuntary clients. Community justice is inherently engaged with practice, and its knowledge, skills and values will determine approaches to working directly with those who have committed offences, those who have been victims and their families.

1 Community justice

Introduction

'Community justice' has become a widely used term over the last decades, and it is used in a variety of ways—some descriptive, some normative and some aspirational. It is increasingly timely to discuss and promote alternative conceptions of justice as the realisation grows that the emphasis on punishment has been both ineffective and expensive (Clear, 2020). The term can be used purely descriptively to refer to anything in the criminal justice system that is not custodial, and it can be used in a way that either specifically excludes the police by concentrating mainly on sentencing and crime prevention initiatives or can deliberately include the police—particularly community policing. Community justice can also be focused on working with people who have committed lower-level offences and general preventive and community-building work. However, community justice can carry much greater meaning than simply a description of where the criminal justice system operates, and this chapter will set the framework for the rest of the book in arguing that, firstly, community justice is a term that makes a claim to promote certain values and, secondly, promoting community justice necessitates an acknowledgement of the severe harm that can be caused by persistent, violent and dangerous offending. In Australia, community justice is a term associated with restorative justice and work with Indigenous communities, but few considered attempts have been made to characterise what the term might mean in an Australian context, particularly with relation to the complexities involved in determining what constitutes an Australian community. It is important to communicate the nature of community justice and community sanctions to the public to build confidence in such approaches (Bartels and Weatherburn, 2020). This book sets out to outline community justice in Australia, and this chapter discusses the meaning of the term. It starts by outlining international conceptions of community before focusing on the Australian context. The chapter refers to related concepts such as restorative justice and transitional justice and provides examples of community justice projects in both Australia and other jurisdictions.

DOI: 10.4324/9781003193814-2

What do we mean by community?

'Community' is a term that is often used but less often unpacked and defined. There are different types of late-modern communities and different ways in which the term is used; these can be summarised as follows (Winstone and Pakes, 2005):

- *Community as a nostalgic indulgence.* This community is one of respectful relationships, mutual sharing and minimal anti-social behaviour. Such a community has almost certainly never existed, but it is an archetype that strongly influences debate;
- *Divided community.* There tends to be a greater focus on community justice in societies that are divided or transitional, such as South Africa and Northern Ireland;
- *Disintegrated community.* A disintegrated community is an outworking of the concept of the nostalgic community, where a community has none of the positive, desirable features. In the same way that the strengths of the nostalgic community are exaggerated, the weaknesses of and lack of support in the disintegrated community can be over-emphasised;
- *Proprietary communities.* These are exclusive and committed to keeping others out. Examples included gated communities with security systems to deter non-community members;
- *Virtual communities.* Some people will gain more significant support and a greater sense of identity from online networks than from real-world relationships, so virtual communities are the groups to which they feel most connected. The distinction between online communities and 'real' communities is breaking down. The virtual community is also, increasingly, a location for offending, such as online theft or fraud or 'revenge porn';
- *Communities of choice.* These are communities that are not determined by location but rather by interest, activity, connection and personal decision. An individual may feel a greater belonging to a church or sports club they have chosen to join than to the neighbourhood where they live.

The association of community with neighbourhood is a strong influence on some understandings of community justice, with an implicit assumption that people living close to each other have enough in common to be classified as a community.

In their discussion of justice reinvestment (JR) (see Box 1.1), Fox, Albertson and Wong (2013: 177ff) outline an understanding of community that links directly into what can be achieved in community justice. They draw on Etzioni's (1995, 1997) concerns with the relationship between the individual and the state, the moral basis of society and the need to put community at the centre. Communitarianism links individual freedom to community obligations, and rights and responsibilities, seeing individuals as essentially interdependent. Fox, Albertson and Wong (2013), however, see Etzioni's communitarianism

Box 1.1

Justice reinvestment

> Justice Reinvestment is not a criminal justice intervention; it is more a way of framing the issues under consideration. At its core it seeks to answer the question society has—indeed all societies have—to address: is there a better way to deliver justice?
>
> (Fox, Albertson and Wong, 2013: 207)

JR is an increasingly important approach to criminal justice policy that brings together insights and approaches from the disciplines of criminology and economics (Fox, Albertson and Wong, 2013). It proposes reallocating funds spent on the punishment of offenders to programs and approaches designed to address underlying causes that are associated with criminal behaviour. It is not led by one department or state agency, but instead it is a cross-disciplinary approach, including health and education, as well as traditional justice agencies. The distinguishing feature of JR approaches is their origin in the discipline of economics and their reliance on economic theory. Indeed, the term 'justice reinvestment' was coined in a paper written for George Soros's Open Society Foundation (Brown, 2013). It is an approach that is driven by data and evidence. Not every community-based approach is JR, for that reason, as a JR approach makes a specific, direct and costed claim to save the state money, as well as promoting a social good. The economic methods used to make these arguments are often complex and necessarily speculative (for example, how do you put a cost on a crime that might, in other circumstances, have occurred but did not now occur?). However, economic arguments are very attractive to policymakers and politicians who have to meet the exorbitant costs of prisons in a climate of public punitiveness and economic constraints. JR is able to attract bipartisan political support, although this has not yet been the case in Australia (Brown, Schwartz and Boseley, 2012). In the same way that not every community-based approach can be described as JR, equally not every economic approach is JR. JR emphasises community involvement, localism and a holistic approach to criminal justice; it is a place-based initiative that should have local leadership (Schwartz, 2010). It should connect criminal justice to wider concerns of social justice, but there is a danger that the reinvestment arguments may simply be reduced to discussions of cost-saving or that JR may become a cover for disinvestment (Schwartz, 2010).

> JR is attracting interest in Australia, particularly with relation to the over-representation of Indigenous people in the justice system (Brown, Schwartz and Boseley, 2012). The Australian Justice Reinvestment Project is looking at ways that international experiences of JR could be relevant to Australia (Justice Reinvestment, 2022). A prominent example of advocacy for Justice Reinvestment in Australia is the Justice Reinvestment Campaign (JRC) for Indigenous young people in New South Wales (Justice Reinvestment Campaign, 2022). The campaign uses the costs of the over-representation of young Indigenous people in custody, along with the high level of disadvantage in Indigenous communities, to argue that that money could be spent more justly and wisely in addressing important issues in Indigenous communities, such as homelessness, child protection and a lack of services. Indigenous young people make up 2 per cent of the population of New South Wales but 50 per cent of the custodial population. The JRC quotes a saving of $3.1million from work in Bourke, more than three times the cost of the program (KPMG, 2018).
>
> *Source:* More information about the New South Wales Justice Reinvestment Campaign is available from its website, http://justicereinvestmentnow.net.au/the-campaign.

as being of limited utility to community justice due to its lack of appreciation of diversity and an understanding of society that places a focus on societal rather than individual needs. They emphasise that a community does not have to be defined by a geographical area: It can be defined in a different way, such as by an organisation, profession or workplace. The understanding of community in restorative justice is also beyond the immediate neighbourhood; instead, it is conceptualised as a community of care (see Richards, 2014a). Fox, Albertson and Wong (2013: 179) draw heavily on Ward and Maruna's (2007) Good Lives Model, a strengths-based rehabilitation theory that guides therapeutic work with people who have committed offences (discussed in Chapter 10), and define community in a way that reflects this model. Their definition of community is a useful starting point for this book's discussion of community justice: 'While it is important … to sustain and build communities able to prevent offending and reduce re-offending, it is also important that those communities are ones which allow and have room to accommodate different conceptions of "Good Life"'. This echoes the capability approach that will support people in achieving their own dignity and well-being (Sen, 1993, 2005). Canadian research into restorative justice processes found that the meaning of 'community' was not well understood by those who had committed offences and that their understanding of the term was very different from that of victims, practitioners and community leaders (Chang, 2017).

The offenders in the study neither felt that they belonged to the community nor felt that the community belonged to them (Chang, 2017).

Defining community in a way that focuses on what it might achieve for an individual is particularly helpful in an Australian context. Community can have a vastly different meaning for different groups of Australians, from Indigenous Australians to descendants of European settlers to more recent immigrant communities with strong connections to their country of origin, such as Pacific Islanders or Chinese groups. Each of these groups contains significant distinctions—for example, the difference between an Indigenous Australian being brought up in a rural environment or an urban environment—and too restrictive a definition can exclude the experience of some individuals. Defining a community as that group that allows an individual to build their own good life acknowledges these differences and brings together concepts of community and justice.

What do we mean by justice?

Often, in the public discussion of criminal justice, the meaning of justice is restricted to the work of the criminal justice system, and achieving justice is discussed as if it is the same as achieving harsh punishment. Community justice requires a wider conception of justice, incorporating fair and just outcomes and social justice that goes beyond the narrow response to a particular behaviour. Faulkner and Burnett (2012) suggest that the philosophical approaches to justice can be divided into rough categories:

- Virtue-based and meritocratic that are concerned with moral desert and purpose;
- Utilitarian approaches that promote the greatest happiness for the greatest number of people;
- Libertarian approaches that are concerned with autonomy and freedom of choice;
- Egalitarian approaches that focus on equal opportunities and fairness;
- Communitarian approaches that see justice as relational and consider that there is a role for the community in regulating conduct.

The authors draw on Aristotle and Aquinas's conceptions of justice as fairness and equality, requiring obligations to others in society. Rawls (1971) expanded on this idea, with the hypothesis of the 'veil of ignorance', requiring everyone to consider the fair society without knowing what role in that society they would perform. More recently, Amartya Sen (Sen, 2009) has encouraged a view of justice more grounded in the reality of people's lives rather than in primary goods or abstract contracts. Sen (2009) sees public debate and an engagement with the many different ways in which justice is perceived within society as a crucial aspect of achieving justice. MacIntyre (2007) again relates justice to the reality of people's lives and the assumption that what is just can be related to what individuals perceive that they deserve. A conception of justice as the common good (Sandel, 2009) is perhaps the interpretation that is most relevant to community justice.

Discussions of justice within a criminal justice setting also must include the crucial concepts of legitimacy and the rule of law. Legitimacy relates to people's perception of their treatment as fair and just and as authority having been exercised properly. It is an important aspect of individuals' engagement with the criminal justice system and their process of desisting from offending that they perceive the institutions with which they engage as holding legitimate authority (discussed further in Chapter 10). The rule of law is defined and explained by Bingham (2010: 8): 'all persons and authorities within the state, whether public or private, should be bound by and entitled to the benefit of laws publicly made, taking effect (generally) in the future and publicly administered by the courts'.

In an Australian context, it is impossible to discuss justice without relating it to history and to the treatment of Indigenous peoples.

What do we mean by community justice in criminal justice?

In bringing together two complex and contested ideas—'community' and 'justice'—it is not surprising that community justice has been understood and interpreted in a variety of ways and that the term is utilised for political and rhetorical purposes. Community justice is not a new concept: The idea of a community-based response to crime has been an attractive option since the 1960s, and the approach has always attracted some attention—as well as some scepticism—from criminological scholars:

> Since the 1960s we have seen the development of one community program after another—community corrections, community policing, punishment in the community, community crime prevention, community prosecution, community justice. 'The community' has become the all-purpose solution to every criminal justice program.
>
> (Garland, 2001: 123)

Stanley Cohen was among the clearest scholars in warning of the attractiveness of community language to policy-makers, as a magic word that could unite administrators and community activists (Cohen, 1985; Maruna, 2002). The lack of specificity in defining what constituted a community allowed the state to control its citizens in a large variety of often-hidden ways (Cohen, 1979). The language of community can also be used in an exclusive way, creating an identity in contrast to that of outsiders and reminding them that they do not belong (Young, 1999).

Alongside this necessarily critical approach, there have been considered attempts to set out a positive outline of what community justice entails.

In accordance with the local emphasis of community justice, these attempts to define it have had some national differences and will be presented in a way that reflects this, starting with community justice in the USA, moving on to community justice in the UK and then considering other national approaches.

Community justice: Neighbourhoods and other communities

The concept of community justice is most closely associated with the work of David Karp and Todd Clear (Karp and Clear, 2000, 2002), who have explored it, both in practice and in academic discourse, across many years. They have defined the term in a number of publications; those definitions include the following:

> Community justice broadly refers to all variants of crime prevention and justice activities that explicitly include the community in their processes and set the enhancement of community quality of life as a goal.
>
> (Karp and Clear, 2000: 323)

> Community justice is a new approach to crime that explicitly includes the community in criminal justice processes. It is expressly concerned with improving the quality of community life and the capacity of local communities to prevent crime and to effectively respond to criminal incidents when they occur.
>
> (Karp and Clear, 2002: xiii)

In Harding's (2007) dictionary entry on community justice, he draws on the four core elements identified by Clear: Community justice operates at a neighbourhood level, it is problem-solving, it has decentralised authority and it includes local citizens. The first of these core elements—that community justice operates at a neighbourhood level—is worth considering in some detail, as it is contained within some, although not all, definitions of community justice.

Community justice operates at the neighbourhood level

The two ways of referring to 'community' in the two quotations above—either in a general sense or in a more specific way, linked to local neighbourhoods—are important variants on how community justice is discussed, particularly in the USA, and it is important to understand how community justice is related particularly to specific neighbourhoods. Clear, Hamilton and Cadora (2011) suggest that two assumptions are inherent in the idea of community justice. Firstly, there are significant and important differences between different communities, and the criminal justice strategy must fit with those differences; although the same criminal law will apply, strategies must take different forms. Secondly, community justice assumes that informal social controls are more important mechanisms of public safety than formal systems of control. Community justice is therefore not simply targeted at individual offenders or victims but rather seeks to build strengths throughout the whole community: 'Community justice, therefore, builds varying strategies of formal social control, depending on the particular problems facing the local area, and always has as one of its main aims strengthening the capacity of informal social control within that location' (2011: 1).

The term 'community' in this sense is used to refer to neighbourhoods but can also refer to groups of people who share common goals or sets of interests, such as a student or business community. In the USA, there are significant differences between the rates of offending and the impacts of criminal behaviour on different neighbourhoods, so community justice initiatives target specific areas where initiatives can have a high impact and produce potentially significant benefits. Community justice will proactively strengthen informal systems and public safety foundations by working in partnership with residents, businesses and other social services. Community justice incorporates the important aspect of promoting social justice.

Community justice and social justice

Community justice has an ethical or values-led component. Clear, Hamilton and Cadora (2011) emphasise the importance of promoting social justice alongside criminal justice. They define criminal justice as the study of rules and social justice as the study of distribution of good resources. Community justice recognises that the criminal justice system is not, on its own, able to respond to offending, so there is a need to build social capital, both the bonding capital that links similar people and the bridging capital that builds links between groups of different people: 'The aim of community justice is not merely to process criminal cases but to restore order, strengthen community cohesion, repair the damage from crime, and build partnerships that nurture a more beneficial community life' (2011: 4).

Community justice seeks a positive outcome of better communities for all who live in them and regards those communities as being able to encourage moral behaviour and to support those who struggle to find the right path. It is associated with the idea of communitarianism: That we are required to fulfil some moral duties, even when there is no immediate benefit to ourselves from doing so.

Crime hot-spots

Central to the idea of the neighbourhood concept of community justice is the acceptance that the impact of crime is not the same in every community and that crime is highly geographically concentrated in some locations.

This understanding has attracted widespread attention in criminology, and Clear, Hamilton and Cadora (2011) identify three main schools of thought regarding how to respond to these so-called crime 'hot-spots':

1. The disorder model states that visible disorder can breed an impression that an area is not cared for and this makes crime more likely. The 'broken windows theory' arises from this disorder model, saying that addressing these minor, but visible, instances of offending makes serious offending less likely to occur;

   - Disorganisation models are influenced by the insights of systemic theory: Poverty, ethnic heterogeneity and mobility make crime more likely. They lead to the idea that 'organising' a community can reduce crime;
   - Informal social control models focus on collective efficacy and argue that crime is reduced when strong forces of informal social control operate in a neighbourhood. Collective efficacy advocates suggest that crime can be reduced by building social relationships in problem neighbourhoods.

The distinctive nature of community justice

There are five main ways in which community-oriented justice strategies are different from traditional criminal justice approaches (Clear, Hamilton and Cadora, 2011):

- Places not cases: Community justice focuses on particular communities or neighbourhoods rather than on individual casework;
- Community justice is proactive, not reactive; it aims to build stronger, safer more resilient communities, not merely to react to offending after it has taken place;
- Community justice seeks to solve the problems of communities—which may not directly be related to crime—rather than simply blame those who have committed offences for their actions;
- The approach of community justice to power and authority is to take a decentralising approach rather than set up a strict hierarchy;
- Like to the approach to authority, community justice also encourages a fluid approach to organisational boundaries rather than setting up a clear fragmentation of responsibilities.

As community justice is a distinctive criminal justice approach with a different philosophy from traditional criminal justice approaches, it needs to be researched and evaluated in a distinctive way. Any evaluation should include community revitalisation and problem-solving and an acknowledgement of the need to establish legitimacy. These perspectives can share in the process of establishing goals and objectives, and research data can then be collected by way of direct observation, focus groups, surveys, official records and social and physical disorder inventories (Clear, Hamilton and Cadora, 2011). A community justice approach cannot simply rely on recidivism data to determine effectiveness, and any evaluation must involve listening to victims, communities and community justice pioneers (Maruna, 2002).

Community justice and criminal justice agencies

Community justice initiatives are identified by a unique set of common concerns: They are proactive, they focus on circumstances of a particular place, they are enacted through collaborations and partnerships and they adopt new priorities that are not necessarily directly related to public safety. Community justice is exhibited in particular ways in different criminal justice organisations.

Policing and community justice

Community policing is perhaps the aspect of the criminal justice system where the use of the word 'community' has become most prevalent. Much of the attention that community justice receives arises from the successes of community policing, and they do share some justifications and objectives. Both community justice and community policing share an intention to promote better community relations and prevent crime. Community-oriented policing includes such approaches as community-building strategies, problem-oriented strategies dealing with the causes of crime and broken windows strategies focusing on crimes of disorder.

There are, however, key differences between community policing and community justice. In particular, community policing has a narrower focus on law enforcement while community justice has a wider ambition to achieve social justice and make changes throughout the criminal justice system (Clear, Hamilton and Cadora, 2011).

The courts and community justice

There are a number of ways in which court processes can be organised in line with community justice, including their location, the work of defenders and prosecutors and their tone and nature. Community courts can be located in particular neighbourhoods, rather than in city centres or out-of-town locations, to allow a greater connection between the work of the judiciary and the concerns of that neighbourhood community. Prosecutors and defenders in such communities also have a closer connection to the neighbourhood, allowing prosecutors to have a greater sense of the needs of that community, including the specific victim, and enabling defenders to think about wider public protection and safety issues, rather than simply the interests of the specific defendant. Such courts will take an informal, inclusive approach and emphasise creative sentencing, prioritising rehabilitation and community needs ahead of punishment. Community courts are often closely associated with restorative justice approaches, such as victim-offender mediation, community reparative boards, family group conferences and circle sentencing, and with courts for specific communities such as drug courts, domestic violence courts and mental health courts. (Restorative justice is discussed further in Chapter 10, and Australian specialist courts are examined in more detail in Chapter 2.)

Corrections and community justice

Perhaps surprisingly, corrections have often been the slowest criminal justice institution to adopt the language and practises of community justice. Although work in the community is central to the work of corrections, it takes a different approach to the individual than community justice:

> Community justice has been slowest to arrive in the correctional field. Perhaps this is because the existing term, 'community corrections', gives the impression of community justice. Under traditional approaches to this field, corrections enters the community, but the community never makes it into corrections.
>
> (Karp and Clear, 2000: 327)

Traditional correctional services have had five main themes: Offender management, risk, treatment, surveillance and control and punishment (Clear, Hamilton and Cadora, 2011), but a community justice approach to corrections would call on different themes as corrections adopt a greater focus on the community rather than the individual:

- *Neighbourhoods and communities.* A community justice approach to corrections is not just about offenders assigned to control but also the places where they live and work. The emphasis of the work is on supporting informal social controls and building up the communities and relationships that are damaged when someone who has offended is excluded.
- *Partnerships.* Corrections agencies are used to working in partnership, but those that have a community justice focus will seek partnerships beyond the criminal justice and statutory sectors and establish alliances with community groups, schools and others.
- *Victims and communities.* Community justice-focused corrections agencies will take a particular and direct interest in victims, families and communities.
- *Problem-solving.* A problem-solving approach is at the heart of community justice, and this is particularly important for corrections, which deals with complex problems where solutions are difficult to find.

- *Restoration.* Community corrections will focus on sanctions that restore the victim while emphasising that restitution is not all one way: The community also needs to give back to the individual who has committed the offence.

It is, however, the location of probation work that most clearly identifies a community approach to corrections. In contrast to the pattern of location probation offices beside courthouses, far away from the communities that they serve—characterised as 'Fortress Probation'—community corrections is located in the neighbourhood, seeking to build support systems for clients. Community corrections will seek to alleviate the disruption in community relationships caused by a period of imprisonment, and its location in the neighbourhood is an important aspect of that service. Community corrections will reintegrate through a combination of treatment and problem-solving while bearing in mind the potential risk posed to the community by the individual. Punishment and surveillance are used, but with the aim of achieving reintegration, not simply as aims in themselves. A community corrections vision for the future would include neighbourhood community justice centres that also include support for employment, health care and housing. The next section considers the wider community justice future vision.

Models for the future of community justice

Clear, Hamilton and Cadora (2011) suggest that any planning for the future of community justice must take account of its three essential aspects:

- *Place.* Community justice has a concrete meaning: It takes place in a designated location;
- *Value.* Community justice requires consideration of people who have committed offences as part of a community and of the wider quality of life of that community;
- *Public safety.* Community justice exists where there is public commerce without personal fear.

Community justice, however, cannot simply be reduced down to a set of techniques: It makes strong claims to values and principles. Karp and Clear (2000) set out the seven principles of community justice. They characterise three principles—norm affirmation, restoration and public safety—as democratic and four—equality, inclusion, mutuality and stewardship—as egalitarian principles. Of these values, the emphasis given to inclusion is perhaps at the very heart of what differentiates community justice from traditional criminal justice approaches:

> The principle of inclusion asserts that communal membership is not cheaply bought or sold. Much of the pressure for longer prison sentences

is predicated on a 'kinds of people' perspective on crime: The world can be cleanly divided into good people and bad people, and the sooner the bad people are removed from the public domain, the better. A community justice approach favours public safety but rejects the simplistic claim that removal of the 'bad guys' is the core strategy for solving community safety problems.

(Karp and Clear, 2000: 335)

Discussion of community justice in England and Wales has taken a different form than that in the USA, but values and principles remain at the heart of the discourse.

Community justice: Alternatives to custody

Although there is a connection between the conception of community justice in England and Wales, and work in particular neighbourhoods, community justice is often defined in a wider, more abstract way:

Community justice comprises working with offenders, crime prevention, community safety as well as working with victims and vulnerable groups. In addition, it is also about revisiting the concept of 'justice' and exploring whether the current arrangements can or will deliver community justice for some or all sections of what we understand to be 'community' (Winstone and Pakes, 2005: 2).

Winstone and Pakes set out three principles of community justice:

1 Community is the ultimate consumer of criminal justice;
2 Community justice is achieved in partnership at a local level;
3 Community justice is problem focused and problems addressed rather than cases processed.

For Winstone and Pakes (2005), the essence of community is distinctiveness—small size, localised interventions and self-sufficiency—but they acknowledge that the language used is not always matched by practice: 'community justice is part substance, part spin ... Not all is well in the world of community justice, and without doubt the strength of rhetoric promoting community justice is rather far removed from the reality of practice in the real world' (2005: 12).

The discussion of community justice in England and Wales has often focused on values and principles and has taken place within a context of great political and organisational upheaval within criminal justice. Community justice is often placed in contrast to other approaches to criminal justice. Some scholars, notably Mike Nellis (2001, 2003, 2005) and Brian Williams (2003, 2005), seek to set out principles of community justice as a way of responding to and challenging other discourses such as managerialism or punishment and exclusion. Community justice, as a term, is visible and often used, notably in the titles of degree programs (Bachelor of Community Justice or Community and Criminal Justice), training organisations (Community Justice National Training Organisation (CJNTO), a journal (the *British Journal of Community Justice*) and an online resource (the Community Justice Portal at Sheffield Hallam University). Nellis (2005) explicitly sees community justice as a way of expressing humanistic values in the criminal justice system—values he characterises as an acknowledgement of the worth of all human beings and a realisation that all are capable of acts of both great good and great evil. Community justice encompasses the ideas of restorative justice, anti-custodialism and community safety and has an advantage over more traditional, liberal approaches—often associated with social work—in that it is able to face up to the reality of the great harm that is done by some people. Nellis's (2000, 2003, 2005) arguments that criminal justice practice is a moral enterprise and that community justice can provide the moral vision at the heart of that enterprise are an important aspect of any vision of community justice. Williams (2003) set out a vision of the meaning of community justice, tracing its origins to the work of Karp and Clear (2000, 2002) in the USA and Nils Christie (1977) in Europe. Williams (2003) characterised community justice as an intention to practise criminal justice—particularly probation work—in a particular way, including an engagement with communities and neighbourhoods. Community justice is a democratic, not an authoritarian, model that has seven characteristics:

- Community justice supports the principle of involving community members in criminal justice;
- Community justice is a way to counter the tendency of criminal justice to over-professionalism;
- Community justice supports the use of informal methods to resolve conflict in the community rather than formal methods that have a tendency to appropriate conflicts;
- Community justice builds upon critiques of remote policing styles and bureaucratic criminal justice agencies and expresses a preference for solutions in the community;
- Community justice necessitates enhanced partnerships between state and non-state agencies;
- Community justice supports a variety of approaches—a 'mixed economy' of informal controls;
- The context within which community justice is developing cannot be ignored.

The imprecision of the term 'community justice' is part of its attraction, and Senior suggested a particularly broad definition of the term: 'I think one definition of community justice would be that you take your direction as an agency from what the community wants from its public sector services' (Senior and Nellis, 2013: 43).

This must be accompanied by the acknowledgement that a community also bears some responsibility for the reintegration of people who have committed offences (Canton and Dominey, 2018). Williams (2005) considers this responsibility, particularly as it applies to victims of crime. He suggests that the authoritarian strand of community justice, which passes responsibility for offending back to communities, has prevailed over the inclusive strand, which emphasises partnerships and community involvement. His suggestion is that the involvement of actual victims is a good barometer for whether a community justice initiative is truly an inclusive approach. However, this attention to victims must be considered with care, and complacency must be avoided; victim involvement and even victim responsibility are often taken for granted, or assumed to bring unconditional benefit, but community justice advocates can sometimes spend little time consulting with victims or evaluating the impact of community justice approaches on victims:

> advocates of community justice blithely argue that it involves new responsibilities as well as new rights both for offenders and for victims ... victims are characterised by some community justice enthusiasts as part of a network of mutual obligations when they have not been consulted about this reorientation of the system and its likely benefits for them are by no means clear.
>
> (Williams, 2005: 128)

The American approach of linking community justice to work in neighbourhoods is present in community justice in England and Wales, and John Harding, then Chief Probation Officer of the London Probation Service, argued that probation work should be based out of offices and outside traditional 9–5 office hour restrictions and should take place in communities, 24 hours a day, with a focus on wider public safety concerns rather than just on individual casework (Harding, 2000, 2007). Community justice approaches are not simply led by criminal justice staff; they require partnerships with community members.

One important criminal justice principle that is supported and promoted by community justice is that of legitimacy: The involvement of lay people as community representatives allows criminal justice organisations to be responsive to the needs of neighbourhoods (Crawford, 2008). Appropriate governance arrangements for probation and community will include a local, neighbourhood element, as it is difficult for community members to feel included by a large, remote bureaucracy (Canton and Dominey, 2018).

Interpretations of community justice

Although community justice has enjoyed the most attention in the USA, and in England and Wales, it has been considered in other jurisdictions, particularly those going through transition or facing challenges relating to relationships between different groups in society. In her overview of community justice in various jurisdictions, Shapland (2008) suggests that the conception of community in each country strongly influences how community justice is considered. In some places, community is considered positively, while in others it is more of a negative, exclusionary concept. Community justice might therefore be positively considered as a form of decentralisation or more negatively seen as a compromise in efficiency or effectiveness. For example, in France, the concept of community is associated with groups trying to set themselves apart, so community justice can be seen as a threat to professionalism—or even to the state itself. In Ireland and Canada, by contrast, decentralisation is regarded positively. Responding to community needs can involve a response to a particular group—an interest group, attachment group or territorial group—and can be an important aspect of building trust and legitimacy, particularly in transitional societies. However, the idea that there should be different justice for different communities is a hard idea for states to accept, in both principle and practice, and the negotiation of the balance between states and communities is not yet resolved: 'the current balance of the tension between justice, civil society and community is not necessarily a stable one or an end point. There is likely to be a continuing tension and continuing movement' (Shapland, 2008: 26).

The Canadian conception of community justice has particular relevance to Australia because of the need to incorporate Indigenous conceptions of justice and the association often made between 'community justice' and Indigenous communities. In Canada, the word 'community' itself is often associated with Indigenous peoples or isolated, rural areas, so it has a connotation close to 'minority' and can be used to separate groups rather than to bring them together (Bartkowiak and Jaccoud, 2008). Steps have been taken to give Indigenous Canadian communities more rights and more involvement in the criminal justice system since the 1960s, and examples of these steps to transfer power to communities include locating courts on reserves, paying lay representatives to participate in government agencies and the use of circle sentencing. These changes have been made by adaption of the system rather than the introduction of formal changes.

Finally, community justice is of particular interest and relevance to states going through a process of political transition. In Northern Ireland, 'community' can have a negative, exclusionary connotation, and 'community justice' can be used as a euphemism for paramilitary punishment. However, this usage can taint genuine community involvement in criminal justice and lead to a construction of the community as dangerous and the state as a benign protector of rights (McEvoy and Eriksson, 2008; Eriksson, 2009). Similarly in the South African transition, there was often a complex relationship between the state and community groups with regard to the administration of justice (Roche, 2003). These debates have relevance to Australia, in that they go to the heart of the discussion of the rights and needs of different groups, the role of the state and responsibility to protect the interests of victims, offenders and the community.

Towards a model of community justice for Australia

The language of community justice is known in Australia, but there have not been the same attempts to set out a coherent community justice model as have occurred in the UK and the USA. In the final section of this chapter, an attempt is made to suggest what a future community justice approach would look like. It is important to note that promoting the values of community justice and achieving community justice goals will take more than an increase in the use of community sanctions. An increase in community sanctions can, on its own, simply lead to an increase overall in the use of punishment and a widening of the power of the state to impose mass supervision, with potentially detrimental impacts on individuals (McNeill, 2019; Clear, 2020; Freiberg and Bartels, 2020). Community sanctions need to be considered to be credible alternatives to imprisonment, and they need to be able to demonstrate their effectiveness in reducing reoffending (Cullen, Lero Jonson and Mears, 2017; Bartels and Weatherburn, 2020). A vision for community justice should follow the Harvard principles (Executive Session on Community Corrections, 2017; Clear, 2020, and see Box 1.3) in promoting principles of well-being, harm-avoidance and human dignity.

Lutze et al. (2012) suggest that there are three ways in which community justice reform can be achieved: Macro-level change, agency-level change and micro-level change.

Macro-level change

The prison debates are different in Australia than in the UK and USA, but there are three characteristics that are shared. Firstly, the prison population is high, particularly compared with jurisdictions with a different discourse, approach and philosophy of incarceration (see Pratt and Eriksson, 2013, for a discussion of these differences). Secondly, prison is still seen as the default response to offending—particularly serious and persistent offending. Debates on offending, particularly in relation to the management and supervision of high-risk offenders, take place on the basis of a key assumption that prison will be required at some point. This focus on prison as the default option in Australia impedes the understanding of community sanctions and limits attempts to promote their greater use (Freiberg and Bartels, 2020). Responses to more serious offending are discussed in more detail in Chapter 6. Thirdly, the disproportionality in the use of incarceration that is particularly apparent in the imprisonment of black people in the USA is also a characteristic of the Australian use of imprisonment with regard to Indigenous peoples. This will be discussed throughout the book.

The discourse on responses to offending in Australia shares some of the same characteristics as that in the UK and USA, with every high-profile serious offence leading to calls for harsher responses. However, even in Australian federal election campaigns, criminal justice is not treated as the same hot political issue as it tends to be in election campaigns in the UK (although in some states—particularly Queensland—politicians do still seek to gain populist support by outlining harsh responses to offending), suggesting that there is, perhaps, greater opportunity to influence the debate. The language of community justice does not simply stand in opposition to the harsh punishment discourse but also contrasts with some traditional, liberal discourses that seem inadequate to respond to the severe harm caused by some offending. Community justice does not take an abolitionist position; it recognises that some people who have committed serious offences require incarceration, but it places the community, not the prison, at the centre of the criminal justice debate.

Evaluation of community justice interventions should focus on the outcome of policy, not its intention. It is unarguable that current Australian criminal justice policies have a disproportionally negative impact on Indigenous peoples. However, other groups within society have different experience of the criminal justice system, including Pacific Islander groups, other racial groups, Islamic groups, young people and women. This is discussed in detail in Chapter 7. Community justice considers the application of corrections approaches to be a human rights issue, so the impact on criminal justice policies on particular groups is a key concern. Community justice values do not simply require that the justice system does not discriminate against particular groups—in intention or outcome—but also rejects a neutral, universal approach. Community justice expects the criminal justice system to promote social justice and to bring positive outcomes to otherwise disadvantaged groups.

Problems confronting people who have committed offences are too great for criminal justice systems alone to manage, and an over-reliance on criminal justice agencies can lead to the oppression of individuals and divert the focus away from important issues of social justice. A community justice approach emphasises partnerships both within and outside the criminal justice sector in response to offending and, importantly, in crime prevention, public protection and proactive community-building. Partnerships with health, education and social services are crucial in all contexts. In rural Australia, criminal justice agencies need to take an imaginative approach to partnership building, developing links with non-traditional, non-statutory agencies as they have the capacity to work within communities in rural settings. In working with Indigenous people, as offenders, victims or as part of affected communities, it is crucial that these partnerships include links with organisations that include these groups.

Agency-level change: Building structural competency and program integrity

It is at this level that values and ethics within the criminal justice system need to be addressed. Community justice advocates that criminal justice responses need to have a moral element and to be driven by humanity and a belief in the possibility of change. Criminal justice should not simply be about the infliction of harm through punishment. However, it is not sufficient for community justice approaches to simply have positive intentions; they also need to have demonstrably effective outcomes for people who have committed offences, victims and communities.

Evidence-based practice is discussed in detail in Chapter 4. A distinction is sometimes drawn between evidence-based approaches and those who promote humanistic or anti-oppressive values within criminal justice. Evidence-based approaches are often associated with quantitative research methods, psychologically based programmatic responses to offending, an uncritical approach to definitions of offending and a focus on reconviction rates alone. Community justice promotes other goals beyond reducing reoffending and acknowledges the constructed reality of offending and the need to address power relations within society—particularly as they relate to the over-representation of particular groups as offenders and victims within the criminal justice system (see Box 1.2). However, community justice also acknowledges the need to produce measurable outcomes.

Box 1.2

Representation of Indigenous people in the criminal justice system

- Indigenous people are more likely to be victims of crime than other groups. They are two to three times more likely to be victims of violence and four to six times more likely to be victims of family violence;
- Indigenous people are imprisoned at 12 times the rate of the rest of the Australian population. They make up less than 3 per cent of the Australian population but comprise more than 40 per cent of the prison population;
- An Indigenous young person between the age of 10 and 17 is more than 24 times more likely to be in prison than another Australian of the same age.

The reasons behind this over-representation are discussed throughout the book, but it can sometimes be difficult to appreciate the human story behind these disturbing statistics. Morseu-Dopp (2013) conveys the impact of this over-representation when she describes working as a criminal justice social worker and visiting an Indigenous woman who was in prison, who asked her to check on the welfare of her daughter and her five sons who were also in detention—seven members of the same Indigenous family incarcerated at the same time.

Source: The statistical material in this box is taken from the Australian Institute of Criminology, www.aic.gov.au. This website is an excellent source of further information about the over-representation of Indigenous peoples within the Australian criminal justice system.

Community justice does accept the utility of programs and the need to ensure that they are based on evidence of effectiveness. However, as discussed in Chapter 10, to support people who have committed offences in the process of desisting from offending, it is important that community justice responses move beyond a simple reliance on programs and seek to support individuals in their integration into the communities.

Micro-level change: Returning community corrections to a human service profession

The agencies that are tasked with leading the state's community justice response in Australia are corrections and youth justice agencies. For community corrections to be successful, they must be seen as human services professions, where the relationship between worker and the individual who has committed the offence is vital. The purpose of the work of these agencies must be clearly identified, and it must be acknowledged that the work is demanding and often stressful so the needs of workers must also be prioritised.

The work and culture of the organisation and the professional and training needs of juvenile justice and corrections staff are dealt with in detail in Chapter 8, as it is important to note that meeting the needs of staff who work in community justice must be connected to their ability to work in an effective manner. There has been some work carried out on probation organisational culture, most recently and prominently by Mawby and Worrall (2013) in the UK, but this has created far less academic interest than police culture research, and there has been little attention given to this issue in Australia. International evidence has highlighted high levels of suicide, misuse of force, substance abuse, post-traumatic stress disorder (PTSD) and employee turnover in corrections staff (Lutze et al., 2012). It is clearly not realistic to expect workers who are stressed, stretched and over-worked to engage individuals effectively, but that issue is rarely acknowledged: 'Taking care of the caretakers of our public safety and community wellness is critical to the future of the justice system' (Lutze et al., 2012: 52).

There need to be realistic expectations and an acceptable level of pressure on community corrections staff. It is important that programs are evaluated and that interventions are based on the best available evidence, but that does not mean that workers should be held entirely accountable for the future offending careers of those they supervise. Community justice accepts the need for accountability but does not require a blame culture; rather, it promotes an approach of positive rewards and incentives for individuals who make positive progress, alongside a similar positive reinforcement of good practice by workers. Community justice agencies should be characterised by an ethics of care (Banks, 2012) for the offenders, victims and communities with whom they work and for their own staff.

A community justice approach focuses on an ethic of care and greater collaboration between agencies. Resources are invested in communities, not incarceration. This book considers different aspects of community justice and management and working with people who have committed offences. The next two chapters look separately at adult and then young people before the book moves on to consider theoretical and research-based approaches to crime and to work with people who have committed offences. The book also considers important contemporary issues in work with people who have committed offences, such as the focus on the management of risk and the use of technology within the criminal justice system. The definition of community justice that has been set out—an approach that supports people who have committed offences in the building of a good life—does influence the choice of subjects to which particular attention is directed in the rest of the book. Taken together, the chapters on values and ethics, diversity, desistance and restorative justice, leading into the chapter on practice skills, build up a picture of what community justice in Australia might look like and how criminal justice practitioners might support those who have offended in building a good life.

Further reading

The Harvard Kennedy consensus paper (Box 1.3) is an excellent place to start with regard to a future vision for community justice. The work of Todd Clear, often with other colleagues, notably David Karp, provides the most

---

Box 1.3

'Harvard Kennedy: Community corrections consensus'

The Harvard Kennedy School brings together individuals based on their expertise and reputation for thoughtfulness to rethink society's response to particular issues. The Executive Session on Community Corrections took three years of deliberation to develop recommendations for a series of necessary paradigm shifts to make community corrections fairer, more humane and just and to contribute to improving well-being and decreasing incarceration. They suggested that micro-level or incremental change would not be enough and that the approach to corrections would need to shift:

- From punishing failure to rewarding success;
- From mass supervision to focused supervision;
- From time-based to goal-based;
- From deficit-based to strengths-based;
- From delayed/arbitrary to swift/certain;
- From offender-focused to victim-centred;

> - From individual-focused to family-inclusive;
> - From isolated to integrated;
> - From fortress to community based;
> - From low profile to high profile;
> - From caseload-funding to performance-based funding;
> - From gut-based to evidence-based;
> - From low-tech to high-tech.
>
> It was the view of the group that the goal of achieving mass decarceration could not be achieved without these shifts and a fundamental realignment to the values of life, liberty and equality before the law.
>
> Source: See full paper at Executive Session on Community Corrections (2017) 'Toward an Approach to Community Corrections for the 21st Century: Consensus Document of the Executive Session on Community Corrections', Program in Criminal Justice Policy and Management, Harvard Kennedy School.

extensive thinking into how community justice might be defined, particularly with regard to local neighbourhoods, and what impact it might have on the working of criminal justice.

Practical task

Imagine you are working with Matthew, a 25-year-old man who has committed a series of property offences. He is not currently working, has no partner or children, and does not have a close relationship with anyone in his family. How would you go about establishing community resources that might support Matthew?

Reflective questions

1.1 How might community justice approaches make a contribution to the work to reduce the over-representation of Indigenous people in the Australian Criminal Justice System?

1.2 Is it useful for Australian criminal justice scholars, students and practitioners to learn from experiences in other jurisdictions? Is there a risk of consciously or unconsciously adopting an Anglo-American bias?

1.3 Reflect on your understanding of the key terms of 'community' and 'justice'. Does justice mean punishment and retribution or is it also associated with fairness? Do you consider yourself to be a member of one or more communities?

2 Adults who have committed offences

Introduction

The history of Australia, since the establishment of the European penal colony, has been bound up with ideas of criminal justice and the treatment of people who have committed offences. A punitive response to offending has always been a part of the Australian regime—whether through deportation, capital punishment, incarceration or corporal punishment—but the country could also claim that it was built by rehabilitated offenders. This chapter focuses on responses to offending within the community. It briefly covers some of the historical and international context to community sanctions in Australia, then considers some of the state responses before concluding with a discussion of what a community justice response to offending might mean in Australia.

Australia was a great penal social experiment in the eighteenth century, with offenders from the UK being transported there as an alternative to capital punishment. Australia was essentially considered to be an open prison (Bull, 2010). The penal regime was a harsh one that only became harsher; in the mid-nineteenth century, the punishment of transportation was more likely to be transportation plus hard labour. Offenders were punished for non-compliance with the regime by banishment to ever-harsher settlements, with the ultimate punishment being transportation to Port Arthur in Van Dieman's Land (Tasmania) (Kornhauser and Laster, 2014). Flogging was a common punishment for any breaking of the rules. This colonial history has meant that Australia's instinctive position in responding to offending is one of punitiveness and general deterrence, and this can be seen both in criminal justice and now in asylum seeker policy (Kornhauser and Laster, 2014).

The end of the transportation policy came about because Australia refused to take any more convicted prisoners from the UK, and Britain sought to find other punishment approaches. Philosopher Jeremy Bentham was one of the leading critics of the transportation approach, saying that a punishment that was so uncertain and so far out of sight could only have limited deterrent effect.

The punitive and exclusionary approach of transportation to Australia did give rise to early rehabilitative approaches to dealing with people who had committed offences in the community. The Ticket of Leave scheme gave freedom to some convicts, allowing them to work and thereby solving some of the acute labour shortages of the time. Pardons were also given to some people who had been convicted of offences, allowing them to build and settle in Australia. This means that, although the UK and USA trace their history of community corrections back to the mid-nineteenth century, Australian history can go back much further than that—even prior to the foundations of Australia's prison building in the early nineteenth century. However, it is only really over the last 40 years that community sentences have become a major part of the Australian correctional system. They have increased in usage due to a disillusionment with the criminal justice system in general and a growing appreciation of the cost and lack of effectiveness of prisons (White and Perrone, 2010). This greater use of community sentences was accompanied by a prison-building scheme that led to more utilisation of both private and public sector prisons. Community-based orders fall into the categories of reparation, supervision and restricted movement and, despite their stated connection with the community, tend to be tightly and directly controlled by the state (White and Perrone, 2010). At the start of the twenty-first century, there was a growing acceptance that some people who had committed offences would be managed better in the community than in custodial settings.

Australia has a high imprisonment rate by international standards; since 2000, the total number of prisoners worldwide has increased at 24%, which is slightly less than the growth in population over that period. The prison rate in Australia has grown by 98% over that period (Fair and Walmsley, 2022). The imprisonment rate in 2021 was 214 prisoners by 100,000 of the adult population (Australian Bureau of Statistics [ABS], 2021). From June 30, 2020 to June 30, 2021, Indigenous prisoners increased by 8% (947) to 13,039, making up 30% of all prisoners. Female prisoners make up 10% of the prison population (ABS, 2021). Attention is given to how women are particularly treated in the Australian criminal justice system in Chapter 5. Cunneen et al. (2013) list some distinctive aspects of the Australian prison regime in the past and present:

- The opening of a facility in Tabalum, NSW, to operate as a sort of pre-prison for Indigenous people who attended on a voluntary basis before sentence;
- The operation of a cruel and brutal regime at Grafton, from the 1940s to the 1970s, as a way of controlling the rest of the NSW prison population;
- Goulburn High Risk Management Unit, which holds the most violent prisoners in NSW. It is not a therapeutic facility; it operates on a system of reward and punishment;

- Victoria has had similar high-security prisons in Victoria, including Pentridge, Jika Jika, Barwon Acacia and Melaleuca. Melaleuca was described by Corrections Victoria as 'super-prison' and the most secure prison in Australia.

Indigenous people make up 2% of the Australian population and 30% of the adult prisoner population (ABS, 2021). There is also a high re-incarceration rate among Indigenous people, with 77% of those in prison having previously been incarcerated (ABS, 2021). The alternative history (Bull, 2010) of the development of the Australian penal settlement and policy is that told from an Indigenous perspective. Indigenous people were racially classified and then segregated from white people in society and in the criminal justice system. The underlying belief was that Indigenous people were inferior and that they would eventually die out. As well as being subject to segregation, they were subject to differential treatment, with flogging being continued for Indigenous people long after it was brought to an end for white Australians. As discussed throughout this chapter, and the remainder of this book, Australian criminal justice interventions bring about negative outcomes for Indigenous people, in design, in effect or both. Even those approaches with seemingly positive or benign intent will have detrimental outcomes:

> The use of diversionary schemes has tended to be biased against Indigenous people, who are drawn into the system much more quickly and more deeply than their non-Indigenous counterparts. Interestingly, Aboriginal young people appear to be under-represented in the use of juvenile diversion schemes.
>
> (White and Perrone, 2010: 542)

Community sanctions are less disproportionate to Indigenous people than custodial sanctions, but the disparities are still stark (Brown, 2020). The over-representation of Indigenous people is the most distinctive aspect of the Australian criminal justice system, so international instruments relating to the rights of this group are relevant to criminal justice. The *International Covenant on the Elimination of all Forms of Racial Discrimination 1969* (Article 2, Part 2) declares that states shall protect all racial groups and guarantee them full enjoyment of human rights and fundamental freedoms. This covenant was ratified by Australia in 1975. The UN Declaration on the Rights of Indigenous Peoples 2007 was not formally ratified by the Australian government, but the government announced its support in 2009. Article 23 of the Declaration states that Indigenous peoples have the right to determine their own priorities and strategies for development, to be involved in developing social programs and to administer those programs through their institutions. Article 34 states that Indigenous peoples have the right to promote and maintain their own traditions, including in judicial systems, in accordance with international human rights standards. Even the basic structure of Australia—the division into states—does not match with the Indigenous understanding of the land, and provisions have been put in place to allow different state jurisdictions to respond to the different understanding of boundaries possessed by Indigenous peoples. See Department of the Attorney-General and Justice NT (2015) and Stout (2014) for a discussion of the Cross-Border Justice Scheme in the Ngaanyatjarra Pitjantjatjara Yankunytjatjara (NPY) region.

The modern sentencing regime and structure are presented below on a state-by-state basis. In this chapter and the next one, on juvenile justice, the intention is not to present a comprehensive, but soon to be outdated, overview of all sentencing options and possibilities, but rather to highlight those that have the most relevance to the discussion of community justice. There is a lack of research into community sanctions in Australia, as compared to similar jurisdictions and Brown (2020: 191) summarises the situation:

> Community sanctions in Australia are similarly largely invisible, characterised as 'not prison', under-researched, lacking in a clear normative foundation, increasingly dominated by risk discourses, and evaluated largely through the lens of recidivism with little appreciation of the lived experience of supervision and its pains.

Australian Capital Territory (ACT)

The ACT has a flexible definition of what it defines as 'custody'. For example, one version of custody is periodic detention, where detainees serve periods of detention over the weekend. This is, however, being phased out, to be replaced by a form of intensive corrections order. Deferred sentence orders are also available, where offenders are convicted and released on bail for up to 12 months, with final sentencing deferred to give the individual the chance to address their offending behaviour. Good behaviour orders can be made as conviction or non-conviction orders, and may include conditions that the individual undertake counselling, a rehabilitation program or community service. The ACT court structure includes the Ngambra Circle Sentencing Court, which is a sentencing court for Indigenous people based on the Circle Court model of Indigenous justice (Marchetti, 2009).

In the ACT, Community Corrections is part of Corrective Services, and has units including the Probation and Parole Unit, the Prisoner Employment Unit, the Corrections Programs Unit and Offender Services. The Probation and Parole Unit will advise courts and refer people who have committed offences to appropriate community resources; the Corrections Programs Unit facilitates specific programs to address identified criminogenic needs.

The ACT has a connection between the justice system and the health system, with the Police and Court Alcohol and Diversion Program diverting people from justice to health.

Box 2.1

Community service orders

Community Service Orders, of some description and sometimes of different titles, are part of the community justice regime of all Australian states. They require sentenced individuals to carry out a set number of hours of community work. Community service is a very popular community sentence across the world: It is easily understood by those subject to it, victims and the public, and represents good value for money—particularly if the work that is done is of use and value to the community. Community service has always tried to incorporate the values of punishment, rehabilitation, reparation and reintegration, and this contributes to its popularity.

Community service punishes by depriving individuals of aspects of their time; it rehabilitates by instilling the discipline of work, and sometimes through the virtue of giving back to the community; it can be indirect reparation to the community at large or even direct reparation to a specific victim (a community service agreement following a victim–offender conference might involve direct reparation); community service can also reintegrate by building links with constructive and positive individuals and community organisations. These values all need to be present in each individual Community Service Scheme for it to be a success, but it can be difficult to hold these in the correct tension.

Where there is a response to public pressure to make community service more punitive (such as stigmatising those subject to it by making them more visible, or allocating work based on its physical demands, rather than its value to the community), that can compromise the rehabilitative or elements. Where rehabilitation or reparation is the main goal, that might not seem sufficiently punitive. For example, if a victim of an attempted burglary asks the offender to repair a fence that was damaged in the attempt, that might meet the victim's desire for reparation and may contribute to rehabilitation, but it may not appear to be a sufficiently punitive response to a serious offence.

New South Wales (NSW)

NSW has the largest prison population in Australia, and it increased by 3% to 13,128 prisoners in 2021 (Australian Bureau of Statistics, 2022). It continues to have a problem with both overcrowding and instances of assault in prison and is investing significantly in prison building (Hall, 2020).

Some of the alternative provision in NSW is presented and described as a form of imprisonment, emphasising the importance of the consideration of custody in thinking about how to respond to offending.

The key legislation in NSW is the *Crimes (Administration of Sentences) Act 1999*, now remade by the *Crimes (Administration of Sentences) Regulations 2014*, which presents four forms of 'imprisonment':

1 *Imprisonment as detention in a correctional centre.* This imprisonment may also include community service work outside the centre.
2 *Imprisonment by way of intensive correction in the community (ICO).* An ICO is a sentence served in the community, with conditions imposed by the judge at the time of sentencing. The conditions can include working or reporting requirements, or community service work. The court can also place restrictions, including the use of electronic monitoring, drug and alcohol testing and restrictions on movement and association.
3 *Imprisonment by way of home detention.* Individuals are strictly supervised, including by the use of electronic monitoring during Home Detention Orders (HDOs). They are required to allow correctional officers to visit and enter their homes at any time for the duration of the order. HDOs also include conditions relating to employment and the completion of community service work.
4 *Imprisonment by the Drug Court.* This refers to compulsory drug treatment in three stages: Closed detention in a Compulsory Drug Treatment Correctional Centre, then semi-open detention, then community custody in approved accommodation. Individuals are issued with a compulsory treatment personal plan, which includes some mandatory conditions as well as personally tailored conditions, which could include employment or education requirements, as well as counselling and drug testing.

Other sentences

Community Service Orders (CSOs) (see Box 2.2) are also available in NSW, and individuals completing other types of sentence, including imprisonment, may be required to complete community service work. Fines and compensation orders are also used, and individuals can be restricted from associating with certain people and/or from attending specific sites or districts.

Other services

In NSW, other non-statutory services have developed to work in the community with people who have committed offences in the community. The Community Restorative Centre (2022) is funded by a number of government agencies and provides a variety of services to prisoners, ex-prisoners, family members and friends, with the aim of reducing crime and preventing return to prison. These services include addressing drug and alcohol

> **Box 2.2**
>
> **Repay SA**
>
> The South Australian Community Service scheme, known as Repay SA, is a good example of how the many objectives of community service need to be held together:
>
> > We are committed to providing an appropriate penalty to offenders via the Community Service Scheme while at the same time offering meaningful work and training opportunities;
> >
> > Community service in South Australia is known as RepaySA. It provides an opportunity for offenders to make a positive contribution to our community;
> >
> > We try to provide skills, training and where appropriate qualifications linked to the community work that offenders undertake. This helps provide offenders with the skills to assist with future employment.
>
> Source: Department for Correctional Services SA, 2022.

problems, unemployment and homelessness, and providing counselling. They provide supported accommodation and counselling as well as referring to other agencies. No Bars is funded by NSW Health and provides information to support provision of alcohol and drugs treatment for released prisoners (No Bars, 2022).

Northern Territory

The issue of Indigenous over-representation in the prison population, which is a problem throughout Australia, is an even more pressing issue in the Northern Territory. The Northern Territory has the highest imprisonment rate in Australia, at 971 per 100,000 of the adult population. Some 86% of those in the Northern Territory's adult prison population are Indigenous people, with an imprisonment rate 15 times higher than the rate for non-Indigenous adults in the Northern Territory: 2390.2 per 100,000 compared with 155.2 per 100,000 (Australian Bureau of Statistics, 2022). Over-representation of Indigenous groups is not just a problem for adults in the Northern Territory; 92% of those in the youth detained population are Indigenous people.

The court structure in the Northern Territory is similar to that described for the states, with the vast majority of cases being dealt with in the Magistrates Court and the Supreme Court being used for more serious offences. A number of specialist courts, including the Community Court, sit within the Magistrates Court structure. The Community Court was established in

34 *Adults who have committed offences*

2005 and provides sentencing hearings for Indigenous people based on Circle Court and Nunga Court models (Marchetti, 2009).

Unlike the states, where there is a focus on drugs, alcohol is the big concern in the Northern Territory. Until 2011, Wholesale Supply of Alcohol statistics were gathered as part of the crime statistics. People can be court-ordered to undergo mandatory alcohol treatment, either residentially or in the community, by the Alcohol Mandatory Treatment Tribunal. In a similar way, the Mental Health Review Tribunal manages involuntary treatment orders.

The Northern Territory has a number of sentencing disposals, described as custodial, that can be served in the community. A Home Detention Order requires the individual to wear a monitoring device and prevents them from leaving the specified premises without permission. A Community Custody Order is a suspended sentence of imprisonment served in the community; as well as strict conditions, this requires participation in prescribed programs.

Community Based Orders place individuals under the supervision of a probation officer with strict reporting guidelines, including the wearing of a monitoring device and the provision of a voice sample to support monitoring. They are also obliged to participate in drug, alcohol or other treatment programs, and may be required to do community work. A community work order can also be imposed, and the purpose is declared to be 'to reflect the public interest in ensuring that a person who commits an offence makes amends to the community for the offence by performing work that is of benefit to the community' (*Sentencing Act 1995*, s 33).

As in other states, there are support services available, some particularly targeted at Indigenous groups. The Community Justice Centre in the Northern Territory provides mediation services and similar Community Justice Centres exist in NSW. The Northern Territory Community Justice Centre has also been involved in Correctional Centre Conferencing for Indigenous people. This supports community integration after serious offences, including murder or manslaughter. The North Australian Aboriginal Justice Agency (NAAJA) (2022) is funded by the Commonwealth and provides civil and criminal legal services to Indigenous people, advocacy and community legal education, and through-care for Indigenous prisoners.

Queensland

Queensland had the largest increase in prison population in 2021, total prisoners increased by 15% to 9,952.

Queensland deals with the vast majority of criminal cases in Magistrates Courts (95% in Queensland) with more serious matters being dealt with in the District or Supreme Court. Queensland previously had a Drugs Court, but closed it in 2013. There is a Mental Health Court, based within the Supreme Court, which provides advice on appropriate outcomes for those who might have a psychiatric disability. The Magistrates Court sits as a Circle Court in a variety of locations across the state, and uses the Circle Court Indigenous justice model.

Queensland has traditional sentencing options, with custodial sentences at one end of the scale and financial penalties at the other. Community sentences in Queensland include Community Service Orders of between 40 and 240 hours and probation orders. Intensive correction orders are prison sentences of one year or less that are served in the community, under intense supervision. Individuals subject to these orders will report regularly to a supervisor, attend rehabilitation programs and counselling, and perform community service. Serious sex offenders can be made subject to electronic monitoring. The programs offered within Queensland for those dealt with by way of community sentences include Turning Point and Making Choices, aimed at general offending behaviour, and Getting Smart, which uses cognitive behavioural therapy (CBT) approaches to enable individuals to abstain from addictive behaviour. The Ending Offending program is designed as a culturally appropriate way of meeting the needs of Indigenous people and Ending Family Violence uses culturally appropriate approaches to address violence within Indigenous families. Queensland operates Indigenous Sentencing Lists in some Magistrates Courts. These sit under the Courts Innovation Program, and the Indigenous Justice Programs both support Indigenous people involved with the Criminal Justice System and work in communities to reduce offending. The Courts Innovation Program also delivers diversionary and referral services.

The Aboriginal and Torres Strait Islander Legal Service (2022) is Commonwealth funded, and provides representation and advice for those Indigenous people in contact with the law.

South Australia

Since 1999, some Magistrates' courts in South Australia have sat as Nunga Courts, providing sentencing based on the Nunga Court model of Indigenous justice (Marchetti, 2009). Again, there is a flexible and innovative approach to custody, with home detention being an option for both young people and adults. Home detention tends not to be used as a primary sentence, but rather as part of a parole release at the end of a period of custodial detention.

The Community Service Program in South Australia is Repay SA (see Box 2.2). There are also intervention programs on which individuals can be sent both prior to and after sentence. The Enhanced Community Corrections Project implements a targeted, risk-based model of offender management, including increased drug and alcohol testing. Community Corrections Centres across the state are staffed by Community Corrections Officers, many of whom are qualified social workers. Electronic monitoring is a part of this project.

The South Australian Department of Corrections takes an integrated offender management approach, so that management and rehabilitation approaches are culturally appropriate, with targeted programs. The programs include Violence Prevention, Sexual Behaviours Clinic, Making Changes Program and Domestic Violence Program. The offence-focused programs are offered alongside vocational education and training, health and nutrition education, and life and social skills, as well as literacy and numeracy programs.

36 *Adults who have committed offences*

The Family Violence Court in South Australia offers support to women and children and gives defendants the opportunity to address violent behaviour by participating in the Abuse Prevention Intervention Program. The Drug Court is non-adversarial and allows defendants the opportunity to address drug dependence and associated criminal behaviour through counselling and rehabilitation, accompanied by random testing, stringent bail conditions and regular court reviews.

As a response to the Royal Commission into Aboriginal Deaths in Custody in 1995, the Aboriginal Services Unit was established to advise on and develop culturally appropriate services for Indigenous prisoners and those who have committed offences. Aboriginal Liaison Officers ensure that prisoners and those under supervision stay connected to their communities while in custody or on a community-based order. Correctional Services commits to providing programs that are culturally competent, and to supporting recruitment and retention strategies for Indigenous staff. South Australia Corrections has constructed Pakani Arangka, an Indigenous accommodation unit at Port Augusta Prison. The justice reinvestment strategy is also part of the attempt to address Indigenous over-representation in the criminal justice system.

Box 2.3

Royal commission into Aboriginal deaths in custody

The Royal Commission into Aboriginal Deaths in Custody (RCIADIC) was instigated in 1987 due to a public concern that Aboriginal people were dying in custody at rates that were far too high, and that the official explanations for this were inadequate. The Commission examined the deaths of 99 Aboriginal people in custody. Their key finding was that Aboriginal people did not die in custody at a higher rate than other people; rather, they were more likely to find themselves in custody or in contact with the police. The RCIADIC made 339 recommendations, some directly relating to the criminal justice system and others addressing wider social issues. Although there has been greater awareness of the issues and greater public concern, the widespread over-representation of Aboriginal people in the criminal justice system, particularly in custody, is still evident today. The recommendation that imprisonment be used as last resort for Aboriginal people did not take effect in Australia's climate of popular punitiveness (Bull, 2010). More than 20 years after the report of the Royal Commission, the incarceration rate in Australia remains high, with the Aboriginal population continuing to be imprisoned in the greatest numbers.

Source: The *Report of the Royal Commission into Aboriginal Deaths in Custody* can be read at www.austlii.edu.au/au/other/IndigLRes/rciadic.

Tasmania

The Tasmanian court structure includes specialist court lists for Court Mandated Diversion and Mental Health and Cognitive Disability Diversion (Magistrates Court of Tasmania, 2022. These focus on treatment and support; dedicated magistrates receive assistance from courtroom teams of health professionals, defence lawyers and prosecutors. They address the low-level nuisance offending of individuals with mental illness or cognitive disabilities in a therapeutic way.

Community sentences in Tasmania include the Community Service Order, which can include work to directly benefit the victim of the offence, and a probation order for up to three years. A Drug Treatment Order provides for an intensive community-based sentence with a custodial sentence attached.

Victoria

The Sentencing Advisory Council Victoria (2014) provides a timeline of the key legislation relating to the community management of those who have committed offences. Some of the most significant landmarks include the provision of alcohol and drug treatment in the *Alcoholics and Drug-Dependent Person Act 1974* (now replaced by the *Severe Substance Dependence Treatment Act, 2010)* and the introduction of periodic detention at attendance centres in The *Social Welfare (Amendment) Act 1975*. Community Service Orders are an important part of any community penalties regime, and these were introduced in Victoria by the *Penalties and Sentences Act 1981*, following the recommendation of the Sentencing Alternatives Committee in 1979. The majority of sentencing (over 90%) occurs in Magistrates Courts in Victoria, with indictable offences being dealt with in the County or Supreme Court.

The most important legislation in Victoria with regard to the treatment of those who have committed offences is the *Sentencing Act 1991*. This Act sets out the sentencing principles and the hierarchy of sanctions and introduced intensive correction orders as a substitute for imprisonment. In 1998, the Act was amended to introduce the combined custody and treatment order for alcohol- and drug-dependent persons. Further sentencing innovations included the confirmation of home detention as a sentencing option in 2006, after a pilot in 2004.

The Victorian government has paid particular attention to the treatment of Indigenous people, particularly since the Royal Commission into Aboriginal Deaths in custody in 1987. The report highlighted the many deficiencies in the treatment of Indigenous people by the justice system and the disproportionate over-representation of this group in Australian prisons. Some 8% of those in Victoria's adult prison population are Indigenous people, the lowest proportion in Australia. However, Indigenous imprisonment in Victoria rose by 6% in 2021, a higher rise than the population as a whole (Australian Bureau of Statistics [ABS], 2021). Koori Courts were established in 2002; they sentence Indigenous people who consent to appearing in the court and admitting the facts of the offence; this regime was extended to the County Court in 2006. The courts seek to reduce Indigenous imprisonment and to increase Indigenous engagement with an ownership of justice processes:

> Sentencing hearings in Koori courts have less formal settings and processes than in other courts. Elders and respected persons from the Koori community participate, not to make sentencing decisions but to talk with the offender about the offence and the effect it has had on the offender's family and the community. This provides a more culturally relevant and inclusive sentencing process for Indigenous people charged with certain offences. A Koori Court Officer, employed by the court, assists these courts.
>
> (Senior and Nellis, 2015)

Evaluations of Koori Courts have shown their success, particularly with regard to the successful completion of orders imposed and the reoffending rates of those sentenced (Senior and Nellis, 2015).

Other additions to the Victorian sentencing landscape have included the introduction of the drug treatment order and the Victorian Drug Court Division of the Magistrates Court in 2002 and the opening of the Neighbourhood Justice Centre in 2004. The Drug Court can sentence those pleading guilty and acknowledging a drug or alcohol problem contributing to their offending. They are then sentenced to a Drug Treatment Order, requiring participation in intensively supervised rehabilitation programs in the community. Victoria also has a Family Violence Court, with staff who are specially trained and able to hear other issues related to family violence, including parenting orders and bail applications (Magistrates Court of Victoria, 2012).

The Neighbourhood Justice Centre in Collingwood (see Box 2.4) uses a problem-solving approach to help people address the problems that have contributed to their offending.

The Drugs Courts are not the only example of provision for people with particular needs or who have committed certain types of offences. Specialist court lists operate alongside general court processes to respond to people charged with particular offences and to link them to the correct services. These lists include a Sexual Offences List, a Court Integrated Services Program (CISP) for those with health and social needs—including homelessness—that might have contributed to their offending and a Mental Health Court Liaison Service that provides court-based assessment and referral for those with mental health conditions.

> **Box 2.4**
>
> **Collingwood Neighbourhood Justice Centre**
>
> The Collingwood Neighbourhood Justice Centre (NJC), in inner-city Melbourne, seeks to work in partnership with local organisations on local justice, crime and community safety issues. It aims to address disadvantage and be proactive in responding to criminal behaviour, rather than reacting to individual acts of criminality after they have occurred. It brings together local service providers into one location. The NJC provides legal advice, victim support, housing advice counselling, alcohol and drug treatment, and support services for Aboriginal and Torres Strait Islander people. Its strategic plan sets out ambitions for expansion both in the geographical area it serves and the offences it deals with.
>
> The NJC is explicitly a community justice initiative, and it interprets community justice as including creative partnerships and problem-solving. Its community justice model is influenced by American understandings of community justice and the centre is based on an approach taken in New York. The model includes the following key elements:
>
> - Places not cases;
> - Strong communities provide the foundations for community safety;
> - Proactive, not just reactive;
> - The court—beyond traditional roles;
> - New organisational structures, not rigid hierarchies;
> - Involving citizens, not just agencies.
>
> *Source:* Information taken from the agency website, https://www.neighbourhoodjustice.vic.gov.au/.

Community corrections orders

In 2012, major changes were introduced to sentencing in Victoria. The opportunity for deferred sentencing was extended and home detention was abolished as an option for sentencing or parole. A new Community Correction Order was created, which replaced the Community Based Order, the Intensive Correction Order and the Combined Custody and Treatment Order. A CCO can be imposed by Magistrates Court or a higher court, and sets standard terms relating to the need to report, comply with directions and avoid further offending. A CCO must also contain an additional term, which may include management by a corrections officer, the completion of unpaid community work or undertaking a program of rehabilitation. The additional terms could also be restrictive ones, including curfews, staying away from named areas, electronic monitoring or the payment of a bond.

Western Australia

Alongside the traditional court structure, Western Australia has a Drugs Court in Perth, which aims to support participants in addressing drug-related problems and the lifestyle associated with them. The court operates a number of programs, both before and after sentence. Similarly, the Family Violence Court provides options for deferred sentence for family violence offenders who have pleaded guilty. People under Community Based Orders must report to a Community Corrections Officer and may have particular requirements relating to supervision or attendance at programs. A community service requirement is another sentencing option.

The rate of imprisonment for Indigenous people is high across Australia, and it increased by 5% in 2021 (Australian Bureau of Statistics [ABS], 2021). Western Australia does offer some initiatives for this group. The Indigenous Diversion Program (IDP) is specifically for people of Indigenous descent, and is available as a regional program in select locations. The Aboriginal Community Court sits as a Magistrates Court, but in a less formal setting, with Aboriginal Elders helping the magistrate. There is a focus on the use of plain language rather than legal terms, and the court is available to Indigenous people who plead guilty to offences. Another project targeted at this group is the Nyoongar Patrol (2013), an outreach service supporting Indigenous people at risk of justice sector involvement.

Western Australia has also developed the Boronia pre-release Centre for Women (WA Department of Corrective Services, 2022a). This is a low-security women's prison embedded in the community in a Perth suburb. The women live in community housing-style accommodation and are supported to reintegrate into the community. They are involved in educational and vocational activities, including voluntary work and are able to experience increased contact with their children and families.

Community justice in working with adults in Australia

Community justice is just one, relatively minor, influence among many on the treatment of adults who have committed offences in Australia. Penal populism, and the need to respond harshly to offenders for reasons of electoral popularity, is a factor in Australia just as it is in other jurisdictions. The particular history of Australia makes this punitive, exclusionary approach a central part of the national narrative. The influence of community justice can be seen, however, in particular responses to offending. Australia is unusual in now moving away from the use of electronic monitoring, something that is discussed further in Chapter 9 with regard to whether this move involves a promotion of community justice or a step away from it. Two other distinctive features of the adult offender regime that link to community justice are the use of particular courts and processes for Indigenous people and the use of tailored processes in work with other groups of people who have committed offences, particularly with regard to mental health, drugs and alcohol, and family violence.

All Australian states and territories recognise the over-representation of Indigenous groups within the criminal justice system, and all have responded to this issue by targeting initiatives at this group. All the initiatives have less formality than standard court processes, respect Indigenous traditions and have the dual intentions of protecting Indigenous communities and responding to Indigenous offending in culturally appropriate ways. However, the rate of Indigenous over-representation in the criminal justice system remains stubbornly high. Those initiatives that have strong links with the community and broader objectives beyond those directly related to criminal justice would seem to have the most chance of success. The recognition that over-representation is not merely a criminal justice issue, but one that relates to wider social disadvantage, is crucial.

The Australian states are also inclined to take creative and innovative approaches to offending that is directly related to drugs and alcohol, or to mental health. The language used for these initiatives is interesting—for example, in NSW, a rigorous drug-treatment program is referred to as 'imprisonment by way of compulsory drug treatment', even though only part of the sentence is served fully residentially. Using harsh penal language to refer to treatment approaches can be effective for introducing innovative rehabilitative measures without significant political cost, but it could alternatively be seen as a missed opportunity to make a case for community justice. Such an approach may backfire when it is realised that measures sold as punitive are not as harsh as was promised. The approach to those who have committed offences who are affected by mental illness is more directly therapeutic, but in some instances—such as Tasmania—diversion for mental health treatment is explicitly restricted to those who have committed low-level, nuisance-type offences.

The strongest examples of community justice values and principles in the response to adult offending are in Community Justice Centres and the Collingwood Neighbourhood Justice Centre. Community Justice Centres do deal with anti-social behaviour and facilitate victim–offender conferences, but they are not concerned primarily with criminal matters. The Collingwood Neighbourhood Justice Centre is more directly focused on the impact of more serious and persistent offending. It is a prominent example of a centre directly based on American concepts and practices of community justice, and is a model that could be replicated.

As in other jurisdictions, some of the most innovative approaches to community justice are targeted at young people, and the Australian approach to youth justice is considered in the next chapter.

Further reading

White and Perrone (2010) and Bull (2010) discuss the treatment of adults who have committed offences in Australia, placing the approach within a historical and cultural context. The Royal Commission into Aboriginal Deaths in Custody, and the follow-up research into its implementation and impact, offer useful insights into the treatment of this group of people and the challenges that have been faced in achieving progress over the last three decades. The websites of Correctional Services and state Departments of Justice, or equivalent, are usually good places to find up-to-date legislation and examples of programs on offer.

Practical task

Mark is a 36-year-old Indigenous Australian, married to Stacy with whom he has three children. They have lived in their current suburb, known for its high crime rate, for the past six years. Mark has been incarcerated for three years on charges of assault, drug abuse and road traffic offences. Early this year, Mark was released to re-integrate into the community. Some residents are concerned about Mark's offences. Mark is determined to rebuild his life and become a responsible community resident.

1. What strategies could Mark employ to build meaningful relationships within the community for purposes of re-integration and acceptance?
2. How best can communities support past offenders like Mark, safely integrate in their localities?
3. Why are Indigenous offenders so over-represented in the Australian adult criminal justice system, and what can be done to address these issues?
4. In your groups, discuss how aspects of community justice can be applied to improve crime in Mark's neighbourhood.

Reflective questions

2.1 It was suggested in the early part of this chapter that the history of Australia has had an influence on modern-day criminal justice policy and attitudes to people who have committed offences. Do you think this is true? If so, in what way?

2.2 Community Service Orders can be rehabilitative, punitive, reintegrative, deterrent or restorative. Which of these functions do you think they most often fulfil in Australia? Which is the most appropriate use of Community Service Orders?

2.3 Why are Indigenous people so over-represented in the Australian adult criminal justice system? What can be done about this?

3 Juvenile justice

Introduction

Sanctions and responses that are applied to adults need to be applied in a different way to young people. Even those who favour a harsh, punitive response to offending acknowledge that young people and adults should be treated in some way differently. Those who take a rehabilitative or restorative approach to offending argue strongly for differential treatment for young people and a focus on meeting their needs, rather than simply seeking to promote more and more punishment. A community justice approach that seeks to build networks of relationships around people who commit offences would be particularly keen to take this approach with young people. This chapter considers some of the wider debate that exists about young offending, and examines responses to youth crime within Australia. It discusses which approaches best meet the needs of young people, including Indigenous young people, and whether they fit with the ideals of community justice.

Treating young people differently: Welfare and justice

One of the key discourses in the argument that young people should be treated differently from adults in the criminal justice system is that of welfare versus justice. While a punitive, justice-based approach may be right for adults, children's welfare needs should be more prominent.

The welfare model associates young people who offend with others in need of care and protection from the state. In Australia, the courts have been able to use welfare approaches to respond to young people who offended, but from the 1970s to the 1990s, there was a concerted move across all states to separate welfare from justice (Cunneen, White and Richards, 2015). Internationally, the welfare approach to young people has been one of treatment, often through large institutions. However, in many jurisdictions—including the UK—the seemingly benign intentions of this approach were not enough to lead to good outcomes for young people: 'Institutions were criticized as stigmatizing, dehumanizing, expensive, brutalizing and as criminogenic rather than rehabilitative agencies' (Muncie, 2009: 274).

DOI: 10.4324/9781003193814-4

44 *Juvenile justice*

The criticism of the consequences of a welfare approach was apparent in many jurisdictions. Criticisms focused on the lack of protection for children's rights and the potential that perceived welfare needs could lead to a child receiving a longer sentence than might have been produced by a justice approach. In Australia, the impact of welfare legislation on Indigenous young people was particularly harsh (see Box 3.1). Expressed welfare concerns for individual young people linked to an approach of destroying a whole culture and way of life for the Indigenous people.

Strongly associated with the welfare approach is the principle of *doli incapax*—the idea that children do not have a full understanding of the difference between right and wrong, so cannot be held fully responsible for their offending actions. *Doli incapax* was abolished in the UK by the *Crime and Disorder Act 1998* in the climate of penal populism following the murder of toddler James Bulger by two ten-year-old boys. In Australia, *doli incapax* is a rebuttable presumption for children aged more than ten but under 14 years of age, meaning that they can be held criminally responsible for their

---

Box 3.1

The stolen generations

A series of legislative measures in Australia in the late nineteenth and early twentieth centuries was designed to prevent Indigenous young people from growing up to identify as Indigenous adults. The legislation included child-protection laws that deemed Indigenous parenting to be deficient, allowing Indigenous children to be removed from families. Indigenous children of mixed descent were placed in white Australian families and were not permitted to practise Indigenous language or culture. The Stolen Generations Inquiry found that in the 60 years of the policy, from 1910 to 1970, between one in three and one in ten Indigenous children were removed. The impact of the policy varied both geographically and across the time of its implementation. Girls were a primary focus of the policy, particularly in the early years. The *Bringing Them Home* report, produced by the National Inquiry into the Separation of Aboriginal and Torres Strait Islander Children and their Families (NISATSIC) (NISATSIC, 1997), was explicit in stating that the removal policy was contrary to international law and met the definition of genocide.

Cunneen, White and Richards (2015) note two particular consequences from this policy that affect contemporary juvenile justice in Australia. Firstly, Indigenous children continue to be over-represented in both the youth justice and the residential welfare systems. Secondly, this unjust and unaccountable policy and practice has led to continuing distrust of police, juvenile justice and welfare officials from Indigenous communities.

actions if the court accepts that they had sufficient maturity and understanding. There have been calls for change to *doli incapax* in Australia, including calls to enshrine it in legislation in every state or to reverse the burden of proof so that the young person has to show that they did not understand right from wrong. At present, *doli incapax* remains a part of the youth justice regime. Evidence from other jurisdictions shows that moves to abolish *doli incapax* usually lead to more children being drawn into the youth justice system (Cunneen, White and Richards, 2015). There is a continued campaign to raise the age of criminal responsibility across Australia, to 14, in line with international standards. In 2021, Australia's Attorney-Generals agreed to raise the age to 12 but, even if and when this implemented, that change will make little difference in most states. Campaigning group Change the Record (2022) state that 499 children aged from 10 to 14 were incarcerated in 2020, and 456 of those were aged from 12 to 14. The ACT and Tasmania have taken a lead in proposals to raise the age to 14.

Internationally, the move away from the welfare model in dealing with young people was part of the same process as the move away from rehabilitation in dealing with adults who commit offences. It was led by a desire to be seen as putting in place popular, punishment-oriented approaches as well as a perception that rehabilitative efforts were inherently ineffective. (The 'nothing works' debate is covered in Chapter 4.) The justice model places the following principles in place in the youth justice regime (Von Hirsch, 1976, cited in Muncie, 2009):

- Proportionality of the punishment to the crime so that there is a connection between offence and sentence;
- Determinacy of sentencing, so there are no more indeterminate sentences justified by a need for further treatment;
- A significant reduction in sentencer discretion;
- An end to disparities between the sentences offered to different people for similar offences;
- The protection of rights through following due process.

There are, however, still considerable overlaps between children defined as being in need of care and protection and those involved in the justice system. This is a connection that is familiar internationally (see, for example, Day, 2021). There is a need, in particular, to coordinate support for young people leaving residential care, as they are significantly over-represented in the criminal justice system (Baidawi, Mendes and Snow, 2014; see Mendes, Snow and Baidawi, 2012 for a discussion of how this issue has been addressed in Victoria). Children who have experienced the child protection system will become involved with the police earlier in life and will experience more serious criminal justice sanctions (Baidawi, 2020). Girls involved in the criminal justice system are more likely to have had an experience of child welfare, and boys involved in child welfare are more likely to go on to offend (Baidawi, Papalia and Featherston, 2021).

New public management

In Australia, the juvenile justice system contains elements of both the justice and the welfare approaches (Cunneen, White and Richards, 2015). The direction of travel, however, has been more towards a justice approach, with an increasing emphasis on accountability, responsibility and the rights of the defendant. In line with a generally increased emphasis on penal populism, the discourse of justice for young people has come to be associated simply with punishment, rather than other aspects of justice such as proportionality, protection of rights or wider social justice goals. However, as Cunneen, White and Richards (2015) argue, the debate between justice and welfare in Australia is pointless and sterile, as interventions led by welfare concerns have also resulted in harsh and unjust outcomes, especially for Indigenous young people:

> Specifically in relation to Indigenous young people, the welfare approach saw large scale social disorganisation imposed on young people and families. Far from any notion of rehabilitation, the system was deliberately and actively destructive.
>
> (Cunneen, White and Richards, 2015: 112)

Cunneen, White and Richards (2015) argue that the important issue to analyse is the practical outworking of the operation of power.

The welfare versus justice debate focuses on the higher-level goals and aspirations that should guide a juvenile justice system. In recent years the advent of New Public Management (NPM) has taken the system away from any aspiration to achieve higher goals, focusing instead on the need for effective organisation and management. In NPM, the criminal justice system is conceptualised as a way of classifying and managing groups of people who commit offences (Feeley and Simon, 1992). Effective and efficient management is not in itself problematic, but it is a replacement for the wider goals of rehabilitation, justice or punishment, and it places a considerable administrative burden on criminal justice agencies (Faulkner and Burnett, 2012).

The emphasis on NPM has a particular impact on young people in many jurisdictions, as they are the most intensely governed group in society (Muncie, 2006). Similar language and techniques as those that might be used to operate a business are now used within juvenile justice. New actuarial techniques associated with NPM include statistical prediction and preventative detention. Finding ways to predict which children might go on to offend at an early stage in their lives, from easily accessible data, remains an attractive but elusive goal (Ringland, Weatherburn and Poynton, 2015). Custody is utilised to manage people who commit offences, rather than rehabilitate or punish. These approaches have an impact on young people: they learn through their experience of juvenile justice that there is no one there to help them—they must simply look after themselves (Phoenix and Kelly, 2013).

The influence of NPM on Australian juvenile justice is seen in the increasing use of fines, infringement notices and administrative sanctions that collectively demonstrates pragmatism with an emphasis on administrative convenience (Bull, 2010). Calls for reform of juvenile justice request greater screening, early intervention and programs tailored to individuals (Weatherburn, McGrath and Bartels, 2012)—yet these too are located within managerialist discourse. Such actuarial approaches can make it acceptable to dispense with concerns about justice and due process in favour of risk-management (Smith, 2006).

Box 3.2

Young people in detention

There is surprisingly little academic literature available about the actual experience of young people in detention in Australia and how the juvenile justice centres manage this challenging group. Two recent, and very different, reports do shed some light on these centres.

Firstly, in 2013 there was an incident of significant disorder in Banksia Hill Juvenile Justice Centre in Western Australia. A group of young inmates escaped from their cells and caused extensive damage (one estimate put the damage at $1.5 million) to the centre. The subsequent inspectorate report into this incident identified problems with the management and culture of the centre, which produced a fragile facility where a major security incident was inevitable (Office of the Inspector of Custodial Services [OICS], 2013). The report recommended the management of juvenile detention be separated from that of adult detention; it also recommended greater private sector involvement in juvenile detention.

Secondly, in 2012 an Australian juvenile justice organisation commissioned a research team to investigate its use of the Detainee Behaviour Implementation Framework (DBIF) (Dadich, Stout and Hosseinzadeh, 2015). This Framework is a group of policies that ensure staff make informed decisions in managing inmate behaviour. The Framework guides decision-making in proactive, active and reactive interventions. The research highlighted the complexity involved in investigating practice within detention facilities, as data were not routinely gathered and recorded, and individual centres implemented policy in different ways. This made it difficult to establish any causal links between policy and practice. Policy implementation in juvenile justice centres is affected by the particular contextual factors within each centre.

Another consequence of this new approach to youth justice is that it is moving increasingly away from social work. Social workers do still work in juvenile justice settings, but it is rare to see a social work qualification being set as essential criteria for such a post. The curriculum standards of the Australian Association of Social Workers (AASW) for qualifying social work programs barely mention correctional settings, in contrast to the detailed stipulations for curriculum content in other fields such as child protection and mental health (AASW, 2021).

A rights-based approach to juvenile justice

The Beijing Rules for the Administration of Justice (Beijing Rules) and the United Nations Convention on the Rights of the Child (UNCRC) both encompass Australia, and there is relevant domestic human rights legislation. The Beijing Rules stipulate that children should be treated differently from adults, and that their needs should be paramount in decisions made about them. The Beijing Rules promote diversion and alternatives to custody. The UNCRC deals with children's rights more generally, and Article 40 deals directly with the rights of children in conflict with the law:

> States Parties recognize the right of every child alleged as, accused of, or recognized as having infringed the penal law to be treated in a manner consistent with the promotion of the child's sense of dignity and worth, which reinforces the child's respect for the human rights and fundamental freedoms of others and which takes into account the child's age and the desirability of promoting the child's reintegration and the child's assuming a constructive role in society.
>
> (UNCRC, Article 40)

There is no national Australian human rights legislation, but the *Human Rights Act 2004* applies to the ACT and the *Charter of Human Rights and Responsibilities Act 2006* applies to Victoria. The ACT Act sets out some specific rights for children involved in the criminal process, including that accused and convicted children must be dealt with in a way that is appropriate for a person of the child's age (Cunneen, White and Richards, 2015).

The UNCRC on its own is not enough to protect the rights of young people: states must take measures to promote diversion and reduce the use of custody (Smith, 2010). The Australian Human Rights Commission (AHRC; formerly the Human Rights and Equal Opportunity Commission, or HREOC) has published briefs on juvenile justice matters highlighting issues of general concern and relevant to particular groups, such as Indigenous young people with cognitive disabilities (Human Rights and Equal Opportunity Commission [HREOC], 2005). The Commission recommended a much greater provision of culturally appropriate diversion services, including conferencing, for this group. In a speech in 2014, AHRC member and National Children's

Commissioner Megan Mitchell called for a national approach promoting greater collaboration between agencies and more use of diversion to ensure that young people were only detained in custody as a last resort (Mitchell, 2014). Diversionary approaches are particularly important for Indigenous young people, but it can be challenging to demonstrate that approaches that clearly meet social need meet an objective standard of effectiveness. An Australian Institute of Criminology team evaluated diversionary approaches across three states but found it difficult to obtain the required data, including baseline data, to show impact. Resource constraints limited both the delivery of the program and the ability to evaluate it effectively (Stewart et al., 2014).

Legislation and policy: State and federal

Although there are regional differences across Australia in terms of the ways in which young people are dealt with in the criminal justice system, these are often differences of policy and practice; the legislation and organisational structures are similar across the country. Young people are, of course, covered by much of the same legislation as anyone else, including the legislation that sets out crimes and offences, but there are also particular processes set in place for young people. This section considers the youth justice context in each state, and begins with some general discussion of context, policy and practice in Australia.

Youth offending has declined in Australia over the last decade, with the rate of young people proceeded against by the police down 36% (Glancey, Wang and Lin, 2020). This is in line with international trends and has a consequent impact on the number of young people entering the youth justice system. The youth justice system has been the focus of considerable attention and a review of recent enquiries suggested that there were six key themes that needed to be considered in focusing on youth justice:

- Vulnerabilities and complex needs;
- Detrimental impacts of detention;
- Indigenous over-representation;
- Detention as a last resort;
- Improving youth justice detention;
- Offenders or victims first?

The age of criminal responsibility is 10 in all Australian states, and young people are dealt with by adult court at the age of 18 everywhere except Queensland, where 17-year-olds are also dealt with in adult courts. The Children's Court is the term used by most Australian jurisdictions (states and territories), with the exception of South Australia and the Northern Territory. In most jurisdictions, a judge heads the Children's Court, but in some (such as the Northern Territory) there is a Children's Magistrate. The Children's Court sits in private and deals with all summary offences. Indictable offences can be dealt with by either the Children's Court or at a higher court, and this is the choice of the young person, subject to the court's acceptance of its jurisdiction. In some states and territories, including NSW and the ACT, there are specific youth drug courts. In NSW, the Youth Drug Court specifically targets injecting drug users aged between 14 and 18.

In most cases that come to the Children's Court, a guilty plea is entered, so the court's role is that of a sentencing body. Pre-sentence reports are normally prepared in cases involving young people. The authors of these reports vary, they can be prepared by juvenile justice staff with various qualifications or by welfare officers, psychologists or even the police.

In some states, including NSW, there is an option to deal with young people who offend by way of a Youth Justice Conference as an alternative to court. This is a restorative approach that aims to involve the community in the process, meet the needs of victims and ensure that the young person takes responsibility for their behaviour. Research has found high levels of participant satisfaction in such approaches, but some evidence suggests that conferences are no more effective than Children's Courts in reducing future offending behaviour (Smith and Weatherburn, 2012a, 2012b).

Generally, the following hierarchy of options is open to the Children's Court (Cunneen et al., 2015):

- Detention, which his can include detention in a juvenile detention centre, home detention, periodic detention or weekend detention;
- Suspended detention;
- Community service and attendance centre orders;
- Probation and other supervised orders;
- A financial penalty, such as a fine, compensation or a good behaviour bond;
- Referral to a youth conferencing scheme;
- A good behaviour bond or recognisance;
- Undertaking to observe certain conditions;
- Dismissal of charges without reprimand or conviction recorded.

Courts are not the only bodies to deal with young people in the criminal justice system. The police have a role in apprehending people who have committed offences in all states, but in some states the police role goes far beyond this and includes the facilitation of conferencing and other diversion schemes. Juvenile Justice Departments are present in some form or another in every state, although there is some variation in terms of whether they are associated with justice and corrections, or welfare and community services. Social workers and other case workers in Juvenile Justice Departments play a significant role in supervising young people in the community, and this role is also supported by the work of some non-government organisations (NGOs). There have been calls for national youth justice standards across Australia, notably from the Australian Law Reform Commission (Australian Law Reform Commission [ALRC], 1997). The Australasian Juvenile Justice Administrators (AJJA) produced an agreed set of standards that all juvenile justice agencies aspire to meet (Australian Juvenile Justice Agency [AJJA], 2009).

Detention remains the most significant intervention in a young person's life available to the courts and there has been some decline in the use of sentenced detention over time, although the rates of unsentenced detention fluctuate, with no clear trend (AIHW, 2021b). On an average night in 2021, there were 819 young people in detention in Australia, with 72% of these unsentenced and 91% of them male (AIHW, 2021b). Half of all young people in detention were Indigenous young people, although these young people only make up 6% of the population: young Indigenous Australians were 20 times more likely to be in detention on an average night in June quarter 2021 (AIHW, 2021b). It is still too early to be certain of the impact of Covid-19 on detention in this time; the courts were not functioning in their usual way and there seemed to be a greater inclination to grant bail (AIHW, 2021b). The Covid-19 pandemic did provide an opportunity to reconceptualise the youth justice system in terms of public health but there are no indications that that opportunity was taken (Gordon, Klose and Storrod, 2021).

Australian Capital Territory (ACT)

The key legislation in the ACT relating to young people includes the *Bail Act 1992*, the *Children and Young People Act 2008*, the *Crimes (Restorative Justice) Act 2004*, the *Crimes (Sentence Administration) Act 2005* and the *Crimes (Sentencing) Act 2005* (AIHW, 2021a).

The ACT enacted the *Human Rights Act* in 2004 and seeks to apply it in all spheres, including in juvenile justice. The ACT government produced a blueprint for youth justice in 2012, setting out its plans for the next decade. The blueprint places a strong emphasis on a whole-of-government and whole-of-community response to youth crime. It specifically seeks to increase diversion, reduce offending and reoffending, and reduce the over-representation of Indigenous young people in the youth justice system (ACT Government, 2012). At the time of writing, however, progress seems to have stalled on proposals to raise the age of criminal responsibility to 14.

The trend in the ACT has been a decline in the already numbers and rates of young people under supervision, both in detention and in the community (AIHW, 2021a).

NSW

The main statute relating to young people who commit offences in NSW is the *Young Offenders Act 1997* and other important legislation includes the *Bail Act 2013*, the *Children (Community Service Orders) Act 1987*, the *Children (Criminal Proceedings) Act 1987*, the *Children (Detention Centres) Act 1987* and the *Children (Interstate Transfer of Offenders) Act 1988* (AIHW, 2021a). The *Young Offenders Act 1997* places diversion at the heart of a very specific tiered system, where court appearance is a last resort, after warnings, cautions and conferences. The Act has made it less likely that young people, including Indigenous young people, will receive a custodial order, and has delayed the time from first court appearance to first custodial sentence (Wan, Moore and Moffatt, 2013).

There is a central Children's Court in NSW, with dedicated magistrates based in Parramatta and Glebe, but generalist magistrates hear cases relating to young people in metropolitan and county courts.

NSW is one of two states where it is particularly difficult for young people to get bail (Cunneen, White and Richards, 2015) and almost half of young people in custody in NSW on any given day are unsentenced (AIHW, 2021a). The recent trend in NSW has been a decline in the number of young people both under community supervision and those in sentenced and unsentenced detention. The rate of Indigenous over-representation has also declined, due to the decline in Indigenous young people under supervision (AIHW, 2021b). Pacific Islander young people have also been over-represented in NSW, and report feeling vilified by police and having difficulties complying with supervision (Ravulo, 2015).

Northern Territory

The youth justice regime in the Northern Territory is governed by the *Youth Justice Act 2006* and the *Bail Act 1982* (AIHW, 2021b). The Territory government introduced the Youth Justice Legislation Amendment Bill in 2021 that strengthened bail laws, expanded prescribed offences and increased the use of electronic monitoring. It also introduced Family Responsibility Orders, giving courts the power to order families to participate in intervention such as training, counselling or programs.

The Northern Territory uses the term 'Youth Justice Court', in contrast to most jurisdictions, which use the term 'Children's Court'. In most jurisdictions, the Children's Court is headed by a judge, but the Northern Territory is one of the jurisdictions where there is a Children's Magistrate.

The Northern Territory has the highest rate of young people under supervision of any of the Australian states and territories, with 50.4 young people per 10,000 under supervision, compared with a national average of 16 per 10,000. Three-quarters of these young people are supervised in the community with the remainder in detention. The rate of Indigenous over-representation is higher than the national trend to the extent that exact rates are not possible to calculate, due to the low numbers of non-Indigenous young people under youth justice supervision (AIHW, 2021b). (See also Box 3.5.)

Queensland

Youth Justice in Queensland is governed by the *Youth Justice Act 1992*, the Youth Justice Regulation 2016, the *Young Offenders (Interstate Transfer) Act Amendment Act 1990*, the *Criminal Law (Rehabilitation of Offenders) Act 1986*, the *Criminal Code Act 1899*, the *Children's Courts Rules 2016*, the *Children's Court Act 1992* and the *Bail Act 1980*. The age of criminal responsibility is 10 in all Australian states, and young people are dealt with by adult court at the age of 18 everywhere except Queensland, where they are dealt with as adults at the age of 17 (AIHW, 2021a).

Of the young people supervised in Queensland, close to nine out of ten are supervised in the community—a higher proportion than the national average. The rates of young people under supervision have been relatively stable in recent years, but the Indigenous over-representation to is higher than the national rate (Australian Institute of Health and Welfare (AIHW), 2021). In 1992, a new model of service delivery was introduced in Queensland, known as the Youth Justice Service, but research into its operation found that it initially had no impact on recidivism (Denning and Homel, 2008).

South Australia

The main legislation in South Australia is the *Bail Act 1985*, the *Criminal Law (Sentencing) Act 1988*, the *Family and Community Services Act 1972*, the *Young Offenders Act 1993*, the *Youth Court Act 1993* and the *Youth Court Administration Act 2016* and the *Youth Justice Administration Regulations 2016* (AIHW, 2021a). South Australia uses the term 'Youth Court'.

The pattern of youth detention in South Australia is higher than the national average, with 21 per 10,000 young people under supervision and 84 per cent of those supervised in the community. The trend is also similar to that found nationally, with a decline in those under supervision in recent years (AIHW, 2021a).

Tasmania

The main statute in Tasmania is the *Youth Justice Act 1997* and other relevant legislation includes the *Bail Act 1994*, the *Children, Young Persons and Their Families Act 1997*, the *Police Offences Act 1935*, the *Sentencing Act 1997* and the *Commissioner for Children and Young People Act 2016* (AIHW, 2021a).

Tasmania has no separate Children's Court with dedicated magistrates; criminal cases relating to young people are heard in a closed hearing by the Youth Justice Division.

Tasmania is one of two states where it is particularly difficult for young people to get bail (Cunneen et al., 2015) and around half of any young people in detention on a given day are unsentenced (AIHW, 2021a). There has been a substantial fall in the rates of young people under supervision in Tasmania in recent years including among Indigenous young people (AIHW, 2021a). In June 2022, the Tasmanian government announced that it would no longer give custodial sentences to young people under the age of 14, although the age of criminal responsibility would remain at 10.

Victoria

The main statute is the *Children and Young Persons Act 2005*; other relevant legislation includes the *Bail Act 1977*, the *Crimes Act 1958* and the *Sentencing Act 1991*. In Victoria, there is a central Children's Court with dedicated magistrates, but most hearings are heard by generalist magistrates in metropolitan and county courts. Magistrates' own understanding of the Children's Court is that it is therapeutic and problem-solving, with an appropriate emphasis on rehabilitation. Magistrates would like to be more directly involved in case management (Borowski and Sheehan, 2013). Victoria also runs youth Koori Courts, an initiative that seeks to make criminal proceedings more meaningful for Indigenous defendants.

Travers (2012) found that there were different sentencing practices in different states and, despite being the only state that did not divert people to restorative conferences, Victoria was the most lenient. It has the lowest rate of imprisonment for both adults and children. A continuous period of Labor government from 1982 to 2010 developed a welfare culture and invested in programs. The difference in sentencing practices was quite striking, and cannot simply be explained by differences in the crime rate:

> In 2008, the rates of sentenced young persons per 100,000 population in detention centres were 50.1 in NSW, 47.6 in Tasmania and 14.3 in Victoria. There were also differences in the over-representation of Indigenous defendants. There was an average rate of 567 in NSW and 166.5 in Victoria.
>
> (Travers, 2012: 175)

The more recent figures reveal a similar pattern, with Victoria showing the lowest rate of young people under supervision (9 in 10,000) and the lowest rate of children in detention (1.9 per 10,000). The figures have dropped in recent years, but the rates of Indigenous over-representation have increased (AIHW, 2021a).

The legislation in Australian states is broadly similar, and the key difference that has led to a lower supervision rate in Victoria is the widespread use of deferral. Travers (2012) found that the variety of programs in Victoria allowed magistrates to try different options, and that the availability of options such as ropes courses (a form of adventure learning activity) meant that court hearings had a lighter, more informal character in Victoria. There was, however, still the potential for young people to be sent to detention—particularly by the County Court, which had fewer options, leading to harsher sentencing. The young people who were perceived as the most difficult—often those who came from the most deprived backgrounds—were sent to detention.

Western Australia

The legislation relating to young people in Western Australia includes the *Young Offenders Act 1994, the Young Offenders Regulations 1995,* the *Sentence Administration Act 2003*, the *Inspector of Custodial Services Act 2003* and the *Bail Act 1982* (AIHW, 2021).

Western Australia is the only state in Australia that retains mandatory sentencing laws for juveniles. Young people who have committed an offence of burglary, or who have assaulted a police or prison officer, can face a mandatory sentence. These sentences are controversial because, by definition, they remove discretion from sentencers, inhibiting their ability to take all relevant factors into account. They also have a particularly detrimental impact on Indigenous young people, as they constitute the group of people most likely to have accrued previous convictions. Mandatory sentences for young people conflict with international law and with human rights principles.

Western Australia has a rate of supervision that is higher than the national average at 23 per 10,000, of which 4 per 10,000 are in detention. There has been a recent decline in the numbers of young people under supervision in Western Australia, but a concomitant increase in the Indigenous over-representation (AIHW, 2021a).

Detention of young people

The numbers of young people in detention in Australia are quite small, with 819 young people in custody on any given night in the June quarter of 2021 (AIHW, 2021b). Before detention is used for young people in Australia, the court must be satisfied that there is no other option available for the young person and it must then set out the reasons for a detention order in writing. However, despite these safeguards, the rate of over-representation of Indigenous young people in detention is still a matter of great concern. The Australian Institute of Health and Welfare (AIHW) reported in 2021 that half of young people in detention were of Indigenous descent. A decline of the total of young people in detention, which has not been fully matched by a decline in Indigenous young people in detention, has led them now to be imprisoned at 20 times the rate of other young people (AIHW, 2021b). This follows a trend identified in 2011: the rate of Indigenous over-representation increases as the reduction in the use of custody for non-Indigenous young people fails to be matched in the sentencing of Indigenous young people (Richards, 2011).

Indigenous young people are over-represented in both sentenced custody and remand custody. It would be wrong, however, to see this over-representation as simply a result of sentencing decisions. The use of diversion and conferencing means that those young people who do appear in court are more likely to have committed more serious offences. Combatting the over-representation of Indigenous young people requires resources being devoted to preventative and diversionary measures. The Australian Institute of Health and Welfare (AIHW, 2012b) found that the over-representation of Indigenous young people was still severe but has been decreasing in recent years. The introduction of diversionary measures has been happening in some states. Cunneen, Russell and Schwartz (2021) recommend nine principles of diversion for Indigenous young people, starting with self-determination and the promotion of cultural safety. Large-scale research in the US found that the impact of diversion on recidivism and future employment was significantly more positive than any alternative responses (Mueller-Smith and Schnepel, 2021).

The experience of custody is not the same for all young people, and nor is it the same for all Indigenous young people. For many, the over-representation of Indigenous young people influences life in the community as well as detention itself: detention in custody is such an expected experience that it is routinised and seen as a rite of passage, a contribution to building a gang culture. Indigenous young people are also over-represented in the care setting, and young people who have been in out-of-home care have a particular experience of custody. Children who have been in care have few visitors, leading to a further degree of isolation. The vast distances in Australia can also increase the isolation of young people, particularly Indigenous young people who live in rural areas (NISATSIC, 1997). A child might be detained many hundreds of kilometres from home, so even those who do have strong family and community support find themselves isolated. This combines with the other challenges faced by young people in rural communities—such as access to education, employment opportunities, recreation and other services—to leave those young people at particular disadvantage (see Barclay, Hogg and Scott, 2007, for a wider discussion of young people, crime and rural communities). Other groups—notably girls—can find it hard to access the necessary support, as there are such small numbers of them in custodial settings. It is also the case that it can be difficult to provide services for particular groups of people, such as those who have committed sexual offences, due to their small numbers.

It has long been accepted by youth justice academics that custody is damaging to young people, to families and to the community:

> Children invariably leave prison not only more damaged but also more angry, more alienated, more expert in the ways of crime and more likely to commit more serious offences—in fact more of everything that the children themselves and the community need much less of.
> (Goldson, 2002: 159–160)

The experience of detention for young people can have some positives. It is certainly true that some young people are safer and better nourished in custody than at home. There are many committed juvenile justice staff working in detention settings and high-quality programs are delivered by those staff and by NGOs. However, the experience of youth detention is isolating and, as demonstrated by a Danish study (Bengtsson, 2012), mainly characterised by boredom. As discussed in Chapter 10, the main impact of custody on the process of desistance is to disrupt it.

Community justice and young people

Young people can be dealt with by the criminal justice system in the community in two ways: either by diversionary measures prior to conviction or as part of a community sentence following conviction. These can be the same, or similar, programs accessed in different ways. The lines between the two might be blurred; sentencers can sometimes use their discretion to suggest a form of diversion even at a late stage in the judicial process.

Diversion is set down in both the Beijing Rules and the Convention on the Rights of the Child as the preferred way of dealing with young people, rather than subjecting them to formal legal processes. It can be carried out in either a formal or an informal way. Approaches to diversion are often a key determinant of what occurs elsewhere in the system; differences in sentencing approaches can be a product of differences in attitudes to diversion. Diversionary measures can also include alternatives to remand in custody, such as those promoted by Jesuit Social Services (2013) in Victoria. Diversion is a term used in a variety of ways, often with little clarity, and can be used to justify both more and less intervention in young people's lives (see Richards, 2014b, for a discussion of the concept of diversion).

Alternatives to custody are sometimes referred to as community corrections or intermediate treatment, and follow the underlying principle that some young people can best be dealt with in a community setting, outside an institution. They are expected to provide an element of both punishment and treatment in a way that both aids rehabilitation and is cost-effective. Responses to offending in young people include fines; good behaviour bonds requiring appropriate behaviour over a specified period of time; suspended or deferred sentences where the young person is asked to do something before sentence imposition (known as a 'Griffiths remand' in NSW); community service orders; youth attendance orders requiring attendance at an activity centre; restorative justice approaches (see Chapter 5) and electronic monitoring (see Chapter 9). Queensland briefly introduced the use of boot camps (see Box 3.3). These are based on the model of the 'short sharp shock' or 'scared straight', the idea being that an early punitive response to young people who offend will deter them from committing further offences, due to fear of the consequences.

Wilderness programs are popular in Australia, and are attractive to sentencers and policy-makers, as they can be used as preventative approaches, diversion or part of a sentence. Some of these wilderness programs are culturally specific and targeted at Indigenous young people. In Tasmania the Lungtalana Project is a residential project on Lungtalana (otherwise known as Clarke Island) for Indigenous young people who participate in culturally appropriate activities. It is targeted at young people either on remand or sentenced to detention, and the assessment is carried out in partnership with the Tasmanian Aboriginal Corporation (TAC) (AIHW, 2014).

The most commonly understood community response to young people who offend is some form of community supervision order. This will often take the form of a case-management approach, with individualised plans for each young person subject to supervision. These plans will involve some direct work with the young people as well as referral to other agencies, including health, education and non-governmental organisations. Older young people are supported in their efforts to seek employment and find accommodation. Probation orders are the best-known form of community supervision, and

Box 3.3

Boot camps in Queensland

The Queensland government introduced two different types of boot camps for young people in 2013. The Early Intervention Youth Boot Camp (EIYBC) was targeted at young people who were assessed as being at high risk of long-term involvement in the criminal justice system. This model required young people to undertake a ten-day camp followed by a community integration phase, ending with another five-day camp. It is possible that this program was an appropriate intervention for some young people, although there was a risk of net-widening and bringing new groups of young people into the criminal justice system (Hutchinson and Richards, 2013)

The Sentenced Youth Boot Camp (SYBC) in Cairns targeted young people facing detention and had a number of phases, including the residential component as well as programmatic and mentoring interventions. The government stated that the needs of Indigenous young people would be met by delivering the program with cultural competence and employing culturally diverse staff.

The Queensland Government produced a summary of the evidence that informed the model (Queensland Government, 2013) and acknowledged that such camps had no success in reducing reoffending. The rationale for the camps, however, was that they sent a message to the public that youth crime was being dealt with. The government stated that boot camps were introduced because of increased community concern about youth crime rather than an actual increase in crime. Their figures show that youth crime was actually decreasing, and that young people were vulnerable to victimisation (Hutchinson and Richards, 2013: 230).

The militaristic language of boot camps is attractive to politicians (Mills and Pini, 2014) and the low cost and flexibility are attractive to policy-makers, but boot camps merely present an illusion of discipline—or a 'penal pedagogy' (Giroux, 2011)—with no effect on recidivism (Meade and Steiner, 2010). A Labor government was elected to Queensland in 2015. It abolished boot camps, describing them as an expensive failure.

they can be explained to young people as a form of support (albeit mandated by the court) rather than punishment:

> Probation provides you with support and supervision on a regular basis but does not interfere in your life too much. It is a chance for you to look at things that are getting you into trouble. Your probation worker

is there to help you change these things if you want, so that you do not end up in more trouble or in court again.

(DHS Victoria, 2014)

Concerns are sometimes expressed about how these supervised orders are used. The quality of supervision and support provided can be variable. The nature of the staff engaged in the work can also vary, and how they are trained and employed varies from state to state, as does the funding available for such programs. In addition, there is always a risk that community interventions will draw more children and young people into the system, at an earlier stage, ultimately increasing the number of young people in custody.

There is a wider acknowledgement of the need for alternatives to custodial approaches in dealing with young people than is apparent in discussions about how adults should be dealt with. Across Australia, there are imaginative responses to young people and a commitment from state governments to early intervention and to developing alternatives to custody. Even controversial punitive measures, such as the boot camps in Queensland, include some community-based programs. Other states have demonstrated commitment and creativity in developing interventions for young people, and examples of this include the Intensive Supervision Program (ISP) in NSW (see Box 3.4) and the Lungtalana project in Tasmania, along with the use of restorative justice interventions discussed in Chapter 5.

Box 3.4

Multi-Systemic Therapy and the intensive supervision program

Although a considerable proportion of work with young people is carried out on an individual basis or in groups with other young people, working with a young person within the context of their family is also a popular approach. This is in line with the Beijing Rules that emphasise the importance of family involvement in working with young people in Juvenile Justice. Research has established links between offending and family factors, including conflict, poor supervision and parents' own behaviour and attitudes (Smith, 2011). Working with families is particularly appropriate where the young person lives with their family and where there seems to be a sharing of values between the family and the worker (Trotter, 2006). Chris Trotter's (2006, 2013a) model of collaborative family work is a home-based model that builds a sense of partnership between the worker, the young person and their family.

The Intensive Supervision Program, implemented by Juvenile Justice NSW. The ISP was a licensed implementation of the American model of Multi-Systemic Therapy (MST), whereby high-risk young people are identified for a three-month intensive intervention from an ISP clinician. This clinician does work with the young person, but the main focus of their work is on the parents and the family as a whole. The clinician provides support for 24 hours a day, seven days a week, with the objective that at the end of the period the parents or caregivers will have learned new parenting skills. MST has received very positive evaluations in the USA, and in NSW it has been evaluated by NSW BOCSAR and from Western Sydney University (WSU) (Poynton and Menendez, 2015; Stout, Schraner and Dalby, 2016). Although the BOCSAR research found little immediate impact on reoffending rates from ISP, beyond what is achieved in other interventions, the WSU evaluation found that the ISP had great success in strengthening family relationships, and building capacity and resilience.

Although both the Collaborative Family Model and the ISP are positive ways of engaging young people and families, such interventions are not always experienced positively. Families can be seen as pathological and as a mechanism for enforcing social control (Smith, 2011). Research in the UK (Evans, 2012) found that where parents were required to attend parenting programs, they experienced this as punitive and reported that the program had little impact on the future behaviour of the young person involved. As such, there is a risk that parenting programs can be experienced as a form of responsibilisation—a way of passing the responsibility for offending away from the state and on to communities, individuals and, in this case, families (see Garland, 2001). Approaches that stigmatise parents and caregivers for the offending behaviour of their children are particularly inappropriate (Smith, 2011). Approaches that provide genuine support are appear to have some impact on future behaviour.

Unfortunately, it remains the case that many children do find themselves spending time in custody after offending, and that too high a proportion of these children come from Indigenous communities. Time in custody disrupts the desistance process for all groups, but this is particularly true for young people. A young person who spends time in custody will experience disruptions in their education, family and peer relationships, and possibly accommodation. The vast geographical areas of Australia can make it particularly difficult for young people in custody to maintain links with home communities while in custody, and this too has a particular impact on Indigenous groups. Promoting community justice in Australia requires more than simply offering diversion options to those considered to be low-risk offenders. It requires a continued

> **Box 3.5**
>
> **Royal commission into juvenile detention in the Northern Territory**
>
> In July 2016 the ABC program, Four Corners, broadcast a program showing the maltreatment of young people in the Don Dale Youth Detention Centre in the Northern Territory. The program showed a teenage boy being restrained, tied to a chair, wearing a spit hoods over his head. Later footage showed other children being sprayed with tear gas. The program described other mistreatment of the children detained in Don Dale, including the use of lengthy periods of solitary confinement in cells with no air conditioning or running water.
>
> The government responded to the program by establishing a Royal Commission into Juvenile Detention in the Northern Territory. The report was presented to Parliament in 2017 and was scathing in its criticism of the welfare, youth justice and detention regimes in the Northern Territory. It recommended the closure of all youth detention facilities in the Northern Territory. It recommended a much greater focus on early intervention with children and young people as well as the creation of Family Support Centres and the use of detention for young people only as a last resort. The Northern Territory Labor Government announced that it would accept the intent and direction of all the recommendations, and put in place a plan of work to implement them.

commitment to finding creative and appropriate alternatives to custody for all levels of people at all points in the criminal justice system.

Further reading

The Australian Institute of Health and Welfare (AIHW, 2021) produces factsheets on youth justice legislation, policy and statistics across Australia, covering the situation in individual states and territories. *Juvenile Justice: Youth and Crime in Australia* by Chris Cunneen, Rob White and Kelly Richards (2015), now in its fifth edition, is the definitive youth justice text in Australia.

Practical task

Daniel is 12 years old and has been getting into increasingly serious trouble at home and at school. He now rarely attends school, he ignores all instructions from his mother (he has no contact with his father) and his disruptive behaviour causes nuisance to local business owners. A series of agencies are involved with Daniel and future possible outcomes include formal involvement in the criminal justice system or a placement in out of home care.

What can be done to support Daniel? At his current age, what are the key protective factors that need to be put in place for him? What professionals and agencies should be involved?

Reflective questions

3.1 What are the potential difficulties in considering young people who offend simply as children in need of welfare support?
3.2 In what circumstances is it right for a child to be sent to custody? If a child is sentenced, what measures can be taken to ensure the minimum disruption to the positive aspects of their life?
3.3 What might make a 'wilderness program' an effective intervention as prevention, diversion or sentence?

4 Theories of offending and evidence-based practice

Introduction

In working with people who have committed offences in the community, it is important to understand some of the theoretical basis to the work as well as the research evidence and theories that inform such direct work. Neither space, nor the focus of this book, permits a comprehensive overview of all the theories of offending here, so the chapter begins with overviews of psychological, sociological and biological explanations of offending, as well as a discussion of how offending behaviour needs to be understood in terms of gender. This discussion is necessarily brief, but at the end of the chapter there is a list of suggested further reading for more detailed information. Community justice approaches rely most on sociological approaches and psychological insights, particularly where they can be applied directly to practice interventions. The second section of the chapter focuses on this applied criminology: The theoretical approaches that have most directly impacted work in the community with people who have committed offences.

Biological theories of offending

Biological explanations for offending behaviour were among the founding contributions to criminology. Early attempts to explain crime by way of dividing people into particular types are now discredited and subject to ridicule or even shame, especially with regard to any association between criminology and eugenics or social engineering (see Newburn, 2012: 133). However, the overall approach of seeking biological explanations for social behaviour has proved to be surprisingly popular and resilient. Biological explanations sit firmly within a positivist tradition, although many psychological and sociological approaches can also be classified as positivist. Positivists assume that society is generally moving forward and that social issues can be improved by scientific study.

The most famous of the early biological criminologists was Cesare Lombroso (1911), who developed a typology of different classes of individual, linking them to stages of evolution. His view was that an offender was born, not made, and that those who were biologically inferior and at an earlier stage of evolution were more likely to commit crime. Lombroso considered that female offending was unnatural, so stated that the female offender was biologically more like a man than a woman. The sexist and racist assumptions make it easy to dismiss Lombroso's theories from a distance, but they need to be understood within their historical context. They built upon scientific advances of the time, and were an attempt to bring scientific hope and optimism to work with people who committed offences and to introduce positive policies (Bradley, 2010). However, some of the racism in Lombroso's work—including that related to Indigenous Australians—still impact on criminal justice approaches today.

Since Lombroso, there have been repeated attempts to explain criminal behaviour in a biological way, including Sheldon's (1940, cited in White, Haines and Asquith, 2012) work on body types. Sheldon classified body types into three categories of physical body build linked to personality traits. The endomorph was soft and round, and likely to be relaxed; the ectomorph was thin and fragile, brainy and artistic; the mesomorph was strong, muscular, energetic and assertive. Criminals were more likely to be mesomorphs.

Recent attempts to find biological explanations for criminal behaviour have focused on genetics and the increasingly detailed and specific knowledge we have about the human genome. Research into possible genetic links to crime and anti-social behaviour is at an emerging stage, but has produced some interesting insights. Early research on genetics was based on adoptive twin studies, where twins who were genetically identical were raised in different environments. These studies provided some evidence for a genetic influence on the commission of property crime, but less evidence for any genetic influence on violent crime. They also provided evidence of the impact of environment, particularly low socio-economic conditions, on offending (Baker, Tuvblad and Raine, 2010). The relationship between genes and environment has been shown to be an indicator of anti-social behaviour, particularly in young people. The next stage of the research into genetic links to offending would be to identify a specific offending gene or genotype, and some progress has been made on this with regard to violent and aggressive behaviour in young men, such as the so-called 'warrior gene' (Gillett and Tamatea, 2012). Again, it is not just the presence of the gene that indicates aggressive behaviour; it is the combination of genetic predisposition with social circumstances and other environmental factors (Baker, Tuvblad and Raine, 2010). An undue and ill-informed focus on genetic explanations can lead to further prejudice against already marginalised groups (Gillett and Tamatea, 2012).

The attractiveness of a biological and physical explanation for crime is seen in a recent suggestion that there has been a link established between the level of lead in drinking water and violent crime. This argument relies on statistics measuring crime trends in the United States in the second half of the twentieth century. Violent crime has dropped significantly since 1990, and this cannot be explained simply by reference to demographics, economic circumstances or the impact of criminal justice interventions. Researchers have mapped data on levels of lead in petrol and paint, which was then ingested by people, and matched that map with crime data to find a strong and, in some cases, exact correlation (Drum, 2013). As always, there is a risk in over-stating or exaggerating such a link, but it does seem to be generally accepted that as ingestion of lead can contribute to health problems and to juvenile delinquency, it can also have an impact on violent crime. There are also recent concerns that young people—particularly boys—with neuro-developmental impairments are more likely to end up in the criminal justice system rather than having their needs met by appropriate support services (Hughes and Chitsabesan, 2015). All biological theories raise the question of how something physical relates to crime, which is both behavioural and socially constructed. Biological theories also generally focus on street crime and violent crime; there seems to be less inclination to seek biological explanations for white-collar or financial offending.

Psychological theories of offending

Psychological theories are becoming more and more popular, and arguably have a dominant place in how some criminal justice institutions respond to crime. Psychological theories also sit within the positivist approach, and seek to explain the behaviour of individuals—although there increasingly has been an attempt to link psychological factors to social and environmental factors. Psychological theories are associated with classicism—the idea that offenders are rational actors who make a free choice to offend (Westmarland, 2006). The emphasis on Cognitive behavioural therapy (CBT) (see Box 4.1) and programs to address offending behaviour originates from a psychological tradition of seeking explanations to criminal behaviour.

White, Haines and Asquith (2012), Hollin (2007) and Newburn (2012) identify the following different perspectives:

- *Psychoanalytical theories* analyse the conscious and unconscious mind and how development and emotional processes affect behaviour. These theories see people as inherently anti-social, so required to regulate their behaviour for the best interests of the group. These theories have had little influence on criminology, as explanations for male offending seem to contradict interpretations of female behaviour and psychoanalysis does not provide an explanation for the variation in offending behaviour across an individual's life and their ultimate desistance from crime;
- *Personality traits*, such as aggression and passivity, influence behaviour. Explanations for offending linked to personality traits originated with Hans Eysenck (1964), and suggest personality types connected to the body types, described in the previous section. Like the body types explanation, these theories tend to be over-simplistic and to over-state the differences between offenders and non-offenders;
- Those who claim a *link between intelligence and offending* focus on the seemingly strong evidence of an association between IQ and offending

Box 4.1

Cognitive behavioural therapy (CBT) and cognitive behavioural theory

The term 'cognitive behavioural' refers firstly to a particular theoretical approach to human behaviour and secondly to a series of intervention methods. It brings together a cognitive approach to change the way the individual thinks with a behavioural approach that focuses on the development of skills and techniques to change actions. CBT methods are highly influential in community justice practice (McGuire, 2007: 45).

A standard part of the rehabilitation process in many jurisdictions is work that addresses the decision-making processes of offenders through cognitive skills training. In the UK, the referral to these programs follows an assessment process based on Ross and Fabiano's (1985) cognitive theory (Newburn, 2012).

The theory behind cognitive behavioural approaches has followed the practice. It is strongly influenced by social learning theory, with an interest in cognition and some elements of Skinner's behaviourism. The terminology of cognitive behavioural theory is used most often by practitioners, and the theory is a meeting point between psychology and criminology. Programs were developed by criminal justice practitioners, particularly in the United States, and in England and Wales, based on what was perceived to lead to effective outcomes with offenders. These were often described as CBT programs, but it is not possible to give a clear definition of what cognitive behavioural theory actually is or to define the theory behind it:

A theory of cognitive behavioural therapy needs to draw on both psychology and criminology, and acknowledge both the personal and environmental factors that contribute to offending. Individual treatment programs need to be seen as part of a wider approach that also addresses the environmental factors that contribute to offending behaviour (Hollin, 2007).

Alongside questions regarding the suitability of CBT for work with offenders, there are also questions about whether it is suitable and culturally appropriate for work with Indigenous Australians. Some have suggested that it might be a promising intervention, while others—including some official guidelines—warn against the use of CBT for Indigenous people, suggesting that narrative therapy is more appropriate (Bennett-Levy et al., 2014). Eight counsellors and academics—seven of whom identify as Indigenous—from a group of Australian universities investigated the appropriateness and effectiveness of CBT with Indigenous clients (Bennett-Levy et al., 2014). They found that CBT was perceived as effective by counsellors, both as an intervention with clients and as a way of managing their own well-being. They found that the elements of CBT that made it effective with Indigenous Australians included its adaptability, pragmatism and empowering nature. The use of visual and pictorial representations was particularly welcomed by Indigenous clients. There were, however, potential adaptations to the CBT approach that would make it particularly appropriate for Indigenous clients, including being fluid to suit social and cultural situations. One suggestion was that running CBT sessions at opportunistic times, in informal settings (such as outdoors), made Indigenous people feel more comfortable (Bennett-Levy et al., 2014). It is crucial that CBT approaches with Indigenous Australians are placed within a culturally responsive context, seen as just one of the tools of a broader framework and utilised with an appreciation of the history of mental health interventions with Indigenous communities (Dudgeon and Kelly, 2014). Similarly, other communities that were over-represented in the Australian prison system, such as recent Sudanese arrivals, may need a response that goes beyond a CBT program, particularly because of the likelihood that those individuals will have had an experience of trauma (see Bartels, 2011, for an outline of crime-prevention programs for diverse communities in Australia).

behaviour (Hirschi and Hindelang, 1977, cited in Newburn, 2012), but the nature of that link remains unclear. Sociological explanations are just as able to explain this link as psychological explanations;

- *Childhood experiences* lead to patterns of personality and behaviour later in life. This approach is most associated with John Bowlby's (1951) theories of maternal deprivation and the idea that disrupted early childhood experiences can lead to problems establishing relationships later in life. Subsequent research has qualified and developed this theory and expanded it beyond just 'deprivation', showing that many childhood experiences can have an impact on later behaviour;
- As a different approach to interpretations that consider background, disposition and childhood experiences, offending has also been considered to be a *rational choice* made by people because it brings them personal gain by way of pleasure or profit (Cornish and Clarke, 1986, cited in Hollin, 2007);
- *Learning theories* see offending as similar to other human behaviour in that it is learnt. These theories originate from the behaviouralist work of

Pavlov, Skinner and others, which suggests that behaviour can be changed through experience. The 'ABC of behaviour' says that antecedents prompt behaviour, which is then followed by consequences. Sutherland's differential association, although it is a sociological approach, also influenced learning theory development. Of most application to work with people who commit offences is Bandura's social learning theory, which acknowledges that learning takes place in a social context and that we learn primarily by observing others. Social learning theory differs from strict behaviourism in that it allows the inclusion of motivation and cognition, thus providing much greater scope to develop approaches to work with people who commit offences. Interventions based on social learning theory include social skills training, social problem-solving training and victim awareness work (Hollin, 2006b);

- *Cognitive theories* have strong links with rational choice theories, and deal with the impact of thinking on the process of committing offences. These theories suggest that it is the decisions made by people that are the key to understanding their offending behaviour.

It is cognitive theories—that have most contemporary influence over work in the community with people who commit offences. As discussed in Box 4.1 above, cognitive behavioural approaches are very popular in work to address offending behaviour in many jurisdictions, and Australia is no exception in its quest to find effective approaches to addressing offending behaviour—see, for example, papers delivered to the annual BOCSAR Applied Criminology Conference, available on the BOCSAR website (Bureau of Crime Statistics and Research [BOCSAR], 2022). Psychological approaches that rely on CBT or programmatic interventions are not necessarily inconsistent with community justice, but can place an over-emphasis on individual factors rather than wider community or societal influences.

Sociological theories of offending

Sociological theories of crime are as wide-ranging as sociology itself, taking in everything from individual street crimes to broad studies of crime patterns across time and countries (Rock, 2007). It is beyond the scope of this chapter to cover all sociological perspectives in detail, but it is useful to identify some of the most dominant sociological approaches that have influenced the study of criminology:

- *Anomie*, or normlessness, is the oldest and most enduring sociological theory of offending. It is associated with the work of Emile Durkheim (1897) and Robert Merton (1938), and relates to structured tension within society—particularly when society is going through great change that leads to criminal behaviour. It influenced the development of strain theory, which focuses on the gap between aspiration and ability

to achieve economic goals; this causes frustration, leading to offending. Offenders choose illegitimate means to achieve their goals because legitimate means are not available to them;
- *Control theories* take a pessimistic view of human nature and say that people will take the opportunity to offend if they are able to do so, if it profits them to do so and if rules are not in place to prevent them from rule-breaking. Control theories pay less attention to the causes of crime and more to the steps we might take to prevent it;
- *Rational choice theory* is influenced by sociology and psychology, as well as by economics. Rational choice theorists say that offenders will commit crime when it is in their interests to do so—that is, when the rewards for offending outweigh the risks. It assumes that choices are made by people who commit offences and others on the basis of what the future might bring;
- In contrast to some theorists who see offenders as being a breed apart from the rest of the population (see, for example, the section on biological theories, above) *routine activities* theorists emphasise the similarities between people who commit offences and the rest of the population. They argue that everyday life simply gives rise to crime, particularly when there is a convergence of an opportunity to offend, a lack of scrutiny and a motivated offender;
- The *Chicago School* was interested in the makeup of the city, particularly in the 'zone of transition' that existed between the CBD and the more settled, suburban areas on the outskirts of the city. The zone of transition had the highest volatility of residents, the greatest number of immigrant groups and the highest rate of criminal, anti-social and delinquent behaviour. For those who lived there, such offending behaviour was simply a normal part of everyday life. Edwin Sutherland's (1933) work on *differential association* arose out of the Chicago School. Differential association says that an individual will become delinquent when there is an excess of definitions favourable to breaking the law, over the definitions favourable to obeying the law;
- The work of *radical criminology* was a response to some of the ways in which other criminological theories seemed to discuss control and state power without any real criticism or scrutiny of such power. Radical criminology focused on how and why some behaviours were defined as criminal and some people were defined as offenders. Radical criminology drew attention to the over-representation of particular groups—especially young, poor, black men—in the criminal justice system. It also drew attention to the crimes of the powerful and how they often received less attention from both state agencies and criminologists than crimes committed by people from lower socio-economic groups;
- One of the best-known sociological approaches to the understanding of crime is *labelling theory*. This theory, most associated with Howard Becker (1963), suggests that there are two aspects to an individual achieving

an identity as an offender: Firstly, they must commit a deviant act; and secondly, this act must be labelled as deviant and treated as an offence. Good young people can become bad young people simply by doing a few bad things, then being labelled as bad young people and continuing in that way;
- Finally, *subcultural theory* suggests that groups of offenders are neither a part of mainstream society nor entirely distinct from it, but rather are a subculture—a small part of society. Subcultures are a solution to the problems created by mainstream society, and the norms and values of these subcultures are different from those in mainstream society.

This brief introduction to sociological explanations for crime raises the question of how these theories are relevant to the work of practitioners in the criminal justice system.

Community justice practitioners might consider that some of the sociological theories are similar to the biological theories in that they do not have an obvious practical application. However, they bring benefit to practitioners by providing some explanation as to why they work so predominantly with the particular group of people they are most likely to encounter. Subcultural theory and differential association can provide explanations of why people who commit offences seem to come from particular small groups or areas, and why many of those people appear to know each other prior to their involvement with the criminal justice system. Radical theories help to explain why the makeup of a particular criminal justice practitioner's caseload might be so different from what would be expected if that group was representative of society as a whole. Some sociological theories can encourage practitioners to reflect on their own role: Are they supporting the rehabilitation of offenders or are they, paradoxically, contributing to a process that labels people—particularly young people—thus entrenching a criminal identity? Practitioners can find themselves in an uncomfortable position where they might naturally be in sympathy with the political and theoretical viewpoint taken by radical criminologists, yet they find themselves working for the state, exerting a considerable amount of social control. The promotion of community justice values can help to resolve this, as practitioners work to build community and promote social justice.

Whether the preferred explanation for offending is biological, psychological or sociological, the one fact that is in no doubt is that offending is primarily a male activity. The next section considers gender-based explanations of offending.

Gender

The links between gender and crime were drawn by Carol Smart (1976), who ensured that attention was drawn to women's experiences as both offenders and victims. Smart and those who followed her sought to increase the visibility of women within the criminal justice system and to address their invisibility in the criminological literature (Walklate, 2007). Smart's work challenged criminology to consider its underlying assumptions and raised fundamental questions about the very nature of the discipline (Walklate, 2010). It opened up a feminist interest in criminology, and Walklate has identified four particular perspectives that bring together feminism and criminology:

- *Liberal feminism* assumes that better scientific approaches are needed to bring more gendered understanding into criminology and that this can be achieved by encouraging more women to carry out criminological research and by ensuring that all research populations include women. This approach is underpinned by an assumption that all should be equal before the law and that research should uncover and then challenge discrimination;
- *Radical feminism* focuses less on societal organisation and more on men's oppression of women. Radical feminists have been most interested in the experience of women as victims—although they prefer the term 'survivor'—and have worked in areas that include rape and other sexual violence, domestic violence and child abuse;
- *Socialist feminists* have been concerned with how race, gender and class interact with each other. Writers and researchers in this group often draw on material outside criminology to find explanations of offending behaviour;
- *Postmodern feminism* celebrates diversity and difference, but has perhaps had the least direct impact on community justice of all feminist perspectives.

Kathleen Daly (2007: 232) summarises a selected set of criminological concepts that have originated in feminism and that give feminist criminology its 'distinctive signature':

- The ethic of care (discussed in detail later in the book);
- The gendered nature of the law itself and of criminal justice organisations;
- The problem of generalising from research carried out just on men and boys, to the whole population; theories of crime that were claimed to be general explanations actually just applied to men and boys;
- Connections between criminalisation and victimisation and the realisation that offenders and victims were overlapping groups. Overwhelmingly, women in prison had experienced being victims in their lives, and for some their experience of victimisation led directly to their offending behaviour;
- The recognition that pathways in and out of crime, the nature of offending and the lives that people live are all gendered. The gendered nature of pathways out of crime is discussed further in Chapter 10. Women also have particular pathways into crime; Daly provides the particular

example of women's law-breaking, whereby a 'street woman' has escaped from an abusive family situation but finds her drug-taking and other behaviour required to survive on the street being criminalised. This is only one among many pathways that women might take into crime.

Although part of the feminist perspective on criminology is to critique how little attention has been paid to questions of gender, arguably this is now less the case with regard to direct work with people who have committed offences. The work on masculinity led by feminist criminologists and the predominantly male nature of offending have had direct practice relevance (Heidensohn and Gelsthorpe, 2007: 387): 'A vital change came in asking what it is about men as men and not as working-class, not as migrants, not as under-privileged individuals but as men, that induces them to "commit crime" (Grosz, 1987)'.

Practitioners have been keen to bring in understandings of gender with regard to both victims and offenders, and to encourage offenders to reflect on how their behaviour is affected by their understanding of masculinity. For example, the Victorian government supports the 'No to Violence' campaign, which runs behaviour-change programs for male perpetrators of domestic violence. This program is explicitly based on pro-feminist principles (No to Violence, 2015). Promotion of social justice principles does require an appreciation of the prevalence and destructiveness of male violence against women. Similarly, work in the community with women who have committed offences requires an appreciation of the fact that responding to women in the criminal justice system is a consequence of failures elsewhere in the social system, and that responding to those women's needs requires a cross-departmental and multi-agency response (Carr, 2022; National Audit Office [NAO], 2022).

Rehabilitation and effective practice

Criminological understanding is important and relevant, but it has never been essential for practitioners to have detailed criminological knowledge. It is difficult to identify any criminal justice organisation, in Australia or elsewhere, that requires a criminology qualification. Criminological or other theoretical knowledge is not unimportant, but the most important thing is for practitioners have an understanding of the work that is of most use to their practice (see Nellis, 2001, for a detailed exposition of this argument in relation to probation officer training in the UK). Practitioners should have an understanding of all the approaches and possible explanations for offending described above, but it is understandable that there should be an instinctive preference in favour of psychological theories. Even if genetic and other biological explanations are fully accepted, they leave no immediately obvious way for practitioners to respond to them. Psychological explanations appear to offer most hope for change: Childhood traumas can be addressed; behaviour that was learned can be unlearned. However, sociological explanations can also influence how practitioners work with people who commit offences in the community, particularly in how they support them in responding to their environment. Understanding of gender and the constructions of masculinity have also influenced direct work that is carried out with people who commit offences, both individually and in programs.

One way of conceptualising this practice-based application of criminological theory is as applied criminology (Canton and Yates, 2008; Stout and Clamp, 2015). Applied criminology is concerned with providing a theoretical basis to those who deal with the 'real-world' problems of crime and criminal justice. It draws on both contemporary academic criminology, which seeks to explore and conceptualise crime, its causes and the responses to it in theoretical terms, and administrative criminology, which has largely become an attempt to 'implement pragmatic means of crime opportunity reduction and to manage crime through situational prevention measures' (Muncie, 1998: 4). Practitioners should engage with criminology in its applied form to compensate for some possible deficiencies in other criminological approaches. Some theoretical approaches to criminology can appear to be detached from real-world concerns and the world of practice. Administrative criminology can be uncritical, beholden to the agenda of the state and can assume that the causes of crime are irrelevant or intractable (see Young, 1988). Applied criminology stays close to practice and takes a critical approach to contemporary responses to offending. The criminology that is of most relevance to practitioners is:

> a criminology which self-consciously and deliberately explores the insights of criminology for their relevance and application to policy and practice' and which 'should have a critical edge, casting a discriminating, analytical gaze over the process of criminalisation, crime enforcement, and the criminal justice system.
>
> (Canton and Yates, 2008: 5–6)

Of most relevance to the topic of this book is the way in which criminological research has informed debates in criminal justice in relation to the topic of what should be done with people who have committed offences. Criminological research has been applied in determining what approach should be taken in effectively rehabilitating people who have committed offences, but this issue has not always been simple or straightforward.

Rehabilitation

Rehabilitation is one of the key aims of the criminal justice system, and is often discussed in counterpoint to other aims such as punishment or, increasingly, restorative justice (see Chapter 7). Rehabilitation stands in opposition to ever-increasing punishment as a response to crime (Hollin, 2006a). As a general objective, it is associated with the idea of restoration, or a return to a former status, and, most narrowly, seen as being achieved when an offender is no longer committing offences (Robinson, 2007). It is then also associated with a return of the offender to their former place within society. Peter Moskos (2011) imagines a device he terms the 'reformatron' (see Box 4.2).

The understanding of rehabilitation evolved over the years to be associated with the treatment model, individual change in individual people and the concept of something being 'done to' an offender, who is characterised as a recipient of treatment. Although treatment approaches can be distinguished from rehabilitative approaches by saying that treatment focuses on the condition but rehabilitation focuses on the person (White and Graham, 2010), the terms do tend to become conflated. As an alternative to the medical discourse, rehabilitation is also sometimes described as a right: Individuals who are punished by the state are seen as having a right to receive rehabilitative services (Robinson, 2007). This is one of the three main motivations for adopting a rehabilitative approach: Rehabilitation is promoted for rights-based reasons but also for pragmatic and fiscal reasons (White and Graham, 2010). The idea of a right to rehabilitation has proved to be a less compelling argument to policy-makers than the pragmatic question of whether it can be achieved successfully. The rise and fall of rehabilitation can be related directly to the general perception of whether attempts to rehabilitate offenders can be measured as effective (Hollin, 2006a) and since the Global Financial Crisis (GFC), fiscal reasons have also led to some shift away from expensive punitive approaches towards cheaper, community-based rehabilitative responses, even in jurisdictions such as the United States, where the unending escalation of punitiveness seemed to be inevitable.

The problems with a dependence on the rhetoric of rehabilitation were highlighted by Pat Carlen in her 2013 Eve Saville Lecture. Rehabilitation seeks to return offenders to the point where they began, but this approach does not recognise the inequities in society. Rehabilitative approaches simply return the poorest in society to where they began, and do little to address the, often far more damaging, offending of wealthy corporate criminals. Rehabilitation is only a justifiable and meaningful doctrine within a context of equality before the law and alongside a commitment to social justice (Carlen, 2013).

Box 4.2

The reformatron

Peter Moskos (2011: 22ff) imagines a perfect rehabilitation device for offenders that he calls the 'reformatron'. A convicted offender would step inside this machine and then step out three seconds later, cured of their criminal tendencies. They could then seek employment, continue their relationships and move on with their life. Moskos invites us to think about whether this would be satisfactory, and also whether it would satisfy our sense of justice. Would a response to offending that just included rehabilitation, with no element of punishment, be sufficient?

Effective practice, 'What works' and responsivity

Discussions of the effectiveness of interventions conventionally start with the notorious meta-analysis of 231 cases to assess the impact of interventions on offenders (Lipton, Martinson and Wilks, 1975) and the conclusion from that analysis that almost nothing works with offenders: 'With few and isolated exceptions, the rehabilitative efforts that have been reported so far have had no appreciable effect on recidivism' (Martinson, 1974: 24).

Robert Martinson was a prison reformer, and initially had intended that the 'nothing works' research would support his anti-custodial arguments. The research was often mischaracterised and was used for political purposes by both left and right (Miller, 1989). Mair and Burke (2012: 120) identify three significant limitations with Martinson's work:

1. It is much more cautious and equivocal in its use of language than many of the people who subsequently interpret it;
2. It relies on recidivism data as a source of data regarding whether an intervention is a success, and such data is methodologically flawed and thus of limited utility;
3. The research does not consider the practical impact of the differences in how programs are actually run—whether they are properly resourced, targeting the right people, run by trained and committed professionals and so on.

Despite its limitations, the 'nothing works' research provided an impetus for the lengthy and ongoing work of establishing what *is* effective in working with offenders. The idea that 'nothing works' had a significant impact on policy-makers and researchers, but much less of an effect on practitioners, who were able to continue with their work in the hope that it would have an impact on rehabilitating offenders (Mair and Burke, 2012) Martinson himself later retracted his 'nothing works' conclusion and accepted that some things work in some circumstances (Martinson, 1979). This has been the focus of the approach in subsequent debates: To determine what works and in what circumstances. More recent community justice work has engaged with social sciences and evaluation approaches, acknowledging the need to demonstrate effectiveness and impact in interventions (Raynor, 2018). There are, however, arguments suggesting that simply asking 'What interventions are effective?' is misdirected and reductive; it is also important to take account of offenders' rights and of the narratives that offenders themselves relate about their desistance from offending. These approaches will be considered in chapter ten. There are particular issues in Australia where local, community-based approaches, working with Indigenous peoples, will not be funded to be evaluated to a standard acceptable to government, so will struggle to be able to satisfactorily demonstrate their value (Cunneen, 2016; Stewart et al., 2014).

Over recent decades, the question of 'what works' or what is sometimes known as 'effective practice' has dominated the application of criminology to work with offenders. Mackenzie (2000) summarised the extent of knowledge by identifying that some of the approaches that worked included the following:

- Rehabilitation programs with particular characteristics;
- Incapacitating offenders who commit crime at high rates;
- Some prison-based therapeutic programs;
- Programs based on the CBT approach;
- Non-prison-based sex offender treatment programs;
- Vocational education programs in prison or other residential settings, and community employment programs.

Mackenzie also identified approaches that had consistently been shown not to work in terms of reducing reoffending. These included specific deterrence programs; interventions based solely on control or surveillance; and boot camps and other wilderness programs. Counselling approaches that were vague and unstructured also had no discernible effect on recidivism rates. Although this summary is now quite dated, it remains an accurate account of the state of the evidence.

This vein of research continues, with increasingly detailed knowledge being produced regarding what is effective in working with offenders. In Australia, the Australian Institute of Criminology's stated aim is to promote evidence-based policy and practice. State institutions publishing crime statistics include the Bureau of Crime Statistics and Research (BOCSAR) in NSW and the South Australian Office of Crime Statistics and Research (OCSAR).

In the UK, the 'What Works' or effective practice initiative was introduced nationally in the late 1990s and early 2000s, seeking to present an evidence-based framework for practice. The approaches relied on meta-analyses from the United States, which identified that cognitive behavioural programs were the best approach to take when working with offenders, but this research was less conclusive than was often claimed and was not strongly supported by non-American studies (Mair and Burke, 2012). The introduction of these programs by the UK Home Office was one of the first attempts at directing probation practice from the centre (Raynor, 2007), and such centralising approaches have dominated community justice and probation approaches in the UK in the decades since then. Most recently, the introduction of a 'Whats Works' Centre for probation research in the UK has been proposed (Sanders, Jones and Briggs, 2021).

The need to deliver interventions that were evidence-based, replicable and capable of being managed and monitored in the UK led to an emphasis on delivering programs and seeking to set up an accreditation regime for such programs. This centralised regime did lead to greater consistency and accountability, but at the cost of some flexibility and independence (Mair and Burke, 2012). The regime was based on three general principles of effective practice, known as risk–need–responsivity (RNR) (Bonta and Andrews, 2010):

- The risk principle was often expressed as 'resources should follow risk', so that those offenders who presented the highest risk of reoffending should receive the most extensive supervision, with lower-risk offenders receiving less attention;
- The needs principle stated that work with offenders should target criminogenic needs—the needs most directly related to offending behaviour;
- The responsivity principle stated that work with offenders should be able to engage them and encourage participation.

The language of effective practice and RNR is known in Australia (see Box 4.3), but rehabilitative approaches have also been discussed in the language of therapeutic jurisprudence (White and Graham, 2010). Therapeutic jurisprudence enables the legal system to focus on the underlying approaches that contribute to an individual's offending. It sees the law as being in a position to promote positive well-being and using the tools of social sciences to promote pro-social lifestyles (Freiberg, 2003). Therapeutic jurisprudence in Australia is particularly associated with problem-solving courts and drugs courts (see Chapters 2 and 3).

Box 4.3

Responsivity

Responsivity is about ensuring that interventions with people who have committed offences are delivered in a way that enables them to engage and participate (Dominey, 2007). Responsivity can be targeted in a general way by designing programs that work best with offender populations or in a specific way that engages the individual, including a focus on their particular characteristics of race, gender or religion. Responsivity is associated with motivational interviewing (discussed in detail in Chapter 12) and sometimes with learning styles. However, the frequently made assumption that offenders have an activist learning style has little foundation to it (Annison, 2006), and achieving responsivity is perhaps better done by workers who have motivational interviewing and other interpersonal skills, as well as an appreciation of the nature of discrimination and diversity (Dominey, 2007). One of the contradictions of the RNR model is that the very nature of a structured model can mitigate against responsivity, in that it can reduce opportunities to tailor interventions to the individual (White and Graham, 2010).

Community justice and evidence-based practice

Community justice approaches have fallen outside the primary attention of criminological researchers, who have focused on largely quantitative studies to determine the effectiveness of particular interventions on changing offender behaviour. These studies have been challenged and criticised on their own terms, with the argument that it is not the content of the programs that impacts on behaviour; it may simply be that the characteristics possessed by individuals who are likely to complete programs are the same as those of people who would cease offending (Hollin, 2007: 68). Completion rates are strongly linked to motivation and motivation is a crucial factor in individuals moving away from offending. Feeley and Simon (1992) identified a new penology with a focus on actuarial and efficient and effective processes that could lower our expectations of the system and become detached from traditional concerns of rehabilitation or punishment. Garland (2001: 19) went further in describing the 'all-pervasive managerialism' that affected all aspects of criminal justice and led to an economic way of reasoning replacing a social way of reasoning. Cohen's (1985) concerns were that an applied criminology could be merely technicist, and that measures ostensibly introduced to help and support an offender could simply become another mechanism of control. If community justice is to be more than merely technicist or administrative, and if it is to promote social justice, then it must address these concerns. There are a number of ways in which this has been done. Community justice is not simply interested in measurable outcomes; it is also concerned with the rights of offenders and with their own self-narratives regarding how they desist from offending, as well as with supporting them to do this.

A simple focus on the effectiveness of programs in addressing offending behaviour can lead to crime being considered a natural disorder, analogous to illness, and can leave crucial questions unexamined. For example, a simple focus on the effectiveness of interventions can ignore the fact that crime, and thus offending behaviour, are socially constructed. It can also neglect questions around the differential representation of particular groups in the criminal justice system, which link to questions of social justice.

In an Australian context, the overwhelming over-representation of Indigenous people in the criminal justice system demands a response that considers social organisation and social justice, just not an inadequate and context-free attention on individual behaviour. Although a rights-based approach has little contemporary attractiveness to policy-makers, viewing rehabilitation as a right, regardless of the effectiveness of particular interventions, can help to address this problem. Rehabilitative and therapeutic services, as well as educational and employment support, can be provided without a need to calculate their effectiveness (Rotman, 1986). Carlen (2013) has gone further, arguing that a focus on rehabilitation is a distraction from the injustices in society and in the criminal justice system. She argues that we need an inclusive social justice that reduces inequality and promotes citizenship. Community justice requires us to consider individual offenders as well as the social context in which they live, and the discourse of 'effective practice' is inadequate in facilitating us to do this. Later chapters will show how concepts of restorative justice, desistance and the Good Lives Model have more to offer with regard to promoting the values and objectives of community justice.

Further reading

The introductions to criminology in this chapter are necessarily brief but comprehensive; introductory texts on criminology are widely available. The third edition of Tim Newburn's (2017) *Criminology* covers all aspects of the criminology discipline and White, Haines and Asquith's (2017) *Crime and Criminology* covers the main issues, bringing in some Australian examples. Hayward, Maruna and Mooney's *Fifty Key Thinkers in Criminology* (2010) outlines the same main points but from a different angle, interestingly providing insights into the life and work of the criminologists as well as their theories. *The Oxford Handbook of Criminology* (Leibling, Maruna and McAra 2017) and *The Sage Handbook of Criminological Theory* (McLaughlin and Newburn, 2010) are also highly recommended for readers who wish to consider some of the criminological perspectives discussed in more detail.

Practical task

You work for a small non-governmental organisation that runs diversionary schemes for young people in the community, in partnerships with schools, religious groups and other community groups. The schemes are popular with young people and families and the organisation's work in providing positive alternatives for young people has the support of the local police. A wealthy philanthropic organisation has indicated that it is prepared to provide funding for your work but has asked you to provide evidence that the work is effective. How would you go about gathering and providing this evidence?

Reflective questions

4.1   This chapter has provided a very brief introduction to some of what criminological theory and research has to say about why people offend and what response is appropriate. Is it important for those who work with offenders to have this theoretical knowledge? Why might it be important for their practice?

4.2   Why is it important that policy and practice with offenders are based on evidence? What might be some of the dangers of an emphasis on evidence-based practice?

4.3   What new research is most needed in community justice in Australia?

5 Restorative justice

Introduction

Restorative Justice is now a central aspect of criminal justice regimes around the world and is integral to the discourse of working in the community with people who have committed offences. In fact, the terms 'restorative justice' and 'community justice' are often used interchangeably, and community justice is strongly associated with restorative justice in the minds of many people: scholars, practitioners and the public. Restorative justice is particularly important to a discussion of community justice in Australia for four reasons, which will be dealt with in turn. Firstly, Australian approaches have been central to discussions of both the recent and ancient use of restorative justice in working with people who have committed offences. Secondly, restorative justice is an important part of the regime of responding to people who have committed offences in work with both adults and young people in Australia. Thirdly, claims are made that restorative justice is an effective and culturally appropriate way of responding to offending from Indigenous people, as well as some other minority communities in Australia. Fourthly, debates about what is meant by restorative justice and what is meant by community justice often cover the same ground and address similar issues about values, so considering restorative justice assists us in considering what is meant by community justice. Restorative justice is considered to be a particularly effective way to include victims in the criminal justice system, so the chapter will conclude with a wider discussion of responses to victims. Firstly, however, it is important to consider what we mean by restorative justice.

What is restorative justice?

Restorative justice is normally presented as an alternative approach to either punitive or rehabilitative responses to offending behaviour, and its perceived strengths are contrasted against the perceived weaknesses of more traditional responses to offending. Bull (2010) presents restorative justice as one of six philosophical approaches that have influenced Australia's responses to offending; restorative justice sits alongside utilitarianism, punishment and reform, incapacitation, just deserts and managerialism. Braithwaite (2003a) warns

DOI: 10.4324/9781003193814-6

that restorative justice needs to set itself apart from the main intellectual traditions concerned with criminal justice: Criminology, jurisprudence and the philosophy of punishment. As discussed later, the tendency to contrast restorative approaches with the perceived failures of other approaches is particularly common in the discussion of responses to offending from Indigenous groups. In defining restorative justice we can consider the two different ways in which it is discussed: As a new paradigm in criminal justice and as a series of techniques particularly associated with conferencing.

The United Nations' definition of restorative justice is of a process 'in which the victim, the offender and/or any other individuals or community members affected by a crime participate actively together in the resolution of matters arising from the crime' (Centre for International Crime Prevention [United Nations] 1999: 482).

Another commonly used definition of restorative justice is Braithwaite's (1999: 5): 'restorative justice is a process in which offenders, victims, their representatives and representatives of the community come together to agree on a response to crime'. This is contrasted with the more traditional criminal justice approaches, where crime is seen as being an infringement of the law and an offence against the state, and as requiring a response where the guilty party is punished (Zehr, 1990). Daly (2016) argues that currently restorative justice can best be conceptualised as a justice mechanism, a form of practice or process.

The well-known work of Norwegian criminologist Nils Christie (1977) was particularly influential in the establishment of this understanding of restorative justice. Christie conceptualised conflicts as property and said the role of the state had often been to steal these conflicts from the parties involved; restorative justice returned the conflict to the parties who owned it. Victims and the wider community are excluded from traditional conceptions of justice, but are critical players in restorative justice.

Reintegrative shaming is a central part of restorative justice, and this involves the denouncement of the actions of the offender without the individual actually being condemned (Braithwaite, 1989). The reintegration aspect of the process places demands on the offender's family, the wider community and sometimes the victim to support the offender in demonstrating their respect for cultural norms and a willingness to put their offending behind him. Restorative justice is important in promoting desistance from offending because it provides a mechanism for managing the feelings of shame that would happen anyway. If carried out in a reintegrative way, shaming can build internal controls and develop a conscience, and can help emphasise to the person involved that, although their actions have caused harm, they are not simply identified by the act they have committed and there are people in their life who care about them:

> Restorative justice interventions are well suited to the task of managing and working constructively with the shame that all parties experience in situations of crime and conflict.
>
> (Harris and Maruna, 2008: 452)

82 *Restorative justice*

Another point of connection between restorative justice and community justice is that it has a strong commitment to a set of values. These values are often claimed to be radical and transformative (Braithwaite, 2003b), and to target the promotion of justice and the good in society. Braithwaite (2003b) divides restorative values into three groups. Constraining values include non-domination, empowerment, honouring a specific limit on sanctions, respectful listening, accountability and respect for fundamental human rights. The values in the second group—such as the prevention of future crime—are not essential, but should be encouraged. The values in the third group are defined as emergent properties and may arise naturally from the restorative process. They include remorse, apology, censure, forgiveness and mercy.

Restorative justice has been particularly attractive to countries with large Indigenous populations, such as Canada and New Zealand, and nations that have undergone significant political transition, such as South Africa and Northern Ireland (see Clamp, 2008; O'Mahony, Doak and Clamp, 2012). Debates around community are particularly important for transitional societies, in that they allow questioning of the state's monopoly on power and justice. This allows a bridging of the gap between the community and the state, empowerment of communities and increased tolerance and respect (Clamp, 2014). However, the community should not always be assumed to necessarily be a positive or benign influence. Restorative justice can be a way of responsibilising particular communities—especially Indigenous communities—and emphasising that it is up to them to deal with their own social problems (see Richards, 2014a, for a discussion of the understanding of community in restorative justice).

Advocates of restorative justice call for its use beyond the realms of responses to offending and speak of its potential to have a transformative systemic and cultural impact on social and political systems (AARJ, 2020). Newburn (2012) identifies five ways in which restorative justice can operate in practice (see also Crawford and Newburn, 2003; Dignan, 2005):

- Court-based restitutive and reparative measures;
- Victim–offender mediation;
- Conferencing;
- Healing and sentencing circles;
- Citizens' panels and community boards.

Origins of restorative justice: Part of Australian history?

The roots of restorative justice can be found in places including abolitionist campaigns, religious influences, communitarianism and connections to Indigenous cultures. The connection between restorative justice and Indigenous cultures has been an important aspect of the development of restorative approaches in Australia, as well as in New Zealand and Canada (Cunneen, 2006). However, these connections are often drawn for rhetorical purposes without any strong evidence to give the claims a historical or factual basis (Cunneen, 2002, 2007). One aspect of the case made to support restorative approaches is the claim that they are traditional and Indigenous, but the search for these traditions has led to over-simplification of Indigenous groups and cultures. The most obvious point to make is that traditions are not simply restorative because they are linked with Indigenous groups—there are Indigenous people living in 70 countries across all continents, and they are associated with a wide variety of justice responses (Cunneen, 2007), not all of which could be described as restorative and many of which have strong retributive and exclusionary elements:

> Indigenous sanctions might include temporary or permanent exile, withdrawal and separation within the community, public shaming of the individual and restitution by the offender and/or his or her kin. Some sanctions may involve physical punishment such as beating or spearing.
> (Cunneen, 2007: 115)

Less contentiously, it is accepted that Australia and New Zealand led the modern introduction of restorative justice, initially through the New Zealand introduction of the *Children, Young Persons and Their Families Act* in 1989. This was the same year as the publication of Braithwaite's (1989) work on reintegrative shaming and together these two initiatives led to the introduction of what became known as the Wagga Wagga model of police-led restorative cautioning in the regional city of Wagga Wagga in NSW (Daly, 2001; Hoyle and Zedner, 2007; Moore and O'Connell, 2003).

Weitekamp (2003) provides an account of the history of restorative justice in non-state societies and includes a discussion of Indigenous societies. Indigenous groups originally formed peaceful, nomadic, ecologically balanced societies with strong family and tribal orientations. White settlers destroyed this lifestyle and culture, and Indigenous groups were forcibly resettled. The criminal justice system was part of this new imposed culture, and was rejected because its formality emphasised process and punishment rather than reconciliation. The geographical and cultural challenges of imposing a Western model of criminal justice on Indigenous communities were an additional problem:

> Imprisonment is not a deterrent and once they are released on parole they cannot be supervised because of the difficult topographical conditions in which they live ... the new approach of the Australian government is to let the Aborigines handle their own problems because all the programs—and there have been many—it has imposed have failed miserably.
> (Weitekamp, 2003: 113)

Origin myths are very important in the promotion of restorative justice, as they allow advocates of this approach to claim that it is consistent with Indigenous justice. They can then go on to claim that they are reclaiming justice from state-sponsored retributivists (Daly, 2003b). These claims are problematic, however, as are the exaggerated claims of success and transformation that are sometimes expressed by restorative justice advocates. Daly argues that to make the claim that restorative justice is rooted in Indigenous justice practice is to take a white-centric view of the world. Daly (2003b) likens some of these origin and outcome claims to a house-builder selling fictional perfect homes; it is more honest and more realistic to base the case for restorative justice on a true account of history and real outcomes from real cases. Daly outlines the four well-known myths of restorative justice that are still evident in some of the way that it is promoted today: That it is the opposite of retributive justice; that it uses Indigenous practices; that it is a feminine, caring approach and that it can produce major change in individuals. At worst, restorative justice advocates can use the Indigenous roots of restorative justice as a selling point, making the interventions more marketable and effectively appropriating Indigenous practices and traditions for policy or financial benefit (see Tauri, 2014).

A more realistic conception of restorative justice is as fragmented justice, bringing together elements of Indigenous justice systems with the more contemporary Western approaches.

Restorative justice in contemporary Australia

Restorative justice has been adopted in each of the Australian states and territories, and Australia is described as a 'world leader in restorative justice' (Maxwell and Hayes, 2007: 524).

Australian Capital Territory

In the ACT, conferencing first began as a police-run scheme in 1994, influenced by Braithwaite's (1989) reintegrative shaming. Both the police and civilians run conferences in the ACT. The research there has shown some lower reoffending rates than for other responses for the particular group of young people who have committed violent offences. Offenders who experienced conferences felt that they were able to make it up to society.

The Canberra Reintegrative Shaming Experiments (RISE) were one of the early restorative approaches and were the subject of considerable interest and research attention (Kurki, 2003). It was found that victims were satisfied, but that victims of violent crime were less satisfied than victims of property crime. A two-year follow-up of young people after the RISE program looked at measures including school completion rates, unemployment, homelessness, divorce, financial problems and serious troubles with others. The results showed few differences between the group of offenders who had undergone a conference and a comparable group of people who had gone through the court process.

Research on RISE found that material compensation was quite rare, but victims said that material restoration was not of primary importance; it was more crucial to them to give an account of how they had been affected by the offence. Some 90% of victims thought that apologies were necessary, and these were present in 82% of conferences but virtually never in court proceedings (Strang, 2003). Victims were also more likely to judge an apology as sincere when it came in a conference, rather than when it was ordered by a court (Strang, 2003).

Braithwaite (2003a) posits three hypotheses to determine whether restorative justice works better than existing criminal justice practices:

1 It better restores and satisfies victims;
2 It better restores and satisfies offenders;
3 It better restores and satisfies communities.

He uses the research from RISE to show that there is very high approval from victims—albeit less high than the approval rates from other participants in the process. Victims believe that restorative justice processes are better at delivering both fairness and satisfaction than non-restorative processes (see also Strang, 2002, 2004).

The details of the process and delivery of restorative justice is very important for victims; they are much less satisfied when conferences are organised and then fall through, or when they have to go both to court and then to a conference. These flaws in process were evident in some of the early work in Canberra, but this was an early, first-level program and subsequent Australian programs have learned from early mistakes (Braithwaite, 2003a). Successful restorative justice conferences contain emotional power: they provide a safe place for emotions to be expressed. Strang (2004) suggests that it is the additional emotional power of conferences concerning offences of violence that influence the lower reoffending rates related to such instances. Later research identified that it was the emotional intensity of the interactions that could distinguish successful conference interventions from less successful conferences (Rossner, 2014).

People who have committed offences also report that the process is fairer and more just than the court process, but there is no strong evidence that restorative justice approaches have a positive impact on reoffending rates (see Box 5.1). This is clearly an important measure for the criminal justice system, but it is important for individual victims too. Research into RISE (Strang, 2004) found that the most frequently discussed justice principle at conferences was the prevention of future offending. Braithwaite (2003a) argues that it would be a mistake simply to measure reoffending rates of restorative justice approaches against the rates from traditional court approaches; it would be more productive to simply take the best aspects of restorative justice and combine them with the best aspects of rehabilitative practice.

The *Crimes (Restorative Justice) Act 2004* has the widest scope of all pieces of Australian restorative justice legislation. It allows less serious offences to be dealt with by restorative justice as diversion, but requires more serious offences to go through criminal proceedings, although the scope of what can be dealt with as restorative justice has expanded in its years of operation. The first phase,

Box 5.1

Is restorative justice effective in promoting rehabilitation?

Although the research shows that victims are generally satisfied with restorative justice interventions, the impact on offenders is more variable. An important factor in holding offenders accountable is to ensure that plans made are followed through. The impact of conferences on reoffending rates is inconsistent, demographic factors remain the most predictive in determining reoffending rates (Maxwell, Morris and Hayes, 2008). Kathleen Daly has found in a number of studies that some elements of restorative justice conferencing are associated with a reduction in crime and that conferencing, at worst, does not increase a risk of reoffending (Hayes and Daly, 2003; Daly et al., 2013). More recent research by BOCSAR in NSW matched offenders sentenced to the restorative justice-based Forum Sentencing with those who would have been eligible for Forum Sentencing but who had been convicted in a court where Forum Sentencing was not operating. They were then followed up for a minimum of six months after the finalisation of the offence. The study found no evidence that those who were sentenced to Forum Sentencing were less likely to reoffend (Poynton, 2013).

Research into the impact of conference on reoffending needs to conceptualise the intervention as a pathway, not a treatment event; a restorative conference is usually preceded by an acknowledgement of responsibility and then followed by some sort of treatment program (Daly et al., 2013). 'The honest answer to the reoffending question is, "we'll probably never know" because the amount of money would be exorbitant and research methods using experimental designs judged too risky in an ethical and political sense' (Daly, 2003a, 2003b: 376).

introduced in 2004, deals with young people and less serious offences. The more radical second phase expanded the scheme to adults who have committed offences, and offences including sexual offences and family violence, and came into operation in 2016. The inclusion of referrals for family violence and sexual was provided for in the third phase, that commenced on November 1, 2018.

NSW

Wagga Wagga in NSW became well known worldwide as the birthplace of the police-led Wagga Wagga model (Moore and O'Connell, 2003). A statutory scheme based on the New Zealand model was introduced in 1998, and conferences were made available throughout NSW. Research into conferencing in NSW found that a large proportion of victims, offenders and supporters classified the procedures as fair. Some early research found that conferencing resulted in a 15 to 20% reduction in the estimated reoffending rate (Luke and Lind, 2002). The Wagga Wagga model is quite a formal, scripted process, led by the police. Reintegrative shaming is a central part of the Wagga Wagga model (Newburn, 2012). The Wagga Wagga model is associated with a high degree of victim satisfaction: over 90% of victims in NSW were satisfied by their experience of a conference (McCold and Wachtel, 2002). The scheme only dealt with juveniles, and exclusively with certain sorts of people who have committed offences. The conferences were soon renamed 'community accountability conferences'.

The New Zealand model, which does not have police leadership, has a less explicit focus on shaming (Young, 2002). The police are not always successful in preventing the shaming being focused on the character of the person who has committed the offence. However, participants have no complaints about the police role: They find the police to be friendly and fair and do not perceive police facilitation to be problematic or illegitimate (Young, 2002).

In NSW, restorative conferences are on offer to young people for the same offences for which they might receive a caution under the *Young Offenders Act 1997*, but they are not designed for people who have committed first-time, minor offences (Larsen, 2014). In contrast to earlier research, an evaluation by BOCSAR in 2012 found that conferences had no significant impact on reoffending rates (Smith and Weatherburn, 2012a, 2012b). Forum sentencing is available for all adults in NSW. More recent research into post-sentence RJ in NSW has identified the skill of the facilitator as a key factor in achieving great conferences (Bolitho and Bruce, 2017).

The Northern Territory

In the Northern Territory, the court established conferencing for young people who committed offences as an alternative to custody in 1999, but it was only made available to a very narrow group of young people: second-time property offenders. The Northern Territory also has a pre-court diversion scheme for non-serious young offenders, which has been in existence since August 2000. Research in the Northern Territory found a high level of satisfaction with restorative approaches and also found that they did have some impact on reoffending rates (Wilczynski et al., 2004). Youth Justice Conferences are available both pre-trial and post-trial under the *Youth Justice Act 2005*. The *Youth Justice Amendment Bill 2021* introduced Family Responsibility Agreements giving courts the power to order families of young people who offended to participate in conferences.

Queensland

In Queensland, the New Zealand model was trialled in 1997 before conference services were expanded throughout the state in 2002. Research showed very high levels of satisfaction with the outcomes of conferences and a general impression of fair treatment, but the reoffending data were more mixed and were associated with offender characteristics. The Justice Mediation Program made conferencing available for adults in Queensland, primarily in relation to less serious offences and for those adults with little or no criminal history (Larsen, 2014). The use of conferencing in Queensland has been influenced by the changes in government and other political considerations and it remains an underutilised aspect of the youth justice regime (Price et al., 2022).

South Australia

South Australia was the first Australian jurisdiction to implement a statutory conferencing scheme. It adopted the New Zealand model where conferences were run and managed by professionals other than the police. As an early adopter of restorative approaches, South Australia attracted considerable research attention (Daly, 2003a) and the researchers found that most participants considered conferences to be procedurally fair. There was some potential to reduce reoffending, but less evidence of 'restoration': the positive movement between victims and offenders. There were some gaps between the ideals and the practice, and young people did not always know their rights, nor did they fully understand the consequences of non-participation. Offenders were generally compliant with the agreements made, but this was not always perceived as reparative by victims. The conference process itself did reduce the anger and fear of victims, and reoffending was less likely in circumstances when those who had committed the offences felt genuinely remorseful. The detailed research into the approach in South Australia Juvenile Justice (SAJJ) at an early stage in the advance of restorative justice was instructive in bringing some more realism into the discussions (Daly, 2003b: 234): 'The nirvana story of restorative justice helps us to imagine what is possible but should not be used as the benchmark for what is practical and achievable'.

South Australia has also piloted the use of adult restorative programs, and research into the findings found that victims valued such approaches (Halsey, Goldsmith and Bamford, 2015). The program did not continue beyond the pilot (Larsen, 2014). Restorative justice is used predominantly with young people in Australia, but using restorative justice approaches with adults is also important to meet the needs of victims.

Tasmania

Tasmania has had a police-run scheme since 1994 and conferencing is one of the options available under the *Youth Justice Act 1997*. Since 2000, this has been a dual system with police using the conferencing scheme to administer formal cautioning and the Department of Health and Human Services (DHHS) also conducting conferences following a police referral.

Victoria

Victoria was the last state in Australia to introduce statutory restorative justice, and initial developments were led outside the state sector. Anglicare Victoria commenced a group conferencing program in 1995. The research into this scheme was consistent with the findings across the other states in that all participants reported satisfaction; young offenders said that the conference had a positive impact upon them; and victims felt that they had been helped and healed. Restorative justice is available for juveniles and governed by the Victorian *Children, Youth and Families Act 2005* and the *Courts Legislation (Neighbourhood Justice Centre) Act 2006*.

The Koori Courts in Victoria are an example of what is sometimes described as a restorative approach. They have been developed in partnership with Indigenous groups and do seem to meet the needs of those groups (Spivakovsky, 2013). The Koori Court sits alongside the Drug Court and the Family Violence Court as a specialised Magistrates Court, as the lowest court in the jurisdiction. However, Koori Courts have a different perspective to drug and family violence courts that still place the law in the role of the therapeutic agent in proceedings and provide little role for the community. Koori Courts have opened up the traditional legal spaces to Indigenous communities.

Koori Courts were established following the Royal Commission into Aboriginal Deaths in Custody (RCDIADIC), which was set up following the deaths of 99 Indigenous people in custody over the space of a decade. The development of these courts specifically addresses the objective of preventing Koori people from having contact with the upper levels of the justice system. The most important initiative of the Koori Courts was to have local Elders sitting in the courts and this has changed the dynamic of the proceedings in three key ways (Spivakovsky, 2013):

1 The offender is seen as a member of the community, not simply a carrier of risk;
2 The Koori community is not seen as simply either vulnerable or dangerous, but as being able to address problematic behaviour in its own community;
3 The formal justice system is not the dominant force, but one voice among many.

The pilot of the two courts found decreased recidivism, and this led to the development of a further five courts. The emphasis was on participation and on the process of conversation, discussion and agreement that can take place between the various stakeholders. Spivakovsky (2013) highlights that one important characteristic in the Koori Courts was in the way they were set up: it was not the arguments of restorative justice advocates that led to their development; it was the influence of outside forces that created the political will to force action and to lead to different conception of the very nature of justice:

> All Victorian practices present the Koori offender as being an inseparable part of the Koori community, and as needing to be reminded that they have a particular role to play in the history of their community. All Victorian practices present the Koori community as capable of contributing to the direction of outcomes for Koori offenders. Finally, all Victorian practices present the formal elements of the justice system as needing to be reduced from the role of sole authority on justice, to just one voice amongst many in a conversation about achieving and delivering justice for Koori people.
> (Spivakovsky, 2013: 473)

Conceptualising Koori Courts as a restorative intervention is not universally accepted, with some scholars (Marchetti and Daly, 2007; Marchetti, 2010) suggesting it is better to consider Koori Courts on their own terms, rather than try to include them in a perhaps unsuitable framework. Koori Courts depart from restorative justice in their primary focus on the offender and in their concern about wider relationships between Indigenous communities and the criminal justice system, rather than simply the present offence.

Western Australia

The proclamation of the *Young Offenders Act 1994* in Western Australia led to the introduction of conferencing. Conferences are convened by Juvenile Justice Teams (JJTs) and young people can be referred as a diversion from court proceedings. The majority of young people who went through the process reported fairness and satisfaction. As in South Australia, conferencing with adults was piloted in Western Australia but, despite positive results, was not introduced beyond the pilot (Larsen, 2014).

Victims of crime

Restorative justice has a concern for victims' rights and needs, but as Hoyle and Zedner (2007) point out in their review of victims' developments, the ascendancy of restorative justice is only one of the changes that has affected victims and brought them to the centre of the criminal justice system. The increased profile given to the victim in criminal justice debates is described as one of the greatest changes in criminal justice in Australia in recent decades (Finnane, 1997; Bull, 2010). However, despite the increased attention paid by both policy-makers and academics to victims' issues, the concept of the victim remains a contested one, and some prefer the use of the term 'survivor'. In public discussions, the figure of the victim is still dominated by the stereotype 'the weak, respectable and innocent party harmed by the big, bad stranger' (Hoyle and Zedner, 2007: 464).

Restorative justice approaches can be appropriate when the dynamics between offender and victim are complex, such as in situations where sons have assaulted mothers. Although no justice processes can fully address the issues in such complex cases, restorative conferencing can have the advantage of ensuring that the victim is heard, as well as the benefit of spending time on the case (Daly and Nancarrow, 2009).

Attention to victims can promote a punitive approach, placing the needs of victims and offenders in opposition to each other and seeming to support victims by 'balancing' the system. Alternatively, there can be a concentration on the provision of emotional and practical support. The most influential of the relevant international instruments is the United Nations Declaration of Basic Principles of Justice for Victims of Crime and Abuse of Power (1985), even though its provisions are not legally binding. The Declaration's principles include access to justice, provision of information, fair treatment and assistance with both formal and informal procedures. This has led in some jurisdictions to victims' charters and victim impact statements, but it can raise an expectation that victims should be treated as consumers and that they might be entitled to a greater influence than they actually possess (see Stout and Clamp, 2015, for a further discussion of this). In Australian restorative justice approaches, the inclusive experience that many victims report is not shared by all, a large number of victims still do not attend (see Maxwell, 2008, for a discussion of this).

Does restorative justice meet the needs of Indigenous groups?

Like the claims about restorative justice having roots in Indigenous practices, restorative justice has also been claimed to have had success in meeting the needs of Indigenous people in contemporary Australia. It is seen to be a more appropriate response than traditional criminal justice approaches. These claims have two aspects (Braithwaite, 2003a). Western traditions should not be considered legitimate because of their historical misuse in Australia and the impact of these approaches is particularly onerous for Indigenous people.

There is considerable optimism about the benefits restorative justice might bring in Australia. Restorative justice has the potential to open up the sentencing process beyond the dominance of professionals and encourage community representative involvement. This is particularly important for Indigenous communities:

> Importantly, restorative justice provides an avenue for opening up the justice system to greater indigenous control. It is an opportunity to reconfigure the justice system with different values, different processes and different sets of accountability.
>
> (Cunneen, 2007: 123)

Examples are available of this greater involvement being encouraged and facilitated, including the introduction of Indigenous courts (such as Murri Courts in Queensland) and the use of circle sentencing for Indigenous offenders in NSW. These courts promote the empowerment of Indigenous communities, bring Elders into the decision-making process and are based on the fundamental premise that it is the community that holds the key to changing attitudes and providing solutions. It should not be assumed, however, that the introduction of such courts provides the whole solution; there is no agreed consensus on what constitutes lawful and right behaviour, so international human rights standards need to be drawn on whenever there is a conflict between state and Indigenous systems (Cunneen, 2007).

Family Group Conferences and other Australian restorative justice approaches have not always had good outcomes for Indigenous young people (Cunneen, 2007), who might be risk-assessed as likely to reoffend, leading them to receive harsh responses and causing them to be excluded from restorative justice approaches while non-Indigenous young people have restorative justice options. If restorative justice is used as diversion and Indigenous young people are less likely to be diverted than other young people, then a focus on restorative justice might even be detrimental to the interests of Indigenous young people. Restorative justice sits within a criminal justice system that is not always perceived as legitimate by Indigenous people, and it is just one of an array of criminal justice options from a varying range of perspectives that are seen as mutually incoherent and contradictory (Cunneen, 2007). Conferencing has offered a hybrid approach, in which the New Zealand system was introduced, but with important aspects not included, such as the initial and ongoing consultation with Indigenous groups:

> provisions in existing or proposed legislation which stipulate that conferencing should be 'culturally appropriate' are nothing more than tokenism if there is no framework provided for significant Indigenous input or control over the form and substance of conferences.
>
> (Cunneen, 1997: 347)

It is also important that Indigenous ways of communicating are taken into account in the running of conferences to ensure that Indigenous young people are fully able to participate in the discussion. The ability to use oral language competently is an important factor in the ability of young people to participate in restorative justice conferences (see Hayes and Snow, 2013). The role of the police was also not given full consideration when the conferencing model was introduced to Australia: Police powers were not reduced and attention was not paid to concerns about the police role in the dispossession of Indigenous communities or the mistrust between the two groups (Blagg, 1997). Blagg's concern was that the element of shaming had enthusiastically been adopted by the police, without any engagement with the wider aspects of the Māori conferencing experience of reflection on the nature of police power.

The United Nations Draft Declaration on the Rights of Indigenous people is an important reference point in discussing the use and relevance of restorative justice processes in working with Indigenous groups in Australia (Cunneen, 2004). It should not simply be assumed that restorative justice processes are appropriate for Indigenous groups; there needs to be a determined attempt to promote human rights through the use of restorative justice. The right to self-determination is particularly important, yet it is often ignored in restorative justice processes. Other critical aspects of using restorative justice with Indigenous groups are the role of the state, the role of the police and the place of restorative justice within a criminal justice system where the assessment of risk and imposition of sanctions are central; assessment tools used to determine risk are often detrimental to Indigenous young people (Cunneen, 2004). The relationship between restorative justice and decolonisation is fundamental (Cunneen, 2002).

The key distinguishing factor between a restorative approach and an Indigenous approach is that a justice approach cannot be truly considered to be an Indigenous approach unless members of the Indigenous group have some power over the decision-making process (Bull, 2010). In Australia, restorative approaches are diverse and, if utilised properly, can respond in a creative and culturally appropriate way to offenders from an Indigenous background, and can link offenders to local Indigenous support workers. However, there are risks involved in setting up such a two-tier justice system, and referring offenders to different systems, depending on their background and on where in Australia they live.

Cunneen (2008) emphasises the importance of a consideration of history in determining the impact of restorative justice on Indigenous communities. From the late 1900s to the mid-1960s, a large number of Indigenous children were raised in institutions and by foster parents in Australia, as part of a policy influenced by ideas of eugenics, assimilation and the absorption of mixed race children (see De Vries et al., 2012, and Box 3.1 in Chapter 3 for a personal account of this experience). The policy breached international obligations on racial discrimination and the Stolen Generations Inquiry in May 1997 determined that basic safeguards had been set aside in the treatment of Indigenous children (NISATSIC, 1997). A restorative approach could have helped to repair relationships, and the acknowledgement of truth is an important first step in this. However, the Australian government, in contrast to approaches taken in Canada and South Africa, ruled out the possibility of compensation even before the process began, and this meant that the ability to address the harm caused was limited (Cunneen, 2008). The experience demonstrates that when utilising restorative justice to work in Indigenous communities, the work must not simply be restricted to narrow conceptions of individual crime. Hakiaha (2004), writing about the Māori in New Zealand, argues that the need to resolve the history of relations between the communities means that Indigenous communities should be given the right to pursue an independent or parallel justice system. The same argument could be applied to Indigenous groups in Australia.

Restorative justice and community justice

The links between restorative and community justice centre on the role and understanding of community and how it can be involved in the justice process. Restorative and community justice have common roots in a clear dissatisfaction with the existing criminal justice system and a desire to soften and humanise it (Clear, 2008; Richards, 2014b). Both are seen as a new lens, through which crime can be seen in a different way (Zehr, 1990; Bazemore and Schiff, 2001). Restorative justice starts from a concern about victims and seeks to move away from the conception of a victim as just someone seeking vengeance. Community justice is concerned about what is happening in and to communities. There are differences of emphasis, with restorative justice seeking to restore an individual and to make right a specific victim, and community justice seeking to restore a whole community. It is this interest in the community as a whole that brings restorative and community justice together. Following Daly (2016), RJ can be seen as a mechanism by which community justice objectives could be achieved.

The popularity of restorative justice can be linked directly to a desire for community life and social unity, even though most offending does not take place in a neighbourhood community-like setting (Walgrave, 2002). The interdependence of relationships within a community is central to the need to produce justice responses, and shaming can only be reintegrative if it takes places within the context of a community that cares about the offender (Braithwaite, 1989). Community justice can help restorative justice to think about these communities and the contexts in which specific victims and offenders live. That some of these environments can barely be described as a community should be seen as an argument in favour of a community justice approach, not against it (Christie, 1977). Shared values of respect, solidarity and responsibility connect community and restorative justice (Walgrave, 2002), and restorative justice does have the potential to build or create community and to bring people together who had not previously been in contact (McCold and Wachtel, 2002). For restorative justice to achieve this, it must move beyond considering the micro-community (those directly impacted by the offence) to looking at the wider macro-community, which has wider concerns about future safety and the prevention of recidivism (McCold, 2004). Restorative justice can play an important part as a pathway to desistance, particularly by allowing offenders to acknowledge wrongdoing and state a public intention to change their behaviour; however, it should not, in isolation, be expected to lead to an immediate cessation of offending.

Debates over the role of criminal justice professionals also provide a link between restorative and community justice, both emphasising the need for some deprofessionalisation, the minimal role of state officials and real encounters between real people (Christie, 1977; McCold and Wachtel, 2003). There is a risk of co-option and of restorative justice approaches simply using community language to extend state power (Cunneen, 2002, following Cohen, 1985). Marchetti's work (Marchetti and Daly, 2007; Marchetti, 2010) also provides a warning that restorative justice advocates can sometimes claim a restorative justice connection from interventions that can more accurately be explained and understood on different terms. However, if professionals are to be involved, they should have the most appropriate background and training. Psychology and particularly social work cover reintegrative concepts and a participatory training approach, while giving trainees input into curriculum design promotes community involvement (Braithwaite, 2003a). If it is accepted that RJ facilitation is a highly skilled role (Bolitho and Bruce, 2017), then it is appropriate to suggest that this work be carried out by trained professionals.

Restorative justice has not yet had the radical, transformative impact on Australian criminal justice that some had expected. Much of the Australian restorative justice literature focuses on early projects and on the pioneering work in restorative justice carried out in the 1990s and Spivakovsky (2013) argues that there has been little development or expansion of restorative justice since that early period. In particular, there has been little expansion into other arenas of the criminal justice system, restorative justice is still seen as an approach suitable for young first-time offenders. This is partly due to the different paradigms and philosophical positions in criminal justice debates: Restorative justice has a very different conception of the offender, the state and the community than that expressed in rehabilitative or risk-management paradigms (Spivakovsky, 2013). Some remain hopeful of a further expansion of restorative justice approaches, and a continuing role as world leaders, with the HAQ Centre for Child Rights recommending both increased development in Australia and implementation of such approaches in India. The Centre recommended a national consolidated framework, more training for all involved, with a view to an expansion to the use of restorative justice for more serious offences (Sewak et al., 2019). The consequence of these different approaches is that it is difficult to bring rehabilitation, reintegration and restoration together, and this has prevented restorative justice from becoming a mainstream approach. Restorative and community justice both strive to promote their values amidst the loud, strong voices of competing punitive and managerialist discourses.

Further reading

Of all the topics in this book, restorative justice is perhaps the subject that has the strongest presence of Australian academics. The work of John Braithwaite and Kathleen Daly has been influential not just in Australia but also in the worldwide development of restorative justice. The work of Chris Cunneen and Elena Marchetti work has taken a critical perspective on the impact on Indigenous groups of approaches described as restorative.

Practical task

12-year-old Daniel has been caught breaking into a local shop. He stole about $200 of cash (that has not been recovered, and that he and his mother say they are not in a position to return) but also caused damage to the shop. the police officer dealing with the case says that the shop owner has a child of about the same age, and is willing to consider a restorative justice response to the matter. The police officer asks your advice on whether such an approach should be adopted.

What factors should be considered in determining whether to proceed by way of RJ in this matter? What would need to be done to maximise the chances of a successful outcome?

Reflective questions

5.1   Why is it important to understand the origins of restorative justice approaches and their links to Indigenous groups throughout the world?
5.2   What are the potential benefits and dangers of involving victims in decisions about how offenders should be dealt with?
5.3   What preparation work should be carried out with young people before they undergo a restorative justice conference to ensure that they can participate fully and that they are treated justly?

6 Risk-management and protection of the public

Introduction

One of the significant developments in community justice over the last few decades has been the emphasis on risk and dangerousness. This has attracted significant research and policy attention from both criminologists and sociologists, as the interest in consideration of risk goes beyond criminal justice into, for example, health, social care and child protection. This chapter sets out the context for a discussion of risk and discusses risk and the management of dangerous offenders in Australia before drawing together concepts of risk with community justice. It uses Western Australia as a case study to discuss the management of sex offenders and Victoria as a case study to discuss the management of dangerous offenders on parole. There can sometimes be a conception that community justice approaches and values apply most appropriately to low-level offending, but this chapter argues the relevance of community justice approaches to even those who have committed the most serious offences.

The risk society

> Today, there is a new and urgent emphasis upon the need for security, the containment of danger, the identification and management of any kind of risk. Protecting the public has become the dominant theme of penal policy.
> (Garland, 2001: 12)

The practitioner approach to risk-assessment must be put in a wider societal context and explained through what has come to be known as the risk society (Beck, 1992; Oldfield, 2007). Crime-control practices have changed fundamentally in line with social, economic and cultural changes (Garland, 2001), and modern crime control focuses on anticipating the future, assessing risks and preventing crime (Newburn, 2012). Living in a risk society means anticipating dangers and taking a calculative attitude to action—both positive and negative (Young, 1999). The growing influence of risk-oriented thinking is seen in increased surveillance, the development of risk-oriented security structures in policing and a growing concern about sex offenders, particularly those who offend against children (O'Malley, 1992). Community programs are conceptualised as risk-management and as controlling unruly groups or dangerous populations, with less connection to wider goals of rehabilitation and reintegration. Considerations of fault or responsibility are replaced by predictions of dangerousness (Feeley and Simon, 1992).

The impact of the risk society can be seen in approaches to offending. Governments are not comfortable in acknowledging uncertainty, or the limits of their powers, leading to an over-emphasis on risk-management and over-confidence in the tools and approaches available (Faulkner and Burnett, 2012). Crime prevention can be carried out at a neighbourhood or community level, but this is work in which correctional workers are less and less involved, as their focus remains mainly at the level of working with individuals (Canton and Dominey, 2018). A further consequence of this approach is that risk is considered merely at an individual level, rather than more holistically, in relation to communities (Faulkner and Burnett, 2012).

Practitioner risk-assessment and risk-management

There have traditionally been two approaches to risk-assessment: clinical and actuarial (Kemshall, 2007). Clinical assessment approaches are based on in-depth interviewing by a practitioner and professional judgement. Their advantage is that they focus on the individual and are a much more effective way of linking an assessment to the planned intervention. Clinical assessments give particular attention to dynamic risk factors that can be addressed (such as attitude, employment status and substance use), and these can then be a focus of intervention (Farrow, Kelly and Wilkinson, 2007). The main reason why clinical assessment is usually less reliable than actuarial judgement is practitioner error or bias, often linked to a practitioner tendency to give insufficient weight to static or demographic factors, such as previous convictions. Practitioner bias can take the form of an over-identification between the practitioner and offender (attribution bias); linking events that are not linked (illusory correlations); giving greater importance to some events than others (selectivity bias); or assumptions based on how an individual has reacted in a previous, similar situation (confirmation bias) (Phillips, 2008). Practitioners might be over-optimistic or over-pessimistic about their ability to bring about change, or may simply make an impaired judgement because they are scared of the individual concerned (Kemshall, Wilkinson and Baker, 2013).

An actuarial approach to risk-assessment relies on statistical techniques, producing a probability score for reoffending. Actuarial tests are more reliable than clinical approaches, but they predict risk for population groups, not for a specific individual. Actuarial instruments do not actually predict specific behaviour from a particular individual, and cannot take account of the relevant situational factors for the particular individual assessed. They also focus on assessing factors where information is easily available, rather than those that have necessarily been shown to have an association with recidivism (Bonta and Andrews, 2010). An actuarial risk-assessment cannot take account of the work of the practitioner in seeking to prevent further offending (Bonta and Andrews, 2010; Canton and Dominey, 2018). Australian forensic psychologists strongly support the use of actuarial risk-assessments, believing that they are much more reliable than clinical assessment (Palk, Freeman and Davey, 2008). Actuarial approaches are attracting increasing interest across the criminal justice including, recently, some exploration of the use of machine-learning to predict high-harm offending by Outlaw Motorcycle Gangs (Cubitt and Morgan, 2022). Actuarial assessments are attractive to managers as they facilitate audit and record-keeping, so even recommendations to divert might require an actuarial assessment.

Third-generation approaches bring together actuarial and clinical approaches. These enable the achievement of an estimate of reconviction, a profile of where best to target interventions and a measure of change and needs during supervision (Moore et al., 2006). Fourth-generation instruments have further integrated broader assessment of risk-need and personal factors, and integrated systematic intervention and monitoring (Bonta and Andrews, 2010). These can be used to measure the effectiveness of interventions by using them again after some time has passed (Robinson and Crow, 2009).

No risk-assessment tool or approach is perfect—the most accurate have around a 70% success rate—and can produce either false positive or false negative effects. A false positive predicts that an individual will reoffend when they do not actually go on to do so. A false negative predicts that someone will not reoffend when they go on to commit further offences. The cautious approach to risk and the potential implications of an error mean that there can often be a preponderance of false positives, leading to an extra burden on the work of agencies, with a consequent damaging effect on prospects of rehabilitation (Faulkner and Burnett, 2012).

Actuarial risk-assessment is based on research done with large population groups, and there can be particular difficulties and controversies with seeking to use instruments tested in one place in a very different setting. In Western Australia, this was addressed directly by the courts in the *Mangolamara case* (McGlade and Hovane, 2007). The judge rejected an application for an order under the *Dangerous Sexual Offenders Act 2006* on the basis that the psychiatric evaluation tools used had not been tested on Indigenous people who have committed offences and that the programs available were not designed or suitable for Indigenous people. There was an urgent need to develop culturally appropriate programs. The decisions in this case and others demonstrate that there is little legal protection in Australia against decisions made on the basis of flawed risk-assessments, including those based on tools that are not culturally appropriate or that have not been tested in Australia (Coyle, 2011; Goodman-Delahunty and O'Brien, 2014). Some Australian assessment instruments have even described Aboriginality as a 'risk factor' (White and Graham, 2010). Some argue that until there is evidence to suggest that these tools are appropriate and effective for use in Australia, they should not be used (Coyle, 2011). Research into the commonly used Static-99 assessment tool following the *Mangolamara case* found that it had poor predictive value with Indigenous people, and recommended that it not be used with this group (Spiranovic, 2012). In the absence of appropriate, locally designed instruments, assessors in Australia are left in a position of either using international material that was developed for sex offenders in a non-Australian context, or using material that was developed in an Australian context but was not designed to be used for sex offenders (Allan and Dawson, 2004). This Australian experience is in line with international findings that risk-assessment does not adequately take account of ethnic diversity because the fundamental factor of racism is not fully acknowledged (Cole, 2008). The blurring of the concepts of risk and needs can lead to an over-inflation of the risk estimates for women and for minority ethnic offenders (Robinson and Crow, 2009).

Polygraph testing is used in some international jurisdictions for both assessment and management in work with sex offenders (see Wood et al., 2010, for a preliminary study of its effectiveness) but has not yet been introduced into Australia. Madsen and Addison (2013) suggest that polygraph testing could be a useful addition to the measures and services already available in Australia.

The assessment of offenders with a history of mental illness presents particular issues, both practically and ethically. Mental health is often associated with risk, and there is a danger that it might stigmatise those who are mentally ill and that responding to concerns might require breaching patient confidentiality. However, when considering tensions between values, the importance of public safety must be given a high priority. Maden (2011) makes the important point that, considering the link between mental health and dangerousness, the comparison to be made is not simply between those who are mentally ill and those who are not, but within the individual between when they are ill and when they are well.

Risk-assessment is associated with the idea of defensible decision-making: The concept that decisions that are made are justifiable (see Box 6.1). This concern relates both to the need to manage the risks posed by individuals and the need to manage organisational risks. However, this can create a culture where decision-making is influenced more by what is defensible than what is right, leading to the making of conservative, risk-averse decisions. Practitioners thus see themselves as fulfilling a professional role but within a need to be procedurally compliant. This can be particularly prevalent in criminal justice, where practitioners find themselves managed by risk-averse managers and accountable to courts and tribunals that also appear to be risk-averse and blame-oriented. Risk of reoffending has become over associated with dangerousness, leading to more offenders being defined as dangerous and defensible decision-making being replaced by defensive decision-making (Nash, 2008). Decision-makers should aspire to be 'optimistic professionally defensible risk takers' (Baker and Wilkinson, 2011) who are able to take decisions that can be positive, yet can withstand scrutiny.

Box 6.1

The metaphors for risk-assessment

The discourse of defensible decision-making is so prevalent that it can be easy to forget that the term 'defensible' is a metaphor, and that it conceptualises the assessment process as some sort of battle. Metaphors play an important role in how people think about crime and how best to respond to offending (Thibodeau and Boroditsky, 2011). Baker and Wilkinson (2011) highlight some of the metaphors used to discuss risk-assessment, including that it is a safety net or a form of protective body armour, and that the assessment tools are some sort of a calculator. These metaphors both reflect the way in which risk-assessment is thought about and create meaning in its practice. Their suggestion is that alternative metaphors might be more helpful and productive, and these could include the risk-assessment process as a symptom checker, a line prompter, a smoke detector or a tourist guidebook. A risk assessment could be seen as a structurally sound foundation for the process of building an intervention. Journey metaphors are popular, and if the desistance process is conceptualised in that way then the risk-assessment might be considered as a map, providing guidance, rather than a sat-nav, providing instruction.

Source: Baker and Wilkinson, 2011.

Risk-management

Risk-management approaches cannot prevent risk; the best that they can do is to reduce the likelihood that the behaviour will occur or reduce the impact when it does occur (Kemshall, 2007). The discussion of risk is sometimes expressed in general, or even unclear, terms; there is a need to ensure that terms like 'risk of harm' and 'risk of serious harm' are used clearly and specifically. It is also important to distinguish between the likelihood of something happening and the potential impact if it does happen. Risk-assessments carry most power when related to potentially dangerous offenders, and such offenders have the potential to cause serious harm to others, even if their likelihood of further offending is less than, for example, property offenders. The term 'dangerous' is usually applied to those who are likely to commit offences of murder, rape or serious assault, and can be a difficult label to lose once it is applied, due to the strong reliance on static factors to assess someone as dangerous. Work with people who have committed such violent offences requires the practitioner to display empathy without being collusive, and to work in a way that both addresses the present behaviour and acknowledges and explores its roots in trauma or abuse (Boswell, 2000; Farrow, Kelly and Wilkinson, 2007).

Community organisations have followed a risk principle (Phillips, 2007), where those who are assessed as being the highest risk to society will attract the greatest amount of resources, and this high risk can relate to either a likelihood of further offending or a potential for serious harm. Although there is a widespread expectation that criminal justice agencies will take steps to protect the public from offenders who might cause serious harm, this approach does conflict with some traditional justice principles, and may potentially be discriminatory. Offenders will be sentenced on the basis of what a professional assessment says that they might do, rather than for what they have actually done.

Similarly to assessment tools, there has been no widespread, systematic development of culturally appropriate programmatic interventions. Programs in Indigenous communities have tended to be adapted versions of those imported from the United States, the UK or Canada, with some additional material for Indigenous communities (Worral, 2000; Harker and Worrall, 2011). The lack of culturally specific programs available can be a factor in the high rate of incarceration for Indigenous people (Worrall, 2000). A review of the research in 2008 found that there was generally a good impact on recidivism from running offender programs in Australia; there was not enough evidence to determine the impact of programs on Indigenous people (Macgregor, 2008). Diversion programs with parents who have committed offences of sexual abuse against their children have shown some success in Australia (Goodman-Delahunty and O'Brien, 2014).

Risk-assessment and management of sex offenders and dangerous offenders in Australia

Although risk-assessment processes can be applied to all people who have committed offences, the issues are most pertinent in relation to sex offenders and others who pose a serious danger to the public, as an erroneous judgement could lead to the most serious consequences.

The Australian Institute of Family Studies (2013b) put together a summary of the offender registration legislation for each state and territory, at the request of the Royal Commission into Institutional Responses to Child Sexual Abuse. All the states have individual reportable information, including phone numbers, email addresses and internet user names. Reporting periods vary from state to state, and there are different periods for different classes of offences, but all states do require lifetime reporting for sexual offences and/or multiple offences. The reporting period for juvenile offenders is usually about half of that for adults. Apart from NSW, all states and territories restrict access to the register, although in practice decisions about access are largely left to the discretion of the police commissioner (Law Council of Australia, 2010a, 2010b). The situation with regard to Western Australia is described below, but there is some variation in the responses of other states too.

- In NSW, the *Crimes (High Risk Offenders) Act 2006* allows for continuing detention orders and extended supervision orders for serious sexual or violent offenders. Corrective Services provides Sex and Violent Offender Therapeutic Programs, offering a range of treatment services for violent

and sex offenders. NSW has also recently strengthened its offender scheduling regimes for electronically monitored offenders;
- In Queensland, the *Dangerous Prisoners (Sexual Offenders) Act 2003* takes a similar approach to that in NSW, allowing for the continuing detention, surveillance and supervision of convicted sex offenders. An Inter-Agency Monitoring Committee was established in 2007 to respond to issues relating to offenders being supervised in the committee. This committee is chaired by Corrections and brings together representatives from the police, the Department of Justice and Attorney-General and the Department of Housing (Queensland Corrective Services, 2007);
- In South Australia, the *Criminal Law (High Risk Offenders) Act 2015* provides for the making of extended supervision orders in relation to serious offenders. It provides for detention, supervision and surveillance, including by electronic monitoring, of high-risk violent and sexual offenders.

The Law Council of Australia (2010a, 2010b, 2019) has expressed some concern about the expansion of the expectation for registration, particularly when it is an automatic process following a conviction for a particular offence. It is the Law Council's position that inclusion on a register should only take place when offenders present a demonstrated risk to children. The Council also recommends a more consistent approach across jurisdictions as to where information from the register is disclosed unlawfully. Box 6.2 examines the Community Sex Offender Notifications Scheme in the UK, known as Sarah's Law.

Box 6.2

The community sex offender notifications scheme in the UK (Sarah's Law)

In the latter half of the 2000s, the UK New Labour government came under sustained media pressure to introduce a version of the American 'Megan's Law', allowing notification of the status and whereabouts of alleged sex offenders. In 2009, this scheme was rolled out as a pilot, evaluated by a team from De Montfort University and then later introduced nationwide. There were many successful aspects to the pilot, due to the limited and managed way in which the scheme was introduced: The police were engaged in the scheme; applicants felt involved in the criminal justice system; previously sceptical NGOs were largely supportive; and the fears about vigilante attacks on convicted sex offenders did not materialise. However, the use of the scheme by members of the public during the pilot scheme was much lower than had been anticipated, and this takeup rate remained low when the scheme was rolled out nationwide. The public appetite to know more about sex offenders had been seriously misjudged, as media pressure was mistaken for public interest by policy-makers (Kemshall, 2014). The marketing strategy had a limited impact because of the restrictions on how it was targeted. The 'Sarah's Law' policy and practice were based on the myth of a rational actor, assuming that sex offenders would weigh up the benefits and losses of their actions, rather than taking into account other information about sex offender behaviour (Kemshall, 2014 and see also O'Malley, 1992).

Sources: For further information, see Kemshall (2010, 2012); Kemshall et al. (2010); Kemshall, Dominey and Hilder (2012); Stout, Kemshall and Wood (2011).

Management of dangerous sex offenders: Western Australia

Western Australia leads the rest of the country in terms of the steps taken to monitor dangerous sex offenders in the community. Legislation provides for controls on individuals who are perceived to be dangerous. The *Community Protection (Offender Reporting) Act 2004* requires certain serious offenders to keep police informed about their whereabouts and other details to reduce the likelihood of reoffending. Further, the *Dangerous Sexual Offenders Act 2006* gives the courts the power to deal with someone by way of a detention or supervision order if it is satisfied that they would commit a serious sexual offence if they were not subject to such an order.

The *Community Protection (Offender Reporting) Act 2004* was key legislation introduced following the 2003 announcement that all states and territories would work together on sex offender registration. The Act created a register of sex offenders and required such individuals to report routinely to the police. The frequency of this reporting varied, depending on the assessment of risk.

Risk-management and inter-agency working have replaced the traditional probation ethos of 'advise, assist and befriend', and Western Australia has modelled its Inter-Agency Public Protection Strategy (IPPS) on the British Multi-Agency Public Protection Arrangements (MAPPA) schemes that facilitate communication between corrections, police and child protection services to manage offenders in the community and support public safety (Harker and Worrall, 2011; Redman, 2011). The Western Australian Inter-Agency Public Protection Committee (IPPC) is the joint agency committee that manages serious offenders in the community. The IPPC meets on a monthly basis to review the circumstances of offenders identified as posing a serious risk to the community, and to share information and plan intervention (Redman, 2011). The police have also set up a dedicated unit, the Sex Offender Management Squad, to manage offenders under the Act. The Act allows courts to make Child Protection Prohibition Orders, prohibiting conduct that would otherwise be lawful.

In 2012, a statutory review was carried out of the *Community Protection (Offender Reporting) Act 2004*. The review considered how young people had been treated under the Act and recommended that the Police Commissioner be allowed to suspend reporting obligations of any young person who is a reportable offender. This allowed the right balance to be struck between protecting children from abuse and ensuring that young people were not unnecessarily drawn into the scheme.

The review considered the concept of risk and the change in the understanding of the role of the court from a body that dealt with events that had already happened to an expectation that it must make predictions about the future. If an individual is to be judged on the basis that they are a risk to others in the future, then that risk must be a substantial one, not merely a minimal or theoretical risk. Courts require access to the expertise of psychologists or psychiatrists to help assess such risks, and those charged with assessing risk—including police officers—must have proper training. The committee considered that the police would be a key agency in managing dangerous offenders in the community, and that a requirement to report to the police, rather than Corrections, would have a greater impact.

The police have a lead role in the management of information-sharing, with officers at inspector rank or greater required to authorise disclosure of information from the Register. In practice, some information is available to general public, authorised by the Minister of Police.

The parliamentary committee considered the expansion of the provisions to include arsonists as well, but determined that this was not appropriate: if arsonists were to be managed in this way, then separate legislation would be required. Individuals who committed sexual offences against adults were found to be more difficult to manage and to require greater police resources.

The Community Protection website in Western Australia (Community Protection Western Australia, 2015) is the most open notification system in Australia, providing information on known sex offenders to the public. The Bill setting up this register was introduced following the public outcry and campaign after the murder of eight-year-old Sofia Rodriguez-Urritia Shu in 2008 (Whitting, Day and Powell, 2014). It is a public register, and has been available since 2012. In other states, the names and addresses of sex offenders on the national register are known only to authorities, but in Western Australia many of these details—including, in some cases, photographs—are publicly available. Western Australia residents are able to access details of convicted sex offenders living in their area simply by entering their details into a website. The register has three tiers of information: firstly, it provides photographs and personal details of offenders who have failed to comply with reporting obligations; secondly, it allows local searches for offenders living in a resident's own suburb; thirdly, it allows for inquiries about a specific person who has regular unsupervised contact with the applicant's children.

Other states will use Western Australia as an exemplar when seeking to bring in more onerous demands on sex offenders. Most recently, there has been interest from NSW regarding on the use of anti-libidinal medication to manage the offending behaviour of the most serious sex offenders, and policy-makers there are seeking to learn from the experience in Western Australia.

The courts are able to order the taking of anti-libidinal medication as part of supervision order, and the individual himself is obliged to undertake the prescribing and managing of this medication through a GP. Monthly blood tests are used to ensure that testosterone is at the required level (WA Department of Corrective Services, 2014).

The public attention given to high-profile serious offences means that communicating decisions about potentially risky offenders to the public is now an important part of risk-management. This communication rarely seems to involve any acceptance or explanation of the limitations of the criminal justice system, despite this being a key recommendation of an earlier inquiry into offender management in Western Australia (Mahoney, 2005).

Victoria: Management of dangerous offenders on parole

In Victoria, the *Serious Sex Offenders (Detention and Supervision) Act 2009* provides for supervision and detention orders, as well as for indefinite sentences in some cases. However, most attention has been given to the supervision and management of individuals on parole.

Similarly to other jurisdictions, policy related to the management of dangerous offenders in the community in Australia has been significantly affected by serious offences, including murder, that have attracted national publicity. In 2013, Jill Meagher was murdered in Melbourne, Victoria by Adrian Bayley, who was both on bail and on parole at the time of the murder. In 2015, 17-year-old Masa Vukotic was murdered by Sean Price when she was walking near her home. It later emerged that Price was on bail and had committed seven previous serious assaults against women. The Victorian Victims of Crime Commissioner, Greg Davies, said that the criminal justice system needed to become more focused on protecting the public than on protecting the rights of one individual. He said that the Price and Bayley cases showed that the system was not working (*ABC News*, 2015).

The Victorian government responded to the murder of Jill Meagher by making immediate changes to the law. Under the new laws, breaching parole would be classified as a separate offence, attracting either a fine or a prison term. The law also gave the police increased power to detain a parolee for breach of their parole. Although the new provisions had widespread public support, the Law Institute of Victoria described the legal changes as unnecessary, saying that what was required was a proper resourcing of the Adult Parole Board (*ABC News*, 2013b; see also Adult Parole Board of Victoria, 2015).

As well as making legal changes, the Victorian government also commissioned a review of the Parole Board, led by former High Court Justice Ian Callinan (*ABC News*, 2013a). The Parole Board admitted that it had made a mistake in not cancelling the parole of Bayley when he had pleaded guilty to an offence of assault, but that did not save it from criticism. The Callinan Report (Callinan, 2013) is scathing both about the decision not to recall Bayley and about the working of the Parole Board in general. The Report criticises the administration and filing systems of the Parole Board.

Justice Callinan (2013) says that the balance of the Parole Board's decision-making has tilted too far in favour of offenders, and that for public safety to be its paramount concern, it needs to become more risk-averse. He particularly draws on the victim's perspective in making this recommendation for greater risk-aversion, as well as recommending better information sharing with victims. Throughout the report, Justice Callinan consistently conveys his view that parole should not be an expectation or a right, but rather a privilege to be earned, including by the completion of relevant programs. The report recommends that attention be given to the recruitment and retention of parole officers, particularly to retaining experienced officers and to ensuring that those who worked with the most dangerous offenders have the proper training to do so. More controversially, Justice Callinan argues that young women should not be supervising the most serious and dangerous offenders—particularly those who have offended against women. The recommendations of the Callinan Report were implemented, with a significant investment in the Victorian Parole Sytem.

Again, the need to reassure the public is central to the working of this process, not just in Victoria but across the country. In NSW, for example, parole decisions are available on the Parole Authority website (for example, see New South Wales Parole Authority, 2013).

When risk assessment goes wrong, this obviously has a detrimental impact on the community, and potentially an extremely tragic impact on a future victim, but it can also damage confidence in the agencies and professionals involved. In the UK, Fitzgibbon (2011) has reviewed two grave and extremely high-profile cases that occurred at around the same time, one involving child protection social services and the other probation agencies (see Box 6.3).

Increasingly, there is an acceptance in Australia of the need to consider other dangerous offenders, particularly those who commit acts of violence

---

Box 6.3

Probation on trial

Peter Connolly was a two-year-old boy murdered by his mother's partner despite extensive involvement in the family from Social Services, health professionals and the police. Laurent Bonomo and Gabriel Ferez were two French students murdered in their flat by a young man, Dano Sonnex, who had recently been released from custody and treated as medium, rather than high, risk. Fitzgibbon (2011) identifies a series of reasons why these incidents occurred, and why the public reaction was so strong, and makes some points about the risk-assessment practices and culture involved. A reliance on actuarial assessment in the Sonnex case meant that information gathered and then shared with other relevant agencies was of low quality and lacking it detail; it was essentially no more than a tick-box assessment. This failing was amplified by a culture of over-reliance on

> such instruments, meaning that inexperienced and under-qualified staff were considered to be sufficiently skilled in such assessments, and given little time or resources to carry out fuller assessments. Skilled workers were replaced with semi-skilled operatives. In both child protection and in criminal justice, it is a mistake to believe that sophisticated instruments do not require the interpretation of skilled practitioners; the interpretation of such instruments and their conversion into action plans are skilled, professional tasks (Fitzgibbon, 2011; Peckover et al., 2011). In addition, workers spent so much of their working lives sitting at computer screens that they did not have the opportunity to gather the social and contextual information needed to provide a full assessment. Similarly, practitioners did not spend the necessary time building relationships with offenders that would both allow fuller assessment and promote desistance.

in the home. A different approach to risk-assessment is taken with regard to intimate partner violence, where the focus is not on the relationship between the offender and the community in general but rather focused on a particular potential victim (Robinson, 2011). In the UK, a challenge in this regard is that there is a lack of consistent training programs and no set minimum qualifications for risk-assessment. In Australia, considerable attention has been paid to offences committed by individuals on parole.

Young people: Risk-assessment and management

There are particular issues in assessing risks for young people, as risk-taking is an inherent part of being young and most young people will not have a long record to allow a pattern of offending behaviour to be described. There are at least four ways in which the concept of risk is applied to young people: in relation to offending behaviour; with regard to access to programs; to determine security rating of young people in custody; and as a generic measure to activate legal intervention (Cunneen, White and Richards, 2015). Risk-taking can be positive for young people, allowing the development of resilience (Titterton, 2011). It is important to balance the need to involve young people in the risk-assessment process with the need to consider them as children in need of care and protection. An approach to risk-assessment that moves away from actuarial calculators and focuses on holistic narratives and life biographies can be appropriate for this work with young people, allowing them to engage in the process and for a true reflection of their lives to be provided. A skilled assessor will bring new meaning and analysis to such stories (Baker and Kelly, 2011). Similarly, a skilled practitioner will allow a young person to take managed risks in an increasingly unsupervised way, particularly when an intervention follows the Good Lives Model philosophy (Titterton, 2011). It can be more inclusive and productive to use the language of vulnerabilities rather than risk factors to refer to school, family and peer issues (Developmental Crime Prevention Consortium, 1999; Cunneen, White and Richards, 2015).

Despite the strong emphasis on public safety, in all Australian states and territories there is recognition of the need to treat juvenile offenders differently from adult offenders (Laub and Sampson, 2010b). In Western Australia, the Police Commissioner decides whether it is appropriate, in individual cases, for children to be entered on the register and to be subject to reporting restrictions. Some offences, when committed by a juvenile—such as the use of a computer for objectionable material—do not lead to inclusion on the register. Similarly, in Queensland, NSW and the ACT, juveniles are not placed on the register for possession of child pornography or lower level acts of indecency. In the Northern Territory and Victoria, if the prescribed offence was committed when the offender was a child, the offender is not subjected to offending requirements or added to the register, unless the court is satisfied that the offender poses a risk to the community.

Juvenile sex offences are a small proportion of the matters dealt with by the Australian courts, and only a small proportion of the offences committed by children are sex offences. However, juveniles do account for a relatively high proportion (about 18%) of the overall total of sex offences committed (Warner and Bartels, 2015). Treatment programs are available, in some places in Australia, for young people who commit sexual offences. Research into one such program—the Griffith Youth Forensic Service—shows promising results regarding its impact on preventing sex offender recidivism in both Indigenous and non-Indigenous populations (Allard et al., 2015).

One particular form of dangerous behaviour in Australia, usually associated with young people, is the act of setting bushfires, as fires spread quickly and cause extensive property damage and sometimes loss of life. The statutory review of the *Community Protection (Offender Reporting) Act 2004* in Western Australia considered whether arsonists should be included in reporting obligations due to the danger of the act and the high risk of both recidivism and escalation. The review recommended that they not be included in the Act, but that any initiative to monitor this group should be undertaken separately.

International experience shows that effective responses to arson require an integrated approach, including the police, fire services and correctional services (Lansdell, Anderson and King, 2011). Western Australia has the highest incidence of suspiciously lit bushfires in the country, and the police take a proactive approach, known as Strike Force Vulcan (Western Australia Police, 2011), to targeting known young people who have previously been involved in fire-setting behaviour. They engage in close surveillance, including by helicopter, of individual young people—particularly on days when the fire risk is assessed as high or catastrophic.

Community justice, risk and dangerousness

Community justice values are challenged by the need to respond to serious and dangerous offenders. Principles of inclusivity are difficult to apply to individuals who have committed the most serious crimes, and who appear to be at risk of further grave offending. It would, however, be a mistake to either suggest that community justice should not apply to all situations or to let discussions of community justice and discussions of risk take place without reference to each other. There are ways to consider and assess risk while still holding to key community justice principles.

Firstly, an important perspective to take on risk-assessment is to ensure that it is both collaborative and linked to treatment plans. Following the Good Lives Model, or other approaches that emphasis the promotion of desistance, does require a collaborative approach to risk-assessment and an assessment of strengths as well as risks (Barnett and Mann, 2011). Such an approach is particularly important in work with sex offenders, when the most effective and ethical approaches will link risk-assessment with the planned treatment. This is better for the intervention, but it also improves the risk-assessment— there is evidence that information gathered by interviews and testing is most accurate and most useful for risk-assessment when it is not perceived by the offender as being gathered simply for risk-assessment (Barnett and Mann, 2011). Collaboration is vital in work with Indigenous offenders; actuarial risk instruments have not been validated with this group, so the only appropriate risk-assessment is a clinical approach that takes individual factors into account.

A planned intervention will take account of strengths as well as risk factors, and will focus on supporting the offender in achieving goals through pro-social, legal means. Interventions need to have a focus on working to strengthen the offender's internal controls (Wood, 2011). Interventions should also support offenders' rights; although giving priority to public protection is crucial, this does not require offender rights to be ignored completely. A risk-assessment carried out using a Good Lives approach will gather similar information about risk factors and protective factors, but the focus on collaborative work and on achieving goals will mean that this assessment will be optimistic and focused on change, so will be experienced very differently by the offender involved (Barnett and Mann, 2011). Working effectively to promote desistance will require not simply risk-avoidance or minimisation, but also the taking of positive risks by practitioners to support personal development and rehabilitation. Practitioners seeking to work in this way must be supported by managers and by their agency as a whole (Kemshall, Wilkinson and Baker, 2013). Risk assessment and the promotion of desistance can be seen as working in tandem towards the overarching goal of promoting public safety (Kemshall, 2021).

Work with high-risk offenders must take place within a context. Community engagement is central in turning community protection into protective communities (Kemshall, 2008). The collaborative approach can be applied to colleagues and other agencies, as well as to offenders. Partnership working is attracting greater interest in Australia, and in some instances agencies are collaborating and sharing information. For example, in South Australia, the Offender Management Plan (OMP) was introduced as a way to enable police and other agencies to treat the offending behaviour of high-risk offenders and to support them to return to the community (Day et al., 2014). However, there is no legislatively supported or consistently implemented multi-agency approach to the management of sex offenders in the community in Australia (Day et al., 2014). Multi-agency working is often introduced for reasons of risk-management and public protection; however, once established, these partnership relationships can make a considerable positive contribution to all aspects of the management of offenders in the community.

All but the most serious offenders will either remain in the community or return to the community after the completion of their sentences. They must therefore be given the opportunity to do so safely, and to maintain the family and community relationships and employment opportunities that support the desistance process. The Good Lives Model (Ward and Maruna, 2007), a strengths-based rehabilitation theory that guides therapeutic work with offenders, has been applied particularly to sex offenders, and it is possible to work with such offenders to promote public safety without undue stigmatisation or labelling. Even surveillance and registration measures that are used to monitor sex offenders in the community can be applied in different ways, with different impacts. The Community Sex Offender Scheme pilot project in the UK was tightly managed and well funded, allowing measures that did not negatively impact on the attempts of offenders to desist from offending to be taken in order to promote public confidence. Other notification schemes, such as those that publish offender details openly or even require signs attached to offenders' houses, present barriers to full offender reintegration, thus seeming to assuage public concern while actually inhibiting longer term safety. It is important that Australian measures that rightly prioritise public safety do not lead to measures that might inhibit offender rehabilitation and reintegration.

Discussions of the most serious cases should not unduly dominate public debate and policy relating to work with offenders. It is absolutely correct and understandable that tragic and violent events should lead to debate about whether the crimes could have been prevented and whether criminal justice agencies could have acted more effectively. However, the answer to this is not always in greater surveillance or more punitive legislation. It is sometimes the case that greater resourcing or more training for staff could have contributed to public safety. Social workers, correctional staff and others who work with offenders in the community are being expected to take on more and more complex work, with often dangerous and violent offenders. It is vital that such staff have the right qualifications and training. Working with risk, violence and dangerousness is skilled and difficult work, and it should not be assumed, or even suggested, that staff with little training can use the instruments (White and Graham, 2010). Efforts to make assessment tools comprehensive should not detract from the need to make them user-friendly, and to allow skilled practitioners to express judgement (Robinson and Crow, 2009).

When Kemshall (2014) reflected on her experience of risk research over 35 years, she used economic terminology and interpreted shifts in policy during that period as a shift from a conception of an abstract rational actor to one of the imperfect actor. When policy-makers wrongly assumed that offenders were rational actors who weighed up the positives and negatives of their actions, offenders responded by adapting their behaviour. Approaches to risk have taken more account of biographical factors, the constraints on offenders' choices and the wider context in which offending behaviour takes place. This context needs to be understood and taken into account by the practitioners who work with such offenders.

As suggested earlier, risk-assessment and risk-management need to take account of the particular, individual factors of the offender and the need for community justice practitioners to take into account the diverse society in which they work. These issues are discussed in the next chapter.

Further reading

Hazel Kemshall is a leading international scholar on the subject of risk and risk-assessment, and her book with Bernadette Wilkinson and Kerry Baker (2013), *Working with Risk*, provides a good overview of the issues in the criminal justice system and other contexts. Day and colleagues (2014) examine risk-assessment practices in an Australian context. Wendy Fitzgibbon's (2011) excellent book, *Probation and Social Work on Trial*, covering two high-profile and very serious cases, contains valuable learning that is applicable beyond the UK environment where the incidents occurred.

Practical task

Look back at the practical task for chapter two, where you were introduced to Mark. If you were working with Mark and carried out an actuarial risk assessment it is likely that he would be assessed as towards the higher end of the risk band. Beyond the score generated by an actuarial assessment, what other factors would you want to take into account in developing a work plan? What might have been either missed, or incorrectly assessed, in an actuarial assessment?

Reflective questions

6.1 Are the values of community justice relevant to work with high-risk and dangerous offenders or are they only applicable to minor offences and lower-risk offenders?
6.2 How might the adoption of a community justice approach affect the possible response to young people suspected of starting fires in Western Australia?
6.3 What training should be provided to practitioners who will carry out risk-assessments on potentially dangerous offenders? Is training in use of the instrument sufficient or do they require wider knowledge and experience?
6.4 What do you think is the most appropriate metaphor for the assessment of risk?

7 Diversity

Introduction

The Australian criminal justice system has a particularly problematic record of engagement with Indigenous people. The declared commitment to social justice within community justice makes it essential to address this issue. There has also been considerable recent attention given to the criminal justice system's failure to respond appropriately to women as victims—particularly as victims of domestic violence. These are not uniquely Australian challenges. Diversity is now considered an important aspect of the discussion of the response to offending and the performance of the criminal justice system. Diversity refers to the visible and non-visible differences between people, and the Parekh Report in the UK provided an important and influential definition (Parekh, 2000):

- *Subcultural diversity* describes group members who share a broad common culture but also create distinct ways of life of their own;
- *Perspectival diversity* refers to, among others, political, religious and environmental groups that criticise and seek to change central societal principles;
- *Communal diversity* are self-conscious, organised communities that live by their own beliefs and practices. Some immigrant groups fit this definition.

The recent attention given to diversity has often been organised around what are sometimes referred to as the six strands of diversity: Age, disability, gender, race, religion and sexuality (see Stout, 2010). This chapter makes reference to these strands, and young people are discussed in Chapter 3. Although issues relating to Indigenous groups and the criminal justice system are dealt with throughout this book, they are of such importance that they are considered in this chapter as well. The chapter also covers the treatment of women in the Australian criminal justice system and the impact of health and disability. It concludes with a more general discussion of diversity in relation to community justice.

DOI: 10.4324/9781003193814-8

Indigenous people

The difficulties and challenges in the relationship between the state—particularly the criminal justice system—and Indigenous people are rooted in Australian history (see Blagg, 2008; Cunneen and Porter, 2017, and Baldry and Cunneen, 2014, for a wider discussion of the links between criminal justice processes and the effects of colonialism). The over-representation of Indigenous people at every stage of the criminal justice system, including prison (Baldry and Sotiri, 2014), is still shockingly high, and is one of many areas of Australian society, such as health and education, where outcomes for Indigenous people are very poor. The Black Lives Matter movement that focussed on policing practice in America drew further attention to Indigenous deaths in custody in Australia. Public campaigns seem to be the only way to get these deaths investigated and prosecuted (Whittaker, 2020). Social work has also had a very difficult history of 'patronising and unjust practices' with Indigenous people that impacts present-day engagement with those groups, and requires learning and reflexivity (Rowe, Baldry and Earles, 2015: 296). In recent years, states, territories and their justice providers have taken steps to engage with Indigenous people. States have responded in their own ways through guiding documents, initiatives, court and conferencing structures, and programs.

One key document in the history of relationships between the Australian criminal justice system and Indigenous people in Western Australia was the Aboriginal Plan introduced by Western Australia in 1996 (see Worrall, 2000). The plan acknowledged four guiding principles for delivering services to Indigenous people:

1. The spiritual relationship to the land is very important to Aboriginal and Torres Strait Islander people;
2. Family relationships are complex and have been disrupted by colonisation, but are very significant to Aboriginal and Torres Strait Islander people;
3. Aboriginal and Torres Strait Islander groups are not homogenous, and attempts to develop services to suit everyone are unlikely to be successful;
4. Customary law should be respected, particularly in remote areas.

These principles are 20 years old, but still provide a useful and relevant guide today. It is the operationalisation of these principles and good intentions that has proved more complex and challenging. Changes and developments elsewhere in the criminal justice system—for example, in staff training, skills development and culture—will impact on outcomes for Indigenous people (see Box 7.1). The de-professionalisation and later re-professionalisation of community corrections in Western Australia had an impact on outcomes for Indigenous people (Harker and Worrall, 2011). Highly skilled practitioners, whose training has included some engagement with issues of discrimination, diversity and Australian history and culture, are more likely to be able to positively engage with people from Indigenous backgrounds.

Diversity   115

> **Box 7.1**
>
> **Marlon Noble**
>
> Marlon Noble is an Indigenous man from Western Australia with an intellectual impairment, originating from a bout of meningitis that he suffered as a child. An assessment carried out when he was a young teenager found that he had literacy and numeracy problems and was well below average intelligence. In 2001, aged 19, Noble was charged with the sexual assault of two children. The court determined that he was unfit to stand trial but, rather than releasing him, the court held him in custody. He was placed under the authority of the Mentally Impaired Accused Review Board, which meant that he remained in custody.
>
> In 2010, a forensic psychologist assessed Noble as being fit to stand trial but the Department of Public Prosecutions (DPP) then withdrew the charges due to the passage of time and the amount of time that Noble had spent in custody. Noble was eventually released in 2011 after spending a decade in prison, despite never being convicted or even facing trial. Despite his release, he was still subject to stringent monitoring conditions, including random drug testing and home detention.
>
> The Disability Rights Commissioner, Graeme Innes, said that the case of Marlon Noble highlights how the Western Australian legislation can discriminate against those with disabilities, facilitating lengthy detention in the absence of a conviction. He said he was aware of other similar cases where people with disabilities were detained for longer than they would have been if they had been convicted of the offence that they were initially alleged to have committed.
>
> In 2016 the Australian government was found to have breached its obligations under the United Nations (UN) Convention on the Rights of People with Disabilities by the UN Committee on the Rights of Persons with Disabilities.
>
> *Sources:* Brull (2011); Aboriginal Disability Justice Campaign (2015); Australian Human Rights Commission (2012); McGaughey, Tulich and Blagg (2017).

Indigenous people who have committed offences need to be treated as a distinct group, with their own needs and their own culture, and some of this difference in approach must relate to differences in practice in rural and urban areas. In Western Australia, most Indigenous people engaged with the criminal justice system are situated far away from Perth. The Mahoney Inquiry recommended that such offenders must be treated differently if prison was to have any effect (Mahoney, 2005). Similarly, Worrall (2000) drew on Harry

Blagg's research (Blagg, 1997) to argue that Indigenous people should be treated as a group of people who have suffered a collective trauma. It is not appropriate to simply import criminal justice interventions from elsewhere and apply them without reference to culture, tradition or history:

> Interventions which fail to take account of dispossession, loss of traditional culture, breakdown of kinship systems and customary law, entrenched poverty and racism, will find program integrity to be but poor compensation.
>
> (Worrall, 2000: 248)

It has been argued that changes to criminal justice and court processes are not sufficient to address Indigenous over-representation, and that what is needed is a strategy that addresses the underlying causes (see Weatherburn, 2014). Respecting culture and responding to Indigenous people in an appropriate way are necessary approaches, but they will not be enough to address injustice and disproportionate impact. Criminal laws that ostensibly apply equally to everyone can have a disproportionate impact on particular groups within the population. The mandatory sentencing laws in Western Australia have a disproportionate impact on Indigenous people (Solonec, 2015). Western Australia has one of the highest rates of imprisonment of Indigenous young people of any of the Australian states, and a government review found that 81% of the young people sentenced under the state's controversial three-strikes burglary law were Indigenous young people, and in 2012 over one-third of the total population of young people in custody in Western Australia were there due to three-strikes laws (Solonec, 2012). This has been criticised by international human rights groups, including the Committee on the Elimination of Racial Discrimination, the Committee Against Torture and the Committee on the Rights of the Child, as it has a racially discriminatory impact (Solonec, 2015). Amnesty International (2015) recommended that mandatory sentencing be abolished and replaced by a justice reinvestment approach and culturally appropriate interventions (Solonec, 2012). The over-representation cannot be explained simply by discrimination in sentencing decisions—in fact, there is some evidence to suggest that Indigenous people are actually treated more leniently at the point of sentencing (Bond and Jeffries, 2012). Indigenous people are also more likely to receive a fine—perhaps because of the perceived difficulties in providing suitable community supervision (Bond and Jeffries, 2012). The causes are complex and require an analysis of inter-connecting issues (Cunneen and Porter, 2017). Addressing Indigenous over-representation and poor outcomes requires scrutiny of how all legislation and policy impacts on these groups.

Indigenous people are more likely to be victims of offences than other groups in the population. The status of victims needs to be properly identified and recorded so that appropriate support facilities can be provided for victims of crime from Indigenous groups (Bryant and Willis, 2008; Hardman, 2010). Within the group of Indigenous people there are also particular groups that have their own needs that are not met; for example, Indigenous people with mental and cognitive disabilities are over-represented and under-supported (Baldry et al., 2016).

Cunneen and Porter (2017) list some examples of community justice initiatives that operate in Indigenous communities and these include mentoring programs such as Tribal Warriors in Redfern and Uncle Alfred's Men's Group, aimed at young men in Townsville, North Queensland.

Culturally and linguistically diverse communities

The history of Australia and the particular criminal justice experiences of people from Indigenous backgrounds mean that Indigenous people need to be considered as distinctly separate groups within Australia, and not simply subsumed into a general discussion about race and religion. However, there are also similarities in the experiences of these groups and those from minority racial or religious groups. In 2011, the Australian Institute of Criminology reviewed the crime prevention programs for what it referred to as culturally and linguistically diverse (sometimes known as CALD) communities in Australia (Bartels, 2011). Although this is a diverse group, with varied needs, its members do share some common factors and some common experiences of the criminal justice system:

- They face difficulties with the criminal justice system, including through perceptions of racism and bias on the part of the police and concerns about over-policing. They are also likely to be less knowledgeable about the law and the workings of the criminal justice system, leading to an under-reporting of victimisation. There can also be difficulties accessing culturally appropriate services;
- They are vulnerable to hate crime, particularly in the form of racially motivated attacks from strangers, and this leads to a particularly high rate of fear of crime;
- Some communities have to deal with issues relating to drug and alcohol abuse, as well as high rates of child abuse and domestic violence. This, however, is not true for all communities—some have much lower rates of alcohol use.

There has long been concern about the relationship between the police and particular communities in Australian society, including those of Indigenous, Asian, Arabic and Pacific Island backgrounds (Mukherjee, 1999). Members of these communities report that they are not treated in the same way as those from an Anglo-Australian background and that there is a low level of trust between them and the police (Mukherjee, 1999). The barriers between communities and the criminal justice system can be cultural, structural or service-related (Sawrikar and Katz, 2008). It is not just in the criminal justice system that community tensions can be observed: Schooling, for example, also has tension with relation to Islamic groups in south-western Sydney (Taylor Webb and Gulson, 2013).

Offending occurs within a cultural context, and there can be specific aspects of offences that occur within particular communities. Fisher (2013) investigated domestic violence within five African refugee communities and how that related to changing expectations of family and gender roles. The study found three dimensions of the relationship between these changing expectations and domestic violence: The male loss of breadwinner role and status; the mismatch between role and expectations; and the changing financial independence of women. These cultural trends are evident throughout Australian society, but have a particular impact on some refugee communities, particularly where those people have travelled from communities with very structured, traditional gender roles.

Engagement with diverse communities in states and territories

Australian states have responded to the diversity of their populations. The Victoria Department of Justice and Regulation (2012) launched a Cultural Diversity Plan to ensure that services were available to those from culturally and linguistically diverse backgrounds. The report sets the context by stating that more than 23% of Victorians speak a language other than English at home (over 230 languages and dialects in total) and that more than 26% of people in the state were born overseas. The plan deals with recruitment and staffing, as well as access to justice. The plan recognises the potential barriers to justice created by issues of communication and understanding. It acknowledges that many people from these communities may have had experiences of displacement and trauma which will also affect their ability to engage with criminal justice services (Victoria Department of Justice and Regulation, 2012). The response of Victoria and the other states and territories has included the development of programs and other interventions for the diversity of people in Australia (Putt, 2010).

Australian Capital Territory

The Multicultural Futsal project was run by the Canberra Police and Citizens Youth Club (PCYC) and allowed young, former refugees to play soccer with other young Australians, including those with backgrounds in other countries. The project included some education about Australian law. This is one of many examples from across Australia of sporting projects being initiated by the police and used as a way of engaging young people. These projects continue to run, although more recently they are led by football authorities and community groups, rather than the police.

NSW

The Vietnamese Transitions Project aimed to prevent both reoffending and relapse into drug use for Vietnamese people who have committed drug offences. It engaged with them prior to their release from custody and provided post-release support in partnership with local Vietnamese community welfare associations. Early evaluations showed that the project had good outcomes, particularly in relation to an impact on reoffending, and it secured further funding. Vietnamese people are less likely than the general Australian population to have problems with drug and alcohol use, but those who do have such problems are less likely to seek help. The program continues to run through the Drug and Alcohol Multicultural Educational Centre (DAMEC) (DAMEC, 2022).

Box 7.2

Responding to the needs of drug users

One group that is significantly represented in the criminal justice system and that does require a response is drug users. As discussed in Chapter 2, states and territories have Drugs Courts to deal with this group, but they also have particular treatment interventions. In NSW, the Compulsory Drug Treatment Correctional Centre provides intensive treatment for and rehabilitation of drug users who are persistent offenders. It seeks to address dynamic risk factors, as well as physical, social and psychological needs. The program has five stages:

- Closed detention, including rehabilitation, treatment, education and vocational training;
- Community access to facilitate reintegration, including social, vocational and employment leave;
- Community custody, including intensive supervision and integration support;
- Parole;
- A voluntary case-management plan.

NSW also offers the Intensive Drug and Alcohol Program (IDATP) at the John Morony Correctional Centre. This is a residential treatment program aimed at those who have a high need for drug and alcohol interventions and who are at a medium to high risk of reoffending. Again, it is aimed at promoting reintegration by addressing drug and alcohol use and offending behaviour, and it includes educational, vocational and therapeutic interventions. It incorporates both education and skills development.

Source: Department of Correctional Services (DCS) (NSW), 2013.

Northern Territory

Another common approach to engaging with communities is the use of police-run residential camps for groups of young people. In 2007 and 2008, the Northern Territory police held 'Knowledge=Power' and 'Respect Yourself' camps for young people from Indigenous and African backgrounds. These camps included activities such as bushwalking and rock-climbing, as well as providing information on health, drug abuse and the law. The camps had a positive impact on education and employment for some of the young people. More recently, diversion schemes have been community based and run in partnership with NGOs, churches and community groups. The Northern Territory Government has produced a strategy on Aboriginal Affairs from 2019–2029 (Northern Territory Government, 2019) and the initiatives include an Aboriginal Justice Agreement. This recognises that an engagement of Indigenous leadership and a shared commitment to addressing underlying factors is required to reduce reoffending and reimprisonment rates.

Queensland

As well as individual projects, organisations within states and territories have also developed resources for their staff and partners to work with groups from diverse communities. The Queensland Police Service developed the *Multicultural Quick Reference Guides*, which give country and community profiles, with examples of common phrases and information about available services. These have been developed for, for example, communities from Samoa, Tonga and Sudan. The information contained is reviewed on an annual basis. In addition, the Multicultural Awareness Online Learning Project (Queensland Police, 2022) aims to increase police awareness and understanding of diversity using an interactive web-based course. The training is compulsory in some areas. The Police in Queensland operate a First Nations and Multicultural Affairs Unit (Queensland Police, 2022).

South Australia

Much of the work in relating to diverse communities is done in partnership with non-governmental or voluntary agencies. For example, the Migrant Resource Centre of South Australia brings together police and community groups in a series of initiatives, and also produces relevant literature (AMRC, 2022). The Centre also works to develop the leadership skills of young people, encouraging them to take up mentorship roles within their communities. The support offered includes advocacy on justice issues. Similar centres operate in other states.

Tasmania

In Tasmania, the 'Hands Across Hobart' program enabled young people from refugee and migrant backgrounds to become involved in community activities, as well as offering work opportunities and referrals to partner organisations. The police continue to employ Multicultural Contact Officers with the aim of ensuring accessibility of services.

Victoria

The police are not the only lead agency in working with diverse communities. In Victoria, Social Services initiated the 'No Excuse for Family Violence' project, which educated the community about family violence, the law and the available services. This initiative included training for staff, programs for men on community corrections orders and refugee women, and media campaigns. The Victorian Police now have a resource on their website where they provide videos in a variety of languages encouraging community members to seek help whenever they are experiencing family violence (Victoria Police, 2022).

Western Australia

In contrast to many of the projects that use sport as a way of bringing people together, in Western Australia the 'Journey Towards Hope (JoTHe) Dance Project' uses dance as a medium for integration. This project is on offer in many countries internationally, and centres on the theme of the United Nations White Ribbon pledge not to commit or condone violence against women and children (see JoTHe, 2022 for more information).

The projects described are a small sample of a wide and diverse group of initiatives—some state led, others initiated within communities, some ongoing, others short-term or temporary seeking to address the long-standing issue of poor outcomes for Indigenous and racially diverse groups in Australia.

Women in the criminal justice system

Offending by women is much rarer than male offending, and women in the criminal justice system will often have particular characteristics and needs. Most young women do not offend, and the main involvement of women in the criminal justice system is as victims, supporters or workers. Australian research has highlighted that girls present with a more concerning background of abuse than boys and have similar patterns of drug and alcohol abuse, but do not commit offences at nearly the same level (Lennings et al., 2007). Substance use in girls is associated with mental illness and gender-specific approaches to responding to this have the greatest positive benefit (Lennings et al., 2007). The vast majority of women in the criminal justice system are there for reasons that would be best dealt with elsewhere, such as in housing, health, education, the welfare system or trauma-informed counselling. Best practice from community justice workers in working with women requires a partnership approach with appropriate agencies (see, for example, Dominey and Gelsthorpe, 2020) for a discussion of the importance of health and housing in resettlement). It is a depressing state of affairs that this fact is well

122 *Diversity*

> **Box 7.3**
>
> **Parramatta Female Factory and Girls' Home**
>
> In their article on colonial patriarchy, Baldry and Cuneen (2014: 285) say that there is no better example of the patriarchal state control of girls in Australia than that of the Parramatta Female Factory and Girls' Home.
>
> The Parramatta Female Factory began in 1821 as a welfare institute for convict women and their children and was also a place of punishment for convict reoffenders. The women were required to work and were treated extremely harshly in very overcrowded conditions. Riots occurred regularly.
>
> In 1841, an orphanage was built next door to the Female Factory in which girls were raised by the Catholic Church. Many of these girls were stolen Indigenous children. The school was dramatically overcrowded, with no proper sanitary or plumbing conditions.
>
> In 1848, the Female Factory was turned into a lunatic asylum, which detained women for 130 years. A large number of the women detained were Indigenous women. The inadequate facilities and poor standard of buildings were criticised from the start.
>
> In 1887, the orphanage became an industrial school for girls, a girls' detention centre that was later known as the Parramatta Girls' Home. It was intended for children who were neglected, abandoned, orphaned or had been convicted of a criminal offence.
>
> The Department of Corrective Services took the centre over in 1980 when it became the Norma Parker Women's Prison.
>
> All iterations of the facility were characterised by physical and sexual abuse and the Royal Commission into Institutionalised Responses to Child Sexual Abuse (RCIRCSA) produced a case study on the Parramatta Training School for Girls that highlighted the particular vulnerability of girls who are in the care of the state (RCIRCSA, 2014).
>
> *Sources:* Information taken from Baldry and Cuneen (2014) and Parragirls (2016).

known and understood but that women continue to be drawn into criminal justice responses (Carr, 2022).

The Corrections Agency in the state of Victoria is investing in services for women, including in Housing, Employment and Community connections for Indigenous women (Corrections Victoria, 2022). Victoria set gender-specific standards for women serving correctional orders in 2009, and these are still applicable today (Corrections Victoria, 2009). These standards lead assessment, management and community work practice. These principles can usefully be followed in all work with women in the community:

- Strengthening relationships—including with children, family members, practitioners and community-based support networks;
- Addressing complex needs in a holistic way, taking account of the impact of abuse, trauma and mental health issues;
- Providing respect and safety through trusting relationships and a safe, supportive environment;
- Creating opportunities by providing choice, maximising individual control and addressing socio-economic and other disadvantage;
- Supporting continuity, using inter-agency partnerships to provide a consistent and coordinated approach to delivering services;
- Responding to the diverse characteristics of individual women and groups of women;
- Staying informed about best practice, knowledge and research, and incorporating monitoring and evaluation into the delivery of service.

Victoria also carried out a review of case management with women who had committed offence, highlighting the lack of research that had been carried out specifically with women and the particular needs of that group (Turner and Trotter, 2010). The review makes two key recommendations in taking a case management approach with women: Firstly, therapy and problem-solving are more effective approaches than discipline and punishment; and secondly, interventions based in the community are preferable to interventions based in custody or other institutions. The review recommends the adoption of the six principles set out by Bloom, Owen and Covington (2005):

- Acknowledge that gender makes a difference;
- Create an environment based on safety, respect and dignity;
- Develop policies, practices and programs that are relational and promote healthy connections to children, family, significant others and the community;
- Address substance abuse, trauma and mental health issues through comprehensive, integrated and culturally relevant services and appropriate supervision;
- Provide women with opportunities to improve their socioeconomic conditions;
- Establish a system of community supervision and reintegration with comprehensive, collaborative services.

The review highlighted the need for staff working in community corrections to be properly trained in working with women.

Interventions with women need to be planned properly, and there should not be an assumption that programs and approaches designed for men and boys can simply be applied in the same way to women and girls. Care needs to be taken even in identifying women and girls for criminal justice intervention. Research shows that the impact of stigmatisation and labelling is different for young women than it is for young men (McGrath, 2010). Young women who felt stigmatised by their experience of the criminal justice system were more likely to commit further offences. The researchers speculate that this linked to a perceived violation of expected gender roles and the greater pressure to conform that is felt by young women. It is also linked to the nature of the population; young women who offend are particularly likely to have experienced a background of victimisation, trauma and abuse (McGrath, 2010). These findings provide strong support for efforts to provide diversionary options for young women.

Restorative approaches are very popular in Australia, particularly for young people, but there are gender differences in the impact of conferences. There are three sets of concerns indicating that young women experience conferencing differently to young men (Alder, 2001, 2003). Firstly, community expectations of young women are different; secondly, girls have different experiences of shame, harm and trust and thirdly, juvenile justice workers perceive girls as being harder to work with than boys (see Baines and Alder, 1996, for further discussion of the perception that girls are more difficult to work with). It can be harder to reintegrate girls who have committed offences back into the community because of community perceptions of girls who offend and greater acceptance of offending by boys (Alder, 2001).

The fact that offending by girls is so rare means that girls who do offend can face an even greater stigma than a boy would do when engaging in exactly the same behaviour, so an approach to reintegration that involves agencies beyond criminal justice is required. In a similar way to the response to women as offenders, the response to women as victims of domestic violence also requires an inter-agency approach and the utilisation of partnerships beyond the criminal justice system (Laing, Irwin and Toivenan, 2012). The use of the Koori Court process for offences of domestic violence allows cultural knowledge to be considered and facilitates taking the victim's voice into account (Marchetti, 2011, 2015).

The principle that gender makes a difference and that it needs to be considered in program design is widely accepted within Australian Corrections. For example, in NSW, many programs on offer are either designed specifically for women, adapted into a male and female version or directly address gender issues. These include (Corrective Services NSW [CSNSW], 2021):

- *Out of the Dark* is a strengths-based program, based on self-determination theory, and it allows facilitators to respond to women as victims as well as offenders (CSNSW, 2021). It is delivered both in custody and the community, and women undertake it before engaging in other programs;

- *Mothering at a Distance* is delivered to women in prison, with their children, to support relationship between mothers and children, in preparation for release;
- *Personal Ownership, Identity and Self-Empowerment (POISE)* is a residential program, delivered to women who have committed offences, targeting drug and alcohol use and the cycle of addiction and offending;
- *The Intensive Drug and Alcohol Treatment Program (ITATP) is delivered separately to men and women, with the womens's program entitled 'Yallul Kaliarna', that translates as 'Always Spread Your Wings';*
- In addition, some programs are targeted solely at men. The Domestic Abuse Program and the Domestic Abuse Maintenance Program are both for men only.

Prison authorities are also becoming better at responding to the needs of their female inmates. The 'Out of the Dark' Program referred to above is delivered in prisons in response to the increasing number of female offenders who enter custody with their own experience of domestic abuse. In Western Australia, the Boronia Pre-Release Centre manages low-security female offenders, with their children, in a community-style setting, enabling a more planned and supported return to the community (WA Department of Corrective Services, 2022a, 2022b).

Transgender prisoners have a difficult and risky experience in custody and are subject to a significantly higher risk of sexual assault (Petersen et al., 1996; Lynch and Bartels, 2017). An international study showed that only about 20% of correctional facilities had formal policies in place for transgender prisoners (Petersen et al., 1996) and there is no consistent sentencing and corrections legislation across Australia (Lynch and Bartels, 2017). One example of such a policy exists in NSW. The NSW Department of Corrective Services recommends that all trans-gender prisoners are case-managed, and decisions are made on an individual basis. The policy states that the only criterion for identification as transgender is self-identification, and that all prisoners have the right to be housed in a facility appropriate to their gender of identification, unless it is determined that they should be housed in a facility matching their biological gender. Such prisoners are housed in single cells until induction screening is complete (DCS, 2022).

Disability and mental health

The needs of people with disabilities in the criminal justice system have sometimes received less attention than is warranted, but there is now a greater focus on this group and a greater realisation of the scope of the issue. In 2014 the Australian Human Rights Commission investigated the experience of the criminal justice system of people with disabilities in Australia (AHRC, 2014a). Disability should not be considered as a discrete issue from the other strands of diversity; disability discrimination intersects with other forms of discrimination in the criminal justice system. Disability is not spread evenly throughout the Australian population: Indigenous people are 1.7 times more likely than non-Indigenous people to be living with disability. As people with disabilities and Indigenous groups are both more likely than the general population to have interaction with the criminal justice system, then there are grounds for serious concern about the over-representation of those Indigenous people who are living with a disability (AHRC, 2014a). This is also true within the prison system, where there is particular concern about the health of Indigenous prisoners. Learning from Indigenous cultures, and their inclusive approach to those in their community with disabilities, could provide a model for the rest of Australian society (Avery, 2018). The main areas of concern with regard to the health of all prisoners within the Australian prison system continue to be mental health issues and risky health behaviours such as tobacco smoking, excessive alcohol consumption and illicit drug use (AIHW, 2015b).

The AHRC Report (AHRC, 2014a) gave some attention to the cost–benefit implications of providing early and appropriate support to people with disabilities (see Box 7.4).

Research into the incidence of intellectual disability in young offenders found that it was a primary risk factor in non-Indigenous young people. For Indigenous young people, also having an intellectual disability did not have the same impact on risk-assessment, but many Indigenous young people in the criminal justice system did have an intellectual disability, and they

Box 7.4

Cost–benefit analysis

There are clearly costs involved in providing access to court buildings, accessible information and access to interpreters. However, investment in early intervention and diversion can provide clear and substantial cost benefits. The difference in costs between custodial corrections and community correction is estimated as $73,365 per person (McCausland, Baldry and Johnson, 2013), and there are diversionary initiatives with people with cognitive impairment and mental health disorders that have shown some evidence of success. A study carried out by a team from the University of NSW estimated that for every dollar spent on early intervention with this group, between $1.40 and $2.40 was saved in the long term (McCausland, Baldry and Johnson, 2013). Similarly, a study carried out by the National Mental Health Commission (2013) estimated that diversion to community-based rehabilitation for substance users led to savings of up to $111,458 per person.

were identified as a group in need of support (Kenny and Frize, 2010). This over-representation can be explained by reference to social and health disadvantages experienced by Indigenous people in Australia. Early intervention diversion work with this group needs to be given a high priority, with services developed to meet the needs of these young people and their families (Kenny and Frize, 2010).

The AHRC report (AHRC, 2014a) found that people with disabilities could encounter the criminal justice system as defendants, victims or witnesses, but that in each of these roles they were at risk of being disbelieved and disrespected. Victims with disabilities were poorly protected, judged as unreliable and at risk of ongoing violence. Offenders with disabilities had a high risk of being imprisoned and of then going on to have repeated contact with the criminal justice system. Police often find themselves in the role of first responders to those with mental health difficulties, but this interaction is frequently marked by difficult communication, leading to poor outcomes. Similarly, court officers have received limited training, so those interactions are also troubled, with equally poor outcomes. Undetected disabilities can lead to disruption to the justice process—for example, through the lack of provision of an interpreter or a lengthy period on remand while disability status is assessed. Again, these situations are likely to have the greatest impact on Indigenous people.

The AHRC Report (2014a) recommends that a Disability Justice Strategy be developed in every state. This strategy should be based on participation, equality and empowerment, and should be developed in consultation with people with disabilities. An appropriate strategy would require better policies and training, better communication and greater accountability.

As well as intersecting with race and identity, disability discrimination also intersects with gender. Women who are identified as having a disability experience violence and abuse at a greater rate than the rest of the population, and this is even greater when such women identify as being of Indigenous descent (Cripps, Miller and Saxton-Barney, 2010). Such women are often more likely to be disbelieved and they face barriers in accessing services and receiving help. The complexity of the needs of this group are experienced by government and service providers as 'too hard to handle' (Cripps, Miller and Saxton-Barney, 2010). Research into the needs of this group found that what was needed was partnership work and follow-up to ensure that requested services were provided, but that this very rarely occurred (Australian Bureau of Statistics [ABS], 2022). Another common issue was funding; services funded to address, for example, domestic violence, were often unable to access the additional funding to provide the additional support for those with disabilities (ABS, 2022).

Offenders with an intellectual disability receive a poor level of support on their release from prison, and struggle particularly in accessing appropriate accommodation. Barriers include poor coordination between agencies, and a lack of properly trained and experienced support staff and advocates (Riches et al., 2006).

There is a need for both specific and appropriate accommodation and community-based therapy services for this group of individuals, the vast majority of whom should be able to be supported effectively in the community (Riches et al., 2006). The responses of the criminal justice system cannot be detached from other societal attitudes to intellectual disability, and the criminal justice system is often required to fill in gaps left by other services. The supervised treatment order (STO) regime in Victoria can use medical diagnosis to determine a legal risk, so that the characteristics that could be used to contribute to a medical diagnosis of intellectual disability become a legal diagnosis of risk and dangerousness (Spivakovsky, 2013).

The criminal justice system responds to individuals with mental health difficulties as both victims and as offenders, but there is also evidence to suggest that the criminal justice system can itself be a cause of mental health problems. Research with male inmates in a NSW prison found that 43 per cent of them reported experiencing a traumatic event while in prison. Such prisoners responded poorly to treatment, were more likely to use heroin in prison and had high recidivism rates (Sindicich et al., 2010). Those who undergo such trauma can be difficult to identify in the prison setting, due to the high rates of mental health challenges within the prison population. Some 38 per cent of prison entrants and 46 per cent of prison dischargees reported that they had been told at least once by a health professional that they had a mental health disorder (AIHW, 2012). This has an impact on the experience of prison but also on release and reintegration. People with disabilities are released with little or no long-term planning with regard to mental health, housing or employment. Indigenous people are, yet again, doubly disadvantaged by a lack of culturally relevant support. This leads to offenders with disabilities cycling in and out of the criminal justice system (AHRC, 2014a).

The needs of groups with disabilities have now received a higher profile, and states and territories are taking steps to address these needs. The NSW Department of Correctional Services now has a number of programs specifically designed and targeted at particular groups (Department of Correctional Services (DCS) (NSW), 2013). These include the Seasons for Growth program, which addresses grief, loss and trauma and is facilitated by the Chaplaincy Service. The Self-Regulation Program is a prison-based program for prisoners who have committed acts of sexual assault and have an intellectual disability or other cognitive impairment. It is offered within a self-contained Additional Support Unit (ASU) therapeutic community-style setting, and includes both individual and group work.

Community justice and diversity

The above sections are not exhaustive, nor are they meant to imply that race, gender and disability are the only relevant diversity issues in the criminal justice system. They do, however, highlight the complexity of the issues and their deep roots, both historically and geographically. Promoting community justice requires an engagement with the complexity of diversity issues and an acknowledgement of the damage caused to individuals associated with particular groups by criminal justice agencies over time. A justice approach must consider diverse groups as victims, offenders, witnesses and family members. The need to give attention to the needs of Indigenous people as offenders in the criminal justice system cannot obscure the fact that they are also extremely prone to victimisation.

Two key points about community justice must be borne in mind in discussions about diversity. Firstly, care must be taken in referring to communities and making assumptions about characteristics that particular individuals might share due to their shared identity. There can be a risk in discussing, for example, the 'Indigenous community' or the 'Muslim community', as that can obscure the differences between individuals or groups of individuals. When discussing Indigenous groups, the differences between the experiences of those in cities and those in rural areas are significant. It is also important to acknowledge the intersection of different strands of diversity as that where the greatest experiences of disadvantage can occur. As discussed above, it might be possible to find resources or services for women or Indigenous groups, but when a service user also has a disability the provided resources might not be sufficient.

Secondly, community is not something that exists or that should be assumed to be present: it is a state to aspire to. This point has been made throughout this book, but it is particularly important in relation to diversity because the term 'community' can sometimes be used in a sentimental or patronising way about particular groups within society. Indigenous people are assumed to belong to a community, but white Australians are not discussed in that way. Equally, an emphasis on community cannot simply be a form of responsibilisation, where the state seems to put both the blame for offending and the responsibility for dealing with it onto community groups that are not resourced for this role.

Diversity within community justice requires a response to and an engagement with some of the most vulnerable groups and individuals in society, at a time when they are most vulnerable—whether as offenders or victims. Correctional agencies within Australian states and territories have taken significant steps to address the disadvantages faced by these groups and have devised innovative and heavily resourced programs and approaches. It is necessary to do this, but it will never be a sufficient approach to expect criminal justice agencies alone to respond to disadvantage and discrimination. When considering diversity, perhaps more than with regard to any other aspect of community justice, it is imperative that community justice be accompanied by social justice.

Further reading

There are considerable online resources available for further information on Indigenous people in the criminal justice system. These include those available from the Australian Institute of Criminology. The Australian Human

Rights Commission also produces information on all aspects of diversity and how people are treated within Australian society.

Practical task

In your work with Mark (introduced in chapter two) you discover that he has some health and disability issues that have previously gone unassessed and unaddressed. It has always been known that he had literacy difficulties but this is now understood to be dyslexia. He has also developed health problems, related partly to his lifestyle choices and partly to his experience of custody. How will this knowledge of his health and disability circumstances affect your work with Mark? Are there services or agencies that might be able to work with you and offer him some support, or is it now too late in his life for him to access such services?

Reflective questions

7.1 Look again at the four guiding principles for delivering services to Indigenous people early in this chapter. How might these principles be operationalised in work with offenders?
7.2 Should people with mental health issues be dealt with by the criminal justice system? Should drug users? If those groups are not appropriately dealt with in the criminal justice system, then how should we respond to them when they commit offences?
7.3 What can be done within the Australian criminal justice system to ensure that violence within the home is responded to as seriously as violent offences committed on the street?

8 Organisation and management

Introduction

The work that community justice workers do with people who have committed offences and victims of offences is located not just within a community but within an organisation. Non-governmental organisations (NGOs) have operated in community justice for many years, and there is an increased role for the private sector; however, it remains the case that most community justice workers are employed within the public sector. This chapter considers what training and qualifications are either useful or required for community justice workers and what the experience and working environment is like for practitioners in this field.

Working in community justice within an organisation

Work with people who have committed offences is emotionally demanding work, and the organisational context can either contribute to these emotional demands or provide a supportive environment for workers. Knight (2014) applied four typologies to emotional work in community justice:

1 *Presentational.* Practitioners are expected to show a positive front, to be positive and warm, and to manage their emotions according to general social rules;
2 *Philanthropic.* Practitioners give their emotional support as a gift to the people with whom they work—for example, by listening patiently to someone who is angry. This is most associated with a traditional, value-based form of community justice;
3 *Prescriptive.* This involves managing emotions according to professional codes of conduct, behaving professionally and reining in emotions. Practitioners are able to take control of a potentially difficult situation by keeping their emotions under control. A bureaucratic, New Public Management approach can see increasing expectations that emotions are kept under control;
4 *Pecuniary.* Emotions are managed for financial gain, this can be seen in the increasing role of the private sector in community work with people who have committed offences.

DOI: 10.4324/9781003193814-9

One way to consider the delivery of work with people who have committed offences is in relation to the idea of capital—a resource that is required to produce the desired outcome. Capital can be political, intellectual, organisational or social. The capacity to manage performance to deliver a quality service can be regarded as organisational capital. In relation to the supervision of people who have committed offences, a critical part of achieving positive outcomes is the capacity to deliver supervision as planned (Chapman, 2010). The work in the community also involves emotional capital. It is an area of work where there is a blurring between private emotions and employer expectations. The worker provides emotional capital, and this is exchanged for other forms of capital, including financial capital. Should this emotional investment be considered a form of labour or a gift offered by the worker to the client (Knight, 2014)? Organisations can expect the display of particular emotions from their staff, and to possess and utilise particular personal qualities in their work. This can be a form of exploitation by the organisation—particularly if workers take on the weight of the emotional demands. The emotional component of the work and the demands that places upon workers cannot be understood without an appreciation of power structures and the gendered nature of emotional labour. Emotional engagement is something that is more important to women and emotional labour is more often expected of women (Knight, 2014).

When community justice workers are based in organisations closely related to prisons, as most statutory workers are in Australia, then there can be an expectation of emotional detachment and difficulties with sharing emotional concerns with senior managers. If emotional support is not available from managers, this leaves practitioners having to find their way through the turmoil of emotions of themselves, and leaves the people who have committed offences on their own. Support through formal debriefing or supervision—an approach traditionally associated with social work—is not routinely offered in community justice settings. Support from line management can be dependent on the personality or inclination of the individual manager. Many organisations provide a confidential counselling service and this is welcomed by practitioners (Knight, 2014). Workers can find that the best source of support comes from their colleagues, and many welcome open-plan offices as a possible way to facilitate this informal support. This is one example of how the physical environment helps an organisation to promote the practice it wishes to encourage and send positive messages to staff (Cherry, 2010).

Although many of those who seek out careers in community justice are motivated by a desire to support others and make a positive contribution to society, the values and characteristics of the organisation where they ultimately work can shape their attitudes and their practices. Government organisations socialise their staff, both overtly and indirectly, and workers take on organisational attitudes and patterns of thought. The values and attitudes of individual workers are a combination of their own dispositions and the impact of the organisation (see Oberfield, 2014, for a study of organisational socialisation in relation to police officers and welfare workers in the United States). The idea that the character of the organisation should reflect the sort of practice that it seeks to promote is presented in Cherry's (2010) understanding of pro-social practice. If practitioners are to be expected to work pro-socially, then managers also need to interact pro-socially with their staff. The supervision relationship should be empathetic, not simply a series of conversations about targeting and monitoring. Managers need to demonstrate the same qualities that are needed in practitioner interaction with people who have committed offences: respect for the individual; punctuality, reliability, consistency, fairness, assertiveness and a willingness to acknowledge mistakes and to put things right (Cherry, 2010). The organisation needs to support deep and high quality relationships between practitioners and those who they supervise (Dominey, 2019). Managers should provide encouragement, offer rewards and demonstrate the behaviours they wish to promote. This is particularly the case with regard to the legitimate use of authority, where managers can demonstrate a clear understanding of their role and set appropriate boundaries to balance the role of colleague and manager, and to protect themselves and staff from risk. When managers need to address performance issues with their staff, they can use similar techniques to those practitioners might use to work pro-socially (Cherry, 2010), including:

- Developing an empathetic relationship with staff members;
- Showing discrepancies between staff members' expressed goals and their current behaviour;
- Avoiding arguments—this breeds resistance with staff members, as it might do with people who have committed offences;
- Rolling with resistance rather than getting into potentially unproductive arguments;
- Developing self-efficacy—this can emphasise skills that the worker has rather than deficiencies.

A fair and equitable approach to providing opportunities will demonstrate justice. If managers attend training programs alongside their staff, this will show their commitment to their own practice and behaviour.

Quality in community justice

A limited amount of research has been carried out regarding quality and effectiveness within community justice organisations, particularly when compared with police or prisons. Leibling (for example, Leibling, Elliott and Arnold, 2001) has carried out research in prisons using an Appreciative Inquiry (AI) approach, and this has been applied to a probation setting too (Robinson et al., 2013, 2014). The focus of an AI approach is relentlessly positive, focusing on best cases and how to enhance what is good and right. AI is similar to restorative justice in its intention to bring about positive affect

(Leibling, Elliott and Arnold, 2001). It is sometimes used as a focus for organisational change, but in other circumstances it is simply a research method.

The AI-based study carried out in probation in the United Kingdom (Robinson et al., 2014) looked at understanding of quality in probation and how it was understood by both managers and practitioners. The researchers found that there were six themes to how quality was understood:

1 *Good working relationships with people who have committed offences* were considered to be most crucial, but networking was a key skill and relationships with colleagues in other agencies were also an important part of quality work;
2 *Resources* were considered to be crucial, with time being the most precious of these;
3 Practitioners also valued being *flexible* enough to respond to the needs of each individual on their caseload, based on how they presented;
4 Practitioners considered both *process* and *outcomes* to be important aspects of probation practice;
5 Practitioners valued the *personal attributes*, *values* and *life experiences* that they brought to their work, considering them to be at least as important as the professional training they had undertaken;
6 Good-quality practice does not occur without *support*, including from colleagues and other agencies. Support from managers was considered to be important, but it was not always provided.

The research found that there was a difference between practitioners' understanding of quality and the corporate understanding of the organisation. Practitioners were aware of this discrepancy, associating quality practice with often-private interactions, while organisational references to quality centred on visible outputs, such as assessment reports (Robinson et al., 2014).

Managerialism and community justice organisations

Managerialism has led to the rationality of the organisation replacing ideas of right and wrong in guiding criminal justice. Responses to people who have committed offences are dominated by evidence-led initiatives and pragmatic concerns (Bull, 2010).

The advent of managerialism can lead to a dangerous and toxic environment for staff, where frontline professionals are held accountable both for their own decisions and for the actions of the people they have assessed or supervised. Calder (2011) introduces the idea of professional dangerousness, where the practitioner is affected, both psychologically and emotionally, by clients, colleagues and the organisation, leading to a destructive personal response. Organisational dangerousness is when the organisation is either complicit in creating this environment or does not address it. It can also lead to a focus on creating an operating model with efficient processes and targets, to the potential determinant both to the experience of those who receive the service and to the morale and wellbeing of practitioners (Robinson, 2019).

One consequence of this culture has been a growth in the role of first-line managers, who can find themselves under significant pressure with little support. The management role, however, is absolutely crucial to the retention and development of staff, as managers need to develop others and be intermediaries between the individual and the organisation. Poor supervision can lead to increased anxiety and reduced confidence in practitioners; poor inter-agency communication and a less satisfactory service to clients (Calder, 2011). Research in both Australia and the United Kingdom has shown that practitioners are able to reconcile the justice and welfare aspects of their work, and are able to cope with the difficult client group, but that they find the demands of the organisation the most likely aspect of their work to lead to burnout (Allard, Wortley and Stewart, 2003; Mawby and Worrall, 2013). Organisational culture has the ability to either constrain or enhance inter-agency work, and those organisations that work with people who have committed offences should seek to display the key components of a learning organisation (Kandola and Fullerton, 2004, cited in Calder, 2011):

- Shared vision;
- Enabling structure;
- Supportive culture;
- Empowering management;
- Motivated workforce;
- Enhanced learning.

Organisations expect accountabilty from their staff, and the increasingly managerialist approach in community justice requires mechanisms to control workers and ensure they are doing what the organisation requires of them (Canton and Dominey, 2018). These mechanisms, and the need to monitor against targets, have in many instances replaced the provision of supervision and emotional support. Performance monitoring can reduce practice to easily measurable tasks, such as the keeping of appointments. However, key aspects of probation practice can be lost by taking an overly managerialist approach. Accountability should mean more than simply ensuring that staff do whatever they are told; there should be an ethical element to it. Workers who understand their accountability to the people who have committed offences with whom they are working, can include a willingness to explain actions, and this contributes to the sense of legitimacy of the intervention (Canton and Dominey, 2018). The understanding of community justice, or probation practice, should lead the organisational structures that are established so that staff are supported in providing flexible practice that demonstrates good judgment and an appreciation of difference (Canton and Dominey, 2018).

Stress and impact on individual staff

Stress can come from within the organisation, from the volume of work and from the type of people with whom practitioners work (Mawby and Worrall, 2013). High workloads will contribute to stress, anxiety and ill health (Ball, Buckley and Moore, 2021). Sometimes a conflict in values can seem to exacerbate this sense of stress. Many practitioners—particularly those trained in social work, are attracted to the work because of a desire to support vulnerable people or to promote social justice. However, there is nothing necessarily inherently progressive or restorative about the work; it is increasingly conceptualised as punishment in the community, with a greater focus on public protection and risk-management than on rehabilitation (White and Graham, 2010). Australian research (Allard, Wortley and Stewart, 2003) found that the expressed preferences of workers as they joined corrections organisations had little bearing on their sense of role conflict or the stress they experienced. Practitioners were able to balance the different aspects and demands of the role, but those who were not able to do so were more likely to experience stress or emotional exhaustion (Allard, Wortley and Stewart, 2003).

Many community justice practitioners have careers that will involve them spending some time working in prisons and other time working in the community. In most organisations in Australia, there is still a pathway from this direct client work to the most senior positions in the organisation, for those who choose to pursue such a career structure. Prison work can be particularly stressful and demanding. Workers in prisons are expected to have specialist expertise while also demonstrating the skills to maintain safety and order in working with the most dangerous individuals. Practitioners who are used to working in community settings—perhaps in agencies led by social work or community welfare values—can find prison work to be difficult and stressful. This may be particularly true for female workers, who can find that both the prisoner and prison officer populations are dominated by men, and that they are constantly made to feel aware of their gender (White and Graham, 2010). In the community, there are more women—both in the population of those who have committed offences and in the staff group. The hours are more social, although there are occasions when evening, weekend or residential work is required.

Individual practitioners need to be able to manage themselves within their organisation and within their professional context. The ability to do this depends upon personal characteristics, including career motivation and professional integrity. Organisations can help by valuing individual good practice. Kemshall, Wilkinson and Baker (2013) propose several sets of personal characteristics that practitioners should seek to develop in working with risk decisions for potentially dangerous offenders:

- Knowledge, skills and ability to engage in reflective practice;
- Resilience and ability to cope with stress;
- Ability to understand and work with your own emotions and those of others.

Stress can be damaging to the individual, but can also lead to destructive patterns of thought that affect decision-making and risk-assessment. Stressed workers can tend to avoid difficult decisions or prioritise their own self-preservation above other factors. Workers need to seek support, both through the formal supervision process and by gaining support from peers, who are often the strongest protectors against stress. Practitioners who are reflective and committed to their own learning will both improve the quality of their practice and protect themselves against stress. Practitioners should also take care of their general well-being and health. It is important for individuals to know when they need to seek help, and for the organisation to be able to provide it (Kemshall, Wilkinson and Baker, 2013: 164).

Ragonese and colleagues (2014), writing about criminal justice careers in the United Kingdom, list the personal attributes and professional skills that they suggest are required for the variety of careers available. Personally, criminal justice staff must be mature and responsible, with integrity and respect for diversity. They must be able to cope with stressful situations. Their professional skills should include both written and oral communication, with the ability to work within a team and to communicate effectively with colleagues and partners from other agencies. Administration and computer skills are now increasingly important.

Mawby and Worrall (2013: 109ff) researched probation organisational culture in the United Kingdom and characterised six responses to organisational stress:

1 *Exit.* A worker might physically leave the organisation or psychologically withdraw from it;
2 *Voice.* Workers might advocate for change, and argue against what they are dissatisfied about;
3 *Loyalty.* Some workers keep faith with the organisation;
4 *Neglect.* Work is performed carelessly, and is of poor quality;
5 *Cynicism.* Workers feel and demonstrate disillusionment and alienation;
6 *Expedience.* Workers bend or exploit rules to achieve goals.

The authors go on to say that these six responses are not sufficient to explain all the organisational dynamics in contemporary community justice work, and that the concept of edgework is also potentially useful.

Community justice in Covid lockdown

Similarly to organisations across society, probation and corrections agencies had to respond to Covid-19 lockdowns by changing the way they work. Researchers in other jurisdictions found that Covid-19 and associated lockdowns impacted both on staff and on the recipients of community justice services. In England and Wales, the National Probation Service (NPS) introduced the Exceptional Delivery Model (EDM). This ended unpaid work, accredited programs and most court-related activities and required that probation practitioners mainly worked from home and engaged people remotely (Phillips et al., 2021). Contact that had previously been face-to-face was now being offered by telephone and very high-risk offenders were checked by doorstep visits. Practitioners were concerned that the measures might not be sufficient to rigorously assess and manage risk and that they might face consequences if those they supervised committed further offences (Phillips et al., 2021). They also found the work challenging both in their ability to supervise effectively and in the potential impact on their home and family life. The work relies on relationships and on judgment and practitioners found it much more difficult to engage with people over the phone (Dominey et al., 2021). They also found it harder to draw boundaries between the demands of community justice work and their home and family life. One example, of many provided, was of a practitioner seeking to supervise a high-risk sex offender while they could hear their own children playing (Phillips et al., 2021). The experience in England and Wales was replicated elsewhere. In Scotland, probationers felt that supervision was less tight but they also generally felt less supported (Casey et al., 2021). In Austria, practitioners were able to stay in regular contact with those they supervised, but found it more difficult to achieve the quality of the relationship required (Stempkowski and Grafl, 2021). Austrian practitioners appreciated the additional flexibility, but missed the experience of working in a team (Stempkowski and Grafl, 2021). The experience in the Netherlands was very similar, and service users there were often positive about the flexibility of remote supervision (Sturm et al., 2021).

It will be important to understand what enduring changes occur as a result of the Covid-19 experience, as sometimes such exceptional circumstances can simply provide an opportunity for an expansion of state power (Carr, 2021). There is an opportunity to reflect on how to build a fair and safe society (Casey et al., 2021). It is clear that telephone supervision is often sufficient for some people, depending on how their risk is assessed and the progress of their order. The flexibility of telephone supervision is appreciated both by practitioners and by service users (Dominey et al., 2021). However, the experience of lockdown showed that community justice practice must focus on the centrality of relationships.

Community justice work as a form of edgework

Working in community justice is difficult and sometimes dangerous. The client group is challenging, the organisational demands can be considerable and the consequences of a wrong decision can be very serious. The work is increasingly multi-disciplinary, so there is a need to understand other professions and working cultures, as well as the worker's own professional background. In some cases, it can be considered to be 'dirty' work: The media and public will perceive it as a socially tainted occupation, working with groups who do not deserve support (Mawby and Worrall, 2013; Worrall and Mawby, 2013). There can be high-profile events, such as riots in custodial settings, or incidents involving dangerous people in the community, but the mundane, everyday routines of the work can also be challenging. Workers need to take care of both themselves and their clients to prevent undue stress, or even burnout.

> Terms such as 'compassion fatigue', 'secondary trauma' and 'vicarious trauma' are used to describe a common phenomenon across the workforce, highlighting the role of governance and structural determinants in sustaining a healthy (or unhealthy) workforce.
>
> (White and Graham, 2010: 235)

Practitioners need to be realistic when taking on the burdens of their clients, and to acknowledge their own need for support—whether from managers, colleagues, personal relationships or through professional help. The reduction of stress and prevention of burnout require both workforce development and a self-management approach.

Box 8.1

Protecting the safety of workers

Organisations are now giving attention to safety of their practitioners, particularly when away from the office and visiting service users or their families. The need to protect worker safety is one of the reasons behind the increased reliance on office visits and the fact that these offices usually have cameras, pass systems and other security measures. These are necessary measures to keep workers safe, but they do have an impact on practice, sending a message to those who visit them that they are dangerous and placing both a symbolic and actual barrier between the community justice organisation and the community it serves.

When home visits are carried out, safety measures are utilised there too. Information about the visit is provided to the manager of the project, including the address and the starting and finishing times. Text messages are sent at the beginning and end of the appointment. There is an agreed process to be followed if the expected text message was not received at the agreed end time, which included phone calls, contact with the local office and, ultimately, a call to the police.

The overwhelming majority of people supervised in the community pose no risk to the staff supervising them, but these measures are important as, in the rare cases where there is danger, staff making home visits can be in a very vulnerable position. Many Australian agencies require home visits to be carried out in pairs.

Somewhat paradoxically, the difficulty and possible danger in community justice work could be factors that attract some individuals to the work and keep them interested and motivated. One important framework for considering the lived experience of working in community justice is to consider it as a form of *edgework*. The definition of the edgework concept comes from Lyng's (1990) research into risk-taking behaviour, notably skydiving. The edge is seen as the boundary between order and disorder; life and death; sanity and insanity. Edgework is a form of action, in that it is undertaken simply for its own sake (Lyng, 2014).

Although initially used beyond an occupational context, the relevance of edgework to the workplace was recognised from the outset. Work can have a high level of emotional intensity, a balance between control and lack of control and, in some cases, a connection to illegality (Milavanovic, 2005). Lyng (2005) made links to high-risk or intensively pressured positions such as emergency workers, investors (see also Smith, 2005), senior managers and lawyers. Others have conceptualised edgework as relating to academic work (Hamm, 2005; Sjoberg, 2005). Mawby and Worrall (2013) extended the use of edgework in their interpretation of criminal justice work. They examined probation organisations in the United Kingdom, interviewing practitioners with experience in custodial and community settings. The practitioners described working in a bureaucratic, administrative setting within tightly controlled boundaries, yet expressed a desire for action and autonomy. They enjoyed working with people who had broken the law, thus attracting society's disapproval, and achieved most job satisfaction from the direct face-to-face work with these people. The 'edge' came from working with these people and seeking to maintain safety, both within the interview itself and in the offender's behaviour in the wider society. They gained satisfaction from using their professional skills to manage behaviour, work quickly to meet important deadlines (such as those set by the court) and work effectively within challenging situations and processes. This could apply equally to juvenile justice work. All community justice work could be described as being 'as much about controlling the boundaries between order and chaos as is police work' (Mawby and Worrall, 2013: 113)

Mawby and Worrall (2013) suggest that there are four aspects to edgework in probation, which could be applied equally to work with adults or young people in the community:

1 Liking offenders, vicarious rule-breaking and the lure of notoriety;
2 Danger and the threat of violence;
3 Its fast and exciting nature (although it is worth noting that community justice work can also be slow and boring);
4 The creativity and intensity of the work and the ambiguity of innovation.

Practitioners in both probation and juvenile justice settings have required the excitement and creativity of edgework to maintain morale and interest in their work. There are, however, roles that are increasingly available that do not have this profile, where the work is more actuarial, without the aspect of personal engagement.

Working in community justice in Australia

Probation supervision in the community is a relatively recent introduction to the Australian criminal justice landscape, particularly when compared with the United Kingdom, where it has been available for over a century. The first Australian probation service was established in Tasmania in 1946, with one officer giving assistance and encouragement to newly released prisoners. Services followed in NSW in 1951, South Australia in 1954, Victoria in 1957, Queensland in 1959 and Western Australia in 1963 (O'Toole, 2006). Most services soon expanded to include parole, then release on licence, then a variety of programs in the community. Early services were based on the English model of advise, assist and befriend. In NSW and other states, the Adult Probation Service provided guidance and support for those released from court and the Parole Service prepared prisoners in custody for release.

Prior to the 1970s, the core function of probation was rehabilitation, but the reorganisation of prison and probation departments into one Department of Corrective Services (in NSW, this happened in 1970; in Victoria, it happened in 1977) was a reflection of a shift in emphasis and priorities. For many years in Australia, services to people who have committed offences were provided by the state or by interested non-governmental organisations, such as St Vincent de Paul, but there is now a private-sector role as well. Borallon in Queensland opened in 1989 as Australia's first private prison, and this was followed by Junee in NSW in 1993, Mount Gambier in South Australia in 1995 and three facilities in Victoria in 1996–1997. There are three ways in which the private sector is able to become involved in corrections: Designing and building prisons, providing health, employment or education services for prisoners and managing facilities under contract (O'Toole, 2006).

There is no clear or stipulated training pathway for those who want to pursue a career in corrections in Australia. This contrasts with the situation in Europe, where training for this work is an important subject of debate and is connected to an understanding of the nature and purpose of probation work. In many European jurisdictions, a social work qualification is required for working in probation or youth justice, and this training might incorporate some specific training input on criminal justice or work with people who have committed offences. In other jurisdictions, such as France, corrections workers are expected to attend a residential training college. In the United Kingdom, specific training has been designed for probation staff, and this is required for appointment to certain positions (see Durnescu and Stout (2011), Knight and Stout (2009) and Nellis (2003) for a wider discussion of probation training in the United Kingdom and Europe). The Council of Europe has recently produced guidelines on the recruitment, training and professional development of probation workers that will contribute to the professionalisation of the work (Council of Europe 2019; Carr, 2020). The next section relates some of the recruitment strategies, and the training and entry stipulations, in Australian states and territories, based on the information provided on the organisations' websites. This information can be limited and dated—for example, one state's Corrective Services website does not seem to have been updated for over three years.

NSW

There is no requirement to hold formal qualifications to work as a probation or parole officer in NSW: informal training is provided on the job. The NSW Department of Correctional Services has worked with Western Sydney University to develop a Diploma of Criminal and Community Justice and a Bachelor of Criminal and Community Justice, but these are not requirements for entry to the organisation. The NSW Department of Communities and Justice (NSW DCJ) has an Aboriginal and Torres Strait Islander employment program, known as Yuranha (CSNSW, 2022). This program seeks to prepare Indigenous students for roles within the Department.

NSW Communities and Justice is seeking to attract those with social work qualifications to consider careers in child protection but does not seem to have the same focus on community justice careers (NSW DCJ, 2022).

Northern Territory

The Northern Territory employs a variety of staff, at a variety of grades, to work with people who have committed offences in the community. Probation and parole support officers and community probation and parole officers (AO3 level) monitor and manage caseloads of adult and young people, including those in regional and remote areas. Probation and parole officers (AO4 level) and probation and parole case managers (AO5 level) also do this work, but have a greater role in assessment, planning and report writing. The team is led by a team leader (AO6 level), who provides supervision and support, as well as managing a small caseload of complex and difficult cases. Similarly, unpaid community work is developed and managed by community work coordinators (AO5) with community work supervisors providing the onsite supervision and management. Probation and Parole officers in the Northern Territory undertake on-the-job training that leads to a Certificate IV in Correctional Practice.

The Northern Territory also seeks to attract and employ Indigenous staff members, primarily through the Indigenous Employment Program, which is designed specifically to attract Indigenous job-seekers (NT DCS, 2022).

Queensland

The vision statement of Queensland Corrective Services does speak to its commitment to equal opportunities, but it does not set out a specific strategy for recruitment of Indigenous staff (Prochaska and DiClemente, 2022). Those who assess and case manage people who have committed offences do need to hold degrees, and these can be in one of a variety of subjects including social work, criminology, behavioural science or education. They provide internal training leading to a Certificate IV in Correctional Practice.

South Australia

South Australia Department for Correctional Services (SA DCS) employs practitioners in a number of roles, including for senior psychologists and social workers. It is relatively unusual for a corrections agency to specifically require a social work qualification, but in South Australia, eligibility for full membership of the AASW is required for appointment to the position of assessment and report writer and they also employ qualified social workers to work in both custodial and community settings. A director of a Sentence Management Unit is required to either hold a social work qualification or current registration as a psychologist (SACS, 2022).

Tasmania

Tasmania offers a number of employment opportunities within corrections, including probation officer, community service supervisor and senior practice consultant. Relevant tertiary or industry qualifications are desirable, but explicitly not required, and it is not specified which qualifications are deemed to be relevant (Tasmania Department of Justice, 2022). The department is committed to providing training and development opportunities for its staff.

Victoria

The Victorian Department of Justice and Community Safety (DJCS) offers a graduate program, with a 12-month training program that can then lead to employment in one of a number of roles. It also runs the Aboriginal and Torres Strait Islander (Koori) Graduate scheme that is a similar program with additional networking opportunities and peer support. Both schemes are open to graduates from any discipline (Corrections Victoria, 2022).

Corrections agencies are keen to ensure that their staff complement includes Indigenous people, particularly to ensure that they are able to provide a culturally appropriate service to Indigenous service-users. Victoria's strategic plan states that people are fundamental to their success (Victoria Department of Justice and Regulation, 2015). The state employs Aboriginal well-being officers and Aboriginal liaison officers who provide well-being support to Indigenous prisoners.

Victoria has set a target to increase its Koori workforce from 1.78% to 2.5% of the total workforce (Victoria Department of Justice and Regulation, 2015). It seeks to do this through a number of initiatives:

- Gateways to Justice raises awareness of career opportunities in justice;
- Koori Graduate Recruitment and Development Scheme (KGRADS) is an employment scheme based on investing in personal development and offered to Koori graduates;
- Koori scholarships give financial support to Indigenous people to undertake studies in justice. Cadetships and the Youth Employment Scheme offer opportunities in a similar way.

Victoria has also adopted a new model of delivering transitional services to those exiting prisons from 2015, using Reconnect Support workers to make connections with the community and to address underlying causes of offending. Again, these staff are not required to hold particular qualifications—just relevant tertiary degrees.

Western Australia

Those who work with young people in Corrective Services in Western Australia (WA Corrective Services, 2022) are not required to hold any particular qualification, or to be trained or registered in a specific discipline. They are simply required to hold, or be working towards, a post-secondary qualification. WA Corrective Services do employ professionals in particular roles, including psychologists and social workers. Corrective Services looks for candidates who are able to communicate, engage young people and families, and work in an ethical manner in a team environment. Those who are appointed to be Community Corrections Officers are expected to undertake nine months of full-time, on-the-job training based between their workplace and at Bentley Academy in Perth. The training is linked to the Certificate III in Correctional Practice (Community) that is a mandatory requirement to work as a Community Corrections Officer in Western Australia.

The organisation and management of community justice in Australia

The structure and organisation of the management of community justice in Australia mean that staff who work in the community with people who have committed offences—particularly in the state sector—work closely with their counterparts in custodial settings. In some cases, staff may be moved between community and custodial settings, and in others staff based in the community and those based in custodial settings are trained together. Compared with the often-heated debates in other jurisdictions, there has been little attention paid in Australia to how community justice staff should be trained and retained, how the workforce should be recruited and what the initial training curriculum should contain.

The training received is a crucial aspect of the professional identity of individual practitioners and the organisation as a whole. Mawby and Worrall's (2013) research in the United Kingdom found that the members of the staff group could be divided into distinct and different organisational groups, based on their qualifying training and its proximity to or distance from social work. More recent research has considered how a professional identity is affected by significant organisational change within justice provision (Robinson, Burke and Millings, 2016). It is crucial that this subject be paid proper attention in Australia; as discussed elsewhere in this book, the skills displayed by the practitioners who assess and manage people who have committed offences are crucial both in the assessment of risk and dangerousness, and in working directly with those people in the community in a way that promotes and supports their desistance (see Box 8.2).

Working in community justice can be difficult, stressful and occasionally dangerous. The experience of stress can be accentuated by organisational structures that may seem to emphasise bureaucratic objectives that don't seem to match the often-messy reality of working with people who can be

---

Box 8.2

Typologies of probation workers

Mawby and Worrall (2013) considered probation occupational culture in the UK by examining what it meant to do probation work from the perspective of probation workers themselves. The three ideal types provide an interesting insight into the changing nature of community justice practitioners and the complexity of an organisation that houses all three groups:

1 *Lifers.* These practitioners are usually over 40 years old and have spent most of their working life in probation. They often have a sense of duty or vocation and may have started their career as a volunteer. They would most likely by influenced by perspectives associated with social work, including accepting a structural view of society and valuing the relationship between worker and client.
2 *Second careerists.* The defining characteristic of this group is that they have followed a previous career in an occupation that is essentially unrelated to their current work. They tend to recognise the welfare-based values at the heart of probation work. They are committed to the relationship with the offender and are able to use the people skills that they may have developed in another setting.
3 *Offender managers.* These are the youngest group in the probation organisation and come with a pragmatic view of work with people who have committed offences, not necessarily expecting to spend their entire career in the organisation. They are comfortable working with technology and with other organisations, and accept that the assessment and management of risk is central to their professional role.

It is the belief in the central importance of the relationship between worker and offender and the belief that people can change that draws these three groups together.

Sources: Material from Mawby and Worrall (2013) and Worrall and Mawby (2014).

both vulnerable and dangerous, and both in need of support and capable of manipulation. Where an organisation is committed to community justice values, and demonstrates those values in its interactions with its staff, this can provide practitioners with both a sense of support and the reassurance that they are working for an organisation that shares the same values as they do. Community justice values are discussed in detail in Chapter 11.

Further reading

The emotional element of working with people who have committed offences has had little attention until recently, but Charlotte Knight's (2014) research focuses on this crucial aspect of practice. The study carried out by Mawby and Worrall (2013) into the occupational culture of probation provides an essential insight into the working experiences of those in community justice roles in the United Kingdom.

Practical task

You work for a small non-governmental organisation that has received funding to develop diversionary interventions for young people and adults who are assessed as being at risk of committing offences in the community. The funding is provided to allow the employment of staff and you have been asked to contribute to developing position descriptions and to join the interview panel. What will you look for in the staff that you wish to recruit? What experience, background and qualifications will they have? What personal qualities will you be seeking and how will you test for these? Will you seek to create a homogenous staff group or will you be looking for a blend of different qualities and profiles?

Reflective questions

8.1 Most readers of this book will either currently work in community justice or will have an interest in doing so in the future. Is this decision influenced by your personal values? Do you think those values are shared by the organisation you work for or that you aspire to work for?

8.2 There is some variation in how community justice workers are trained in the different Australian states and territories. Which training arrangements do you think are most appropriate?

8.3 Knight describes the emotional demands of community justice work as 'gendered'. Does that match your experience? Are there different expectations of how men and women are expected to respond to emotionally significant work?

9 Technology and community justice

Introduction

This chapter considers the use of technology in Australian community justice, primarily with regard to tracking and tagging technology and with brief reference to how the increased popularity and use of social media have impacted on Australian community justice. The chapter contains a brief description of how technology is used in criminal justice across each state and territory of Australia.

Electronic monitoring devices have been used throughout Australia in a variety of ways, with some differences between states and some general themes. Electronic monitoring (EM) was initially promoted as an alternative to custody, but it was never fully accepted as sufficiently punitive so lost popularity and was phased out in some states. Global Positioning System (GPS) tracking is now growing in popularity, particularly as a way of managing those who have committed sex offences and others who are assessed to be dangerous when they are released from custody. These alternative options for how EM is conceptualised—as punishment or as surveillance—constitute a theme throughout the worldwide research and literature on EM, and are explored throughout the chapter. 'Electronic monitoring' is used as a generic term for a variety of remote surveillance technologies, including radio frequency checking, biometric voice verification, remote alcohol monitoring and GPS satellite tracking (Nellis, 2013a, 2013b). It is commonly acknowledged that EM tagging was first introduced in 1983, in the USA, after a judge in New Mexico saw something similar in a Superman comic book (see, for example, Black and Smith, 2003; Goeghegan, 2012). It is now in use in over 30 countries worldwide, and in many jurisdictions it has become a mainstream measure (Nellis, Beyens and Kaminski, 2013). It is very attractive to governments as it helps them to show that they are serious about crime and are part of the digital age (Daems, 2020). It can be used pre- or post-trial, or post-custody as a measure enabling return to the community, on its own or in combination with another sentence. Some forms of EM require considerable cooperation from the individual—for example, by charging the device every day and communicating with the

DOI: 10.4324/9781003193814-10

EM operatives on a regular basis. Other, more recent, technologies require less involvement from the subject. There are a variety of competing rationales for the use of EM; it can be used as an additional punishment, an aid to a community sentence or a further layer of control and surveillance (Nellis, 2013a). Its growth in popularity as a sentence has accompanied a growing managerial approach in community justice, where New Public Management approaches have seen a greater involvement of the private sector (see Chapter 8). Australia is not unusual in initially justifying EM as a way of addressing a growing prison population, but then later explaining it as an additional form of surveillance. EM advances have been led by private sector innovation, but they need to be understood not just as technological innovation but also as a response to offending embedded in a social and political context (Nellis, 2009a).

The use of technology in community justice in Australia

Australia considers itself to be a leader in the adoption of technology in criminal justice, so was keen to adopt EM technology as soon as it became available in the early 1990s. It was portrayed as a way of getting tougher in sentencing and structuring the time of those subject to monitoring. EM programs have been conducted in partnership with private sector companies since that time in NSW, Queensland, South Australia, the Northern Territory and Western Australia (Smith and Gibbs, 2013). EM was used to monitor curfews, prohibit entry to certain places and track movements. The initial justification was that EM would be a form of punishment, but this surveillance function has come to dominate in recent years. The introduction of GPS tracking in Australia, initially in Queensland, Victoria and NSW, was led by the release from custody of high-profile child sex offenders and the need to assure public safety (Martinovic and Schluter, 2012). There was some concern expressed that these measures would not reduce reoffending (Szego, 2005), but the measures were introduced quickly without extensive public debate. There were also concerns about the extension of punishment and the potential for net-widening (Black and Smith, 2003). The use of GPS technology to monitor domestic violence perpetrators has attracted greater discussion (Martinovic and Schluter, 2012), and in 2015 then Prime Minister Tony Abbott proposed a national approach to monitoring repeat high-risk perpetrators of domestic violence by GPS (Maiden, 2015). One victim of domestic violence who participated in a trial of the technology described the combination of a personal alarm and the GPS tracking of her former partner as a huge deterrent that kept her safe (Carter, 2015). EM, usually in the form of GPS (see Box 9.1), can also be used to monitor suspected terrorists on control orders.

The next section provides some examples of the use of EM in different states, noting that the Australian Bureau of Statistics does not provide data on those subject to monitoring, so the exact picture is more difficult to present.

Box 9.1

What is GPS tracking technology?

The US Department of Defense created the GPS in the late 1970s for military purposes. It is made up of a series of satellites 11,000 miles above the Earth that are used to pinpoint the location of an individual on the Earth. GPS tracking is based on a process of tri-location, whereby a device can calculate its location on the basis of its distance from three different satellites. GPS tracking is in widespread, creative and varied use in both the military and civilian worlds, but was relatively late to be used in work with offenders. The pattern taken in Australia is a familiar one throughout the world, where radio frequency EM is used first and then later replaced by GPS tracking. The move from radio technology to GPS technology is often accompanied by a change in the discourse from one of punishment to one of surveillance.

Australian Capital Territory (ACT)

In the ACT, restricted movement orders (a form of home detention) were introduced in 2001, available from 2002 but then removed in 2005. The first-stage report of the ACT Justice Reform Strategy (discussed in Box 2.1 in Chapter 2) makes a number of references to electronic monitoring, as currently used in the Northern Territory and elsewhere in Australia. Importantly, it recommends that future use of electronic monitoring would need to be in conjunction with treatment to provide real benefit.

NSW

NSW introduced home detention, supported by EM, in 1997 and this move was explicitly designed to be a rigorous, punitive response and a direct alternative to custody. It was an expensive measure, but the costs were justified by the state government in light of the savings that could be made in diverting some convicted offenders from custody (Studerus, 1997). In 2014, the state moved forward in the use of GPS equipment, allowing spot location checks for people released from custody. Initial trials of GPS technology in both NSW and Victoria proved disappointing, with movements not tracked in real time and buildings blocking the signal (Smith and Gibbs, 2013), but the provisions were introduced anyway. Unlike some other states, NSW went straight to the use of GPS EM; it did not start with radio frequency monitoring. As well as strengthening the hardware, making it more difficult to pull off, the change to a GPS-based technology allowed the mapping of 'heat zones' of the areas most often visited by those subject to monitoring and the monitoring of whether two or more offenders were meeting up (NSW Department of Justice, 2014). Currently in NSW, convicted offenders may be made subject to electronic monitoring as part of an Intensive Correction Order (ICO) in the community or as part of their imprisonment by way of home detention. The use of home detention in NSW has been increasing since 2016 (Bartels and Martinovic, 2017).

Northern Territory

The Northern Territory currently operates electronic monitoring both in the community and for prisoners in the Tennant Creek work camp. Home detention with EM can be a primary sentence. Corrections in the Northern Territory uses surveillance transmitters and voice recognition technology to allow it to monitor the behaviour and location of people on community orders, and it uses G4S tracking to monitor them in the community. A press release in 2011 (NT DCS, 2022), announced the $1.46 million investment in electronic surveillance equipment as part of an investment in rehabilitation. In 2014, the Northern Territory government trialled technology that could detect whether the person monitored had alcohol in their system alongside location tracking-based technology (Dunlevie, 2014). This was rolled out more broadly in 2016, but the use of EM in the Northern Territory continues to be modest (Bartels and Martinovic, 2017).

Queensland

The Queensland EM home detention program was one of the first to be introduced, but was abolished in 2006 (Martinovic, 2014). As in other states, in Queensland there is now less of a focus on using EM as punishment; instead, it is used as a surveillance mechanism for people assessed to be dangerous offenders. EM is a standard feature of Dangerous Prisoners (Sexual Offenders) Supervision Orders, and is used post-custody. Two different types of EM are used. Firstly, radio frequency devices that monitor whether individuals remain in their homes, but cannot track their whereabouts when they leave, were introduced in 2007 after a 2006 amendment to the *Dangerous Prisoners (Sexual Offenders) Act 2003*. GPS devices are also now used, and they do record and report the location of individuals (Prochaska and DiClemente, 2015a). The GPS tracking technology was introduced in 2011 after a media campaign, highlighting the limitations of an EM technology that could simply identify when an individual was not at home but not locate them further (see, for example, O'Loan, 2011). Queensland uses two different sorts of GPS device, one a handheld device requiring cooperation from the individual and the other based in an ankle bracelet (Prochaska and DiClemente, 2015a).

South Australia

Home detention, supported by EM (see Box 9.2), is available as a sentence for adults in South Australia if a custodial sentence would make imprisonment 'unduly harsh' on health or other grounds. It is also available for some

Box 9.2

3M and G4S

The development of EM, internationally, has been led by innovation within the private sector and in Australia two large, multinational companies dominate. 3M provides a range of tools for EM and for communication, allowing operators to choose both the nature and the intensity of the supervision required. They provide both landline-based and cell phone-based technology as well as a voice verification scheme. Voice verification is used by some banks and by the Tax Office, but is not yet utilised within the criminal justice system. 3M also offers GPS tracking, including an option that includes voice verification. A combination of the available technologies can provide a domestic violence proximity notification system, informing both the authorities and the identified victim if the offender enters the prescribed exclusion zone. The Remote Alcohol Monitoring System allows offenders' alcohol intake to be measured remotely, potentially as part of home detention. 3M has signed a contract to provide EM service to New Zealand Corrections.

G4S provides GPS, radio frequency and biometric technology to government customers, and responds to changing demands by providing new technologies such as alcohol monitoring. Its transdermal bracelets detect alcohol intake through the skin. G4S's technology is in widespread use across Australia, including in South Australia, the largest EM program in the country. South Australia uses G4S as its technology provider for electronic monitoring and recently awarded the provider a new contract to run until 2017. In the Northern Territory, its technology is also used to monitor prisoners at the Tennant Creek work camp.

Sources: 3M Electronic Monitoring (2015); G4S Electronic Monitoring Services (2015).

people on parole (Attorney-General's Department South Australia, 2022a). The state is Australia's largest user of EM and its programs cover both adults and juveniles on court orders, as well as at a pre-trial stage. In March 2015 there were 471 people being electronically monitored by Department for Correctional Services South Australia, representing a steady increase on previous year's figures (Attorney-General's Department South Australia, 2022b). South Australia is working with G4S to expand electronic monitoring into alcohol monitoring and domestic violence. South Australia trialled a bracelet that tests instantly whether the wearer has been drinking alcohol and then sends a signal to a monitoring system (Hunt, 2015). South Australia has also commenced the use of GPS tracking to monitor serious sex offenders released from custody at the end of their sentences (Dillon, 2015), following a 2012 amendment to the *Correctional Services Act 1982*. South Australia does use EM more than other states, with a particular tendency to use it for those on bail (Bartels and Martinovic, 2017).

Tasmania

'Breaking the Cycle', the Tasmanian Strategic Plan for Corrections 2011–20, makes reference to electronic monitoring. It recommends the investigation of options for introducing electronic monitoring as compliance monitoring for people supervised in the community as well as working with the police to propose a trial for accused people on bail. The plan also recommends carrying out a feasibility study of home detention with electronic monitoring as a sentencing option.

Victoria

The Community Corrections Order in Victoria has a number of additional conditions that may be imposed by a judge, including electronic monitoring. Individuals may also be subject to EM when released on parole. Victoria receives supplies from G4S for those being monitored in the community and in other Corrections facilities. The service also includes alcohol monitoring that uses bracelets to measure alcohol intake through the skin. Victoria introduced GPS monitoring for convicted sex offenders in 2013, having previously used radio frequency EM. This use now includes an accommodation facility where convicted offenders can live and work but where their access to children is restricted (Smith and Gibbs, 2013; Bartels and Martinovic, 2017). The technology used enabled the ankle bracelets to also monitor blood alcohol content, so those whose orders included alcohol bans could be monitored (O'Donahue, 2013).

Home detention was abolished in Victoria in 2011 by the state's Liberal–National Coalition government, which portrayed it as a soft-on-crime approach that passed both costs and pressure on to families from the state. The media contributed to this conception of home detention—for example, by portraying those subject to electronically monitored home detention as mainly wealthy 'couch criminals' subject to a 'go-to-your-room attitude' (Mickleberg, 2010). The media have been critical of the perceived softness of home detention, but are more positive about the potential for GPS to be used to track sex offenders (see, for example, O'Loan, 2011). Martinovic (2014) argues that the abolition of EM in Victoria is connected to its lack of acceptance as a punitive response; home detention is not seen as a severe enough punishment in a 'tough on crime' political climate. The number of people subject to EM is low, but it is increasing (Bartels and Martinovic, 2017) and there is limited stakeholder support due to the lack of engagement and consultation that has taken place (Martinovic, 2014).

Western Australia

Western Australia is another state where EM has fallen out of favour as a form of punishment, but GPS surveillance is now playing a role in the system. The state did have a home detention program, using home detention as a primary sentence or at a pre-trial stage, but abolished it in 2003 following negative media reports portraying home detention as a soft option (Martinovic, 2014). It also specifically provided for electronic monitoring at the pre-trial stage in the *Bail Act 1982* (Black and Smith, 2003). Western Australia introduced new laws in 2013 to allow it to track the movements of sex offenders, classified under the *Dangerous Sexual Offenders Act 2006*, released back into the community (Dollery, 2013). The then Corrective Service Minister said that if it worked effectively, it could be expanded for use with those convicted of other offences, including domestic violence or arson (Dollery, 2013).

Electronic monitoring: Punishment or surveillance?

EM's use in Australia has had mixed results and mixed responses. Its initial popularity waned as the arguments used to justify it as a punitive response were undermined by its portrayal as soft option, allowing wealthy criminals to serve sentences in their comfortable homes. However, the advances of GPS technology have made that form of electronic monitoring more popular again, as it seems to be able to protect the public from convicted sex offenders and other violent offenders.

This debate between the use of electronic monitoring for punishment or for surveillance has also occurred in other jurisdictions. Although the worldwide conception of electronic monitoring has been as a form of confinement, it is better understood as a form of surveillance (Nellis, 2009a). It has more in common with community sentences than with imprisonment (Hucklesby, 2013). The electronic monitor controls the person's body, not their mind, there is no need for them to reflect on or to think about their behaviour. Offenders are controlled: They adapt their behaviour to the demands of the monitor rather than to wider demands of the law or society (Nellis, 2009a).

The electronic tag has even more of an impact on personal space and on family life than other community offences. It turns the home into a prison and can inhibit the wearer in carrying out basic household tasks, such as childcare or gardening. Some families report that they feel as if they too are subject to a curfew (Nellis, 2009b). Those who lived with someone subject to EM reported that they felt as if their role was somewhere between a convict and a controller; they were both being punished and playing an active role in the administration of punishment (Vanhaelemeesch and Vander Beken, 2014). The imposition of EM can have a positive impact on family life, in that the subject is more available, more predictable and less likely to stay out late and drink to excess. However, families found the experience stressful—particularly when the family had to take a lead in ensuring compliance. Family members found their lives to be more constrained and less spontaneous, and that they needed to take on additional roles, such as walking the dog, taking children to school or putting out the bins. However, overall, family members felt that this burden was a price worth paying, to ensure that the offender was at home rather than in custody (Vanhaelemeesch and Vander Beken, 2014).

The experience of what it is like for a subject to wear a GPS tracking device is not widely researched, but one Australian researcher did wear a device for two weeks and reported on the experience (Martinovic and Schluter, 2012). She found that there were physical and psychological effects associated with wearing the device, but that these lessened over time and that there were simple strategies that could be taken to reduce the impact. The wearing of the device was a reminder to comply with the GPS requirements, and the support of family and friends could help with the completion of an order (Martinovic and Schluter, 2012). More recently, researchers in NSW who interviewed perpetrators of Domestic Violence who were being monitored, found that the experience of being monitored impacted on all aspects of the subjects' lives including both work and personal lives, and could create a feeling of social exclusion. They were constantly aware of being monitored both because of the need to charge the device regularly and the physical weight of it (Hwang, Simpson and Butler, 2021).

As well as the use of GPS technology, another technological innovation to affect community justice in Australia is the increasing use and prevalence of social media (see Box 9.3 for how social media is used by criminal justice agencies). The impact of the surveillance society and the easy accessibility of

---

Box 9.3

Community justice and social media

There has been a relatively limited engagement with social media in community justice, and it is used much more for publicity and communication between organisations and the public than in community supervision or in engagement with communities and families.

The social media policies of justice organisations tend to be conservative and risk-averse, with restrictions placed both on who can use official social media accounts and what they can say. For example, the NSW Department of Justice's social media policy (DoJ NSW, 2022) requires approval from a head of division or office before using social media as a departmental representative. These authorised representatives are not permitted to use social media to engage with current or former clients where that might bring the department or the employee into disrepute. This also applies to personal use of social media for all staff and contractors. Employees are not permitted to publish content that is offensive, defamatory or obscene, even in their personal lives or on their own time, on their own social media accounts. Other Australian states have very similar social media policies.

There are examples of innovative use of social media within the justice system—for example, the approach of using social media networks to promote health and safety messages (Informa Australia, 2013). However, negative, reactive stories are more common. Corrections in ACT was subject to media criticism when prison inmates used social media to publicise fights and upload 'selfie' photographs (Willis and Osborne, 2014; Reinfrank, 2015). The best-known social media instance to affect Corrections was the case of the so-called 'Facebook Six' in NSW. Six prison officers set up a Facebook site and posted comments that their employers described as being bullying and harassment. The Industrial Relations Commission ruled that Corrections were unable to take disciplinary action against the six men, due to the way that it carried out the investigation and the fact that, at the time, it did not have a social media policy in place (Moses, 2010).

Other organisations have been proactive in their engagement with social media. The police use social media—mainly Facebook and Twitter—for recruitment, public relations and community engagement (McGovern, 2010, 2014b; Kelly, 2014a; New South Wales Police Force, 2012; Commissioner for Law Enforcement Data Security Victoria, 2013). Seemingly in contrast to the tight central control of social media postings exerted by Corrections, the police allow individual police officers, at the community level, to manage and administer Facebook sites (Kelly, 2014b). The Australian Federal Police (AFP, 2015) hosts a site aimed at young people, as well as a site to inform adults of how young people use social media. The police also scan social media accounts of suspected terrorists, an approach that is generally accepted and approved of by the public (Wroe, 2015).

Social work practitioners and academics have engaged extensively with social media in recent years, with considerable attention being given to the practical and ethical issues of engaging with clients, accessing social media accounts and maintaining proper professional boundaries (see, for example, Fang et al., 2014; Westwood, 2014; Cooner, Knowles and Stout, 2015). A successful app has been developed to support the training of social work students in engaging with these ethical issues (Cooner, Knowles and Stout, 2015). Although there is no direct community justice element to this work, the issues covered are clearly as of much relevance to work with those who have committed offences, victims and communities as to other areas of social work.

digital records—which may not be ever deleted, and are not always correct—can make it very difficult for individuals to put an offending history behind them (Lageson, 2020). This can be exacerbated by naming and shaming practices by self-appointed community vigilantes who will draw attention to offending behaviour on social media (Dunsby and Howes, 2019).

Is the use of electronic monitoring effective?

Despite the prevalence and popularity of the use of Electronic Monitoring there has been limited research into its impact and effectiveness. A systematic review carried out by British and Australian researchers under the auspices of the 'What works Centre for Crime Reduction' in the UK both suggested a program logic and presented some evidence of impact and effectiveness (Belura et al., 2020). The researchers suggested that the logic behind the use of EM to reduce reoffending followed a number of assertions:

- EM increases the risks for the individual of further offending, in that it is more likely that they will be detected;
- EM increases the effort required in offending, particularly where the individual has to remove the device;
- EM reduces the rewards of committing crime;
- EM removes excuses for the commission of further offending, particularly where there are restrictions on the use of drugs or alcohol;
- EM reduces the provocations for offending, by imposing curfews and geographical restrictions that minimise the opportunity for peer pressure.

Their review of research to date on the impact of EM on reoffending found that there was evidence that it was effective in work with sex offenders, particularly in Europe, and there were important contextual factors that affected its impact on reoffending (Belura et al., 2020).

Technology and community justice: Parallel tracks

The use of Electronic Monitoring, GPS and other forms of surveillance have, largely, developed separately from wider community justice debates, along 'parallel tracks' (Mair and Nellis, 2013). This is partly due to the different origins and lead agencies, with electronic monitoring innovation led by the private sector and community justice approaches largely led within the public sector. The private sector dominance of electronic monitoring technology is part of a wider trend towards the commercialisation of criminal justice and the expansion of the crime control system, to incorporate the private sector first in transportation, then in prisons and now in electronic monitoring (Paterson, 2013). The development along parallel tracks should be seen as a missed opportunity to integrate the two approaches, and to link spatial or temporal control with work to support desistance. Although, internationally and particularly in the UK, some social work and probation agencies have opposed the introduction of EM, seeing it as a challenge to their values and ethos, there is potential for integration between a monitoring approach and community justice responses. There is some evidence that EM can bring stability to the lives of offenders, enabling them to participate fully with community orders (Nellis, 2010). The imposition of home confinement or a curfew supported by EM can act as a brake on offending and can provide a legitimate reason for subjects to disassociate themselves from offending acquaintances and stay clear of offending venues. This can provide opportunity for reflection and the opportunity to cooperate with a community order. This is crucial if EM is to have success beyond enabling a short, closely watched break from offending, and if it is to support desistance in the long term (Nellis, 2010). Desistance does sometimes require a sanction element as well as support and encouragement.

A second reason for the parallel tracks development of community justice interventions and technological innovation is the leadership from different professional groups, with little overlap in knowledge or values. Community justice interventions are led by practitioners who traditionally are lacking in technological skill and suspicious of technology-led approaches. Those who have led on technological innovation have little grounding in the ethical issues of community justice. Nellis (2013a, 2013b) argues for the need for an ethical component to the further development of technological approaches to prevent the possibility of ever more repressive approaches. Ethical issues raised by the use of EM include the validity of consent, the human rights implications of increasingly invasive approaches and the possible gender differences in the impact felt by EM (Smith and Gibbs, 2013). EM had a more negative impact on women than it had on men, and they found themselves burdened with most of the housework (Renzema, 2013). The use of EM, properly imposed, can be ethically justified; however, in order to be constructive and effective, it needs to be offered as an accompaniment to other interventions.

A partnership with social work can both reduce the negative impact of EM on people who have committed offences and their families, and can help those to gain meaning from the program and support them in rehabilitation and reform (Nellis, 2013a). In the UK, there has been some frustration about the approach of separating EM from wider community justice approaches and interventions: 'Each and every review of electronic monitoring has consistently identified the problem that EM is not sufficiently integrated or embedded within day-to-day offender management' (Goeghegan, 2012: 12).

There are some Australian examples of the positive use of technology to support good practice in community justice. A scheme in South Australia used a chatbot facility to support women gaining ID on their release from custody (Jarldorn and Emery, 2022). During the Covid-19 lockdowns the use of virtual courts kept the justice system functioning (Rossner et al., 2021).

It is difficult to be optimistic about the prospect of EM replacing custodial sentences in a widespread way. Advocates for the use of EM-supported home detention as an alternative to custody argue that it is still punitive but less expensive, as it passes costs and control from the jail to the home (Kornhauser and Laster, 2014). It should have the potential to increase the possibility of rehabilitation, as a reduction in the use of incarceration will allow individuals to remain at home, maintaining employment and family connections (Black and Smith, 2003). It does have the flexibility of being able to be used pre-trial, as a sentence or post-custody, and it can provide punishment and at least temporary protection of the community by way of incapacitation. The visibility of the punishment can be a deterrent, particularly as punishment can be swiftly applied (Kornhauser and Laster, 2014). However, those subject to monitoring did not attribute any deterrent impact to the experience (Hwang et al., 2021). There would need to be a significant change in the popular punitive discourse to allow a significant move away from prison sentences as a primary means of punishment. Arguments relying on the sophistication of the technology and the potential for cost-savings are unlikely to be successful on their own: 'If moral argument and political strategies alone cannot galvanize commitment to reduced prison use, the availability of a new technology (at least this technology, in this context) cannot, by itself, be of help' (Mair and Nellis, 2013: 78).

There is potential for EM to have a positive effect on long-term desistance, but only if it is used in partnership with other community sentences. Judging whether EM is a success requires us to define what success might constitute (Daems, 2020), but the promotion of long-term desistance has to be a part of it. Legislation in some Australian states, such as the Community Corrections Order in Victoria, could facilitate this. Desisters report that a curfew can help in the desistance process, but only if they are already predisposed to make efforts themselves (Hucklesby, 2013). A review of the research available found that EM had the most impact on mid-range offenders, with more influence on older than younger people (Renzema, 2013). However, EM restrictions can have a negative impact on employment opportunities, particularly for shift workers, so restrictions need to be managed as part of an intervention plan if they are to provide a longer term support to the desistance process. Ensuring compliance, particularly in a way that will support long-term change, will best be achieved in partnership with some sort of social work intervention (Nellis, 2013a, 2013b). Individuals find the routine imposed by EM to be helpful, but that needs to be accompanied by work to address their thinking and behaviour, and to support their ongoing desistance. Those who have committed offences should be partners in the process, embrace the demands made by EM and cooperate with the accompanying work to challenge their offending thinking and behaviour (Nellis, 2009a). Those who do not wish to comply will usually be quickly detected, although, with commitment, it is possible to find a way to subvert even sophisticated systems; Goffman (2014) provides an account of a young man who offered a service of voice impersonation to subvert a phone-based system. Compliance is not static: Even those who do not initially comply with EM can be supported to do so, through work to uncover the reasons for resisting (Martinovic, 2010).

Technology can have unexpected impacts, and can affect not just what we do, but who we are (Turkle, 2011). As society gets more and more used to regular and consistent surveillance of all of our actions, it will increasingly be understood and expected that offenders will be watched. It is how this is done, and the values that guide it, that will determine whether community justice objectives can be met:

> The egalitarian and humanistic values that have informed penal reform in the past—commitment to social justice, respect for personal dignity, care and understanding of the vulnerable, censure of violence and confidence that people can be helped to change for the better—can never be dispensed with; there can never be purely technocratic solutions to engrained structural and cultural problems.
>
> (Nellis, Beyens and Kaminski, 2013: 16)

The work of community justice to support desistance will be covered in the next chapter, followed by a more detailed discussion of community justice values in Chapter 11.

Further reading

Technology and criminal justice is a subject that has not yet attracted an extensive academic literature, but Nellis, Beyens and Kaminski's (2013) edited collection, *Electronically Monitored Punishment*, provides a good overview of the main issues and of the international adoption of technologies. Kornhauser and Laster (2014) probably provide the most detailed engagement with the possibility of electronic monitoring leading to decarceration in Australia.

Practical task

You are working with Suzy, a small business owner who has previously been convicted of offences related to financial irregularities. Unpaid creditors, including some victims of her previous offending, have used social media to publicise her behaviour and express their anger towards her. Suzy now regrets her earlier behaviour and is keen to make a success of her legitimate business but feels constrained by the reputational damage to her online profile. How would you advise and support Suzy?

Reflective questions

9.1 One researcher wore an electronic device for a short period and wrote about the experience (Martinovic and Schluter, 2012). What do you think of the benefits and challenges of this as a research technique?

9.2 Try to think about the next ten years in criminal justice. Can you predict any new technologies that might be introduced? Would the introduction of such technologies be likely to make the system more or less punitive?

9.3 How might the imposition of electronic monitoring impact differently on men and women?

10 Facilitating desistance and building good lives

Introduction

A desistance approach to work with people who have committed offences involves a shift from an emphasis on programmatic interventions to one underpinned by relational and social contexts (McNeill, 2006; Weaver, 2014). Desistance approaches fit very closely with community justice values, as they emphasise long-term sustainable change, seeing the individual as a whole person, rather than just through their offending behaviour, and working within a context of community and relationships. They are relevant to both adults and young people, and move beyond a strict emphasis on programmatic interventions and short-term impact on reconviction. Desistance is defined as the process by which people stop and sustain the cessation of offending, and it can occur with or without the intervention of criminal justice agencies (Weaver and McNeill, 2007a). It consists of a primary component—when an individual is not offending—and a secondary component—when the individual has taken on a new, non-offending identity (Maruna, 2006). It can be a difficult concept to define, as it relates to the absence rather than the presence of something (Weaver and McNeill, 2007b), and the confident description of an individual as a desister requires a prediction that they will not offend again in the future. This chapter explores the implications of taking a desistance approach on work with people who have committed offences and on the role of the practitioner. It pays particular attention to desistance research in Australia and concludes by drawing connections between desistance and community justice.

Promoting desistance by asking a different question

Desistance approaches have attracted considerable attention in recent years, mainly in relation to the management in the community of people who have committed offences in the community but also now in policing (see, for example, Sherman and Neyroud, 2012). The focus on desistance processes is both a development of the Risk Needs Responsivity (RNR) model and a reaction to it. The RNR model was associated with the 'What Works'

DOI: 10.4324/9781003193814-11

movement (see Chapter 4) and led to both a particular approach to the work with people who have committed offences and to evaluating and researching that work. The RNR model focused on the development of accredited programs; individuals were assessed and allocated to these programs; and quantitative models were used to determine the success or otherwise of these interventions on reoffending rates. 'What Works' approaches and desistance approaches do not need to be set in competition with each other and can be best considered complementary approaches, sharing the same belief in the capacity of an individual to change, but preferencing different research approaches (Maruna and Mann, 2019).

This approach has had a very beneficial impact on work with people who have committed offences —particularly in dissipating some of the pessimism associated with 'nothing works' (Martinson, 1974). However, it has not always matched with the lived experience of work with people who have committed offences, the complexity of their lives or the reality of workers' interventions with them (Ward and Maruna, 2007). In work with young people, studies have shown that contact with the criminal justice system can itself be damaging, and even the best programs will have only a marginal beneficial impact on offending as a whole (McAra and McVie, 2011). A desistance approach involves a change in focus, from thinking about programs to thinking about lives and about social institutions (Farrall and Calverley, 2006; Maruna and Lebel, 2010). Desistance studies ask, 'Why do people stop offending?' and then 'What can the criminal justice system do to aid these processes?' (Farrall, 2007).

Desistance approaches can often be explained in terms of three broad perspectives (see, for example, McCulloch and McNeill, 2009):

1 *Maturational reform theory*: There is a correlation between age and criminal behaviour;
2 *Social bonds theory:* The varying ties to family, employment and so on in early adulthood affect desistance from crime;
3 *Narrative approaches:* These explain desistance by a subjective change in person's sense of self: The acceptance of redemption script rather than condemnation script.

These broad perspectives can be identified in the discussion of desistance throughout this chapter, particularly in the outline of different desistance approaches in the next section.

Perhaps the clearest summary of the shift in ethos from the RNR model to a desistance approach is encapsulated in Ward and Maruna's (2007: 12) suggestion that a subtly different question should be asked:

> As numerous observers have argued over the years, 'What Works?' is probably the 'wrong question' for the important issue of offender rehabilitation. Imagine, after all, that rather than asking 'What Works?' Martinson had asked 'What helps people go straight?' The difference in word choice

is subtle enough. Presumably the two phrases mean essentially the same thing. Yet the difference in impact between the two questions is substantial.

Desistance approaches emphasise relational and social context. The process of desistance is not owned by the practitioner or expert, but by the desisting individual and their community. The role of the practitioner is one of support (McNeill, 2006; Weaver, 2014).

Different desistance approaches

A desistance approach emphasises the impact of life events and achievements in the move away from offending (see Box 10.1). The four main such life transitions are spirituality, marriage, parenthood and employment

> **Box 10.1**
>
> **Desistance and life events**
>
> The idea that individuals simply grow out of crime, and cease offending when they reach a certain age, is compelling but is an over-simplistic way to explain complex processes of desistance. Robert Sampson and John Laub's research on the offending life course (Sampson and Laub, 1993; Laub and Sampson, 2003) found that key points in individuals' lives could precipitate desistance decisions. It was the bond between the individual and society that determined whether an individual was likely to be engaged in offending behaviour or to seek to desist from it. One of these points could be military service, but the three more universal turning points were marriage, the birth of children and the securing of employment. These researchers' early work was criticised for relying too heavily on an argument that external social forces were what was responsible for desistance, and they did later give a greater weight to human agency (see Farrall et al. [2014] for a discussion of how this work relates to other approaches to desistance).
>
> The work of Sampson and Laub was initially based on their analysis of data gathered by their predecessors, the Gluecks, and then on their own work in following up the cohort of individuals interviewed (see Bottoms, 2008, for an account of their methodological approach). This longitudinal approach allowed for a detailed and theoretically informed connection to be drawn between the account the interviewees gave of their own lives and the events of those lives. Like much of the desistance research, Sampson and Laub's research does present a challenge to criminal justice practitioners, in that it links desistance to wider social forces, not to actions carried out within the criminal justice system.

(Weaver, 2014). There are clear links between these: Employment can lead to financial stability, making marriage and parenthood more likely and attractive. There can be challenges for those with convictions to find employment but there are some employers who have a commitment to social justice who will employ those with criminal records, and they achieve both commercial benefit and a committed workforce by doing so (Atherton and Buck, 2021). For girls and young women, pregnancy may bring an abrupt end to offending behaviour, as desistance in girls is often associated with the taking on of parental responsibility (Sharpe, 2012; Weaver and McNeill, 2007b). However, depending on circumstances, pregnancy and childbirth may place different constraints on young women's lives (Sharpe, 2012). The complex pathway to desistance for women can sometimes be experienced as uncanny or frightening (Fredriksson and Galnander, 2020). Australian research found that women responded positively to strengths-based work delivered by workers who were reliable and developed positive working relationships with them (Trotter, McIvor and Sheehan, 2012). Any desistance work with women needs to take consideration of the impact of shame and stigmatisation (Rutter and Barr, 2021).

In considering these different forms of desistance, Farrall et al.'s (2014) conception of different models of desistance for different groups of people who have committed offences is most helpful:

- *Rational choice theory.* This is the idea that ex-offenders make a deliberate, conscious and rational choice to stop offending. Like the idea that the choice to commence offending is a deliberate and rational one, this idea has largely been rejected.
- *Age invariance theory.* The opportunity to offend becomes less as people age. This has also largely been rejected.
- *Sampson and Laub's (1993) age-graded theory of social control.* This is one of the best-known theories of desistance, and it highlights the bond between an individual and society. It suggests that key events and turning points (most notably marriage) can influence the pattern of both offending and the avoidance of offending.
- *Moffit's (1994) dual taxonomy theory.* This theory suggests that there are two different sorts of offenders: Those who persist throughout life and those who just offend in adolescence. This theory has little empirical support.
- *Maruna's phenomenology of desistance.* Desisters need to see themselves as fundamentally good people who have done bad things. Ex-offenders need to develop a coherent pro-social model identity for themselves—a positive narrative.
- *Giordina, Cernkovich and Rudolph's (2002) theory of cognitive transformation.* This theory focuses on cognitive shifts as the main drivers of desistance;

offenders who desist change their outlook and their thinking. A period of reflection and reassessment is important in the early stages of desistance, but this needs to be accompanied by an opportunity to change, such as a job offer.

- *Gadd's (2004) psycho-social theory of desistance and reform.* This theory highlights the importance of unconscious motivation. Desisters want certain things but are not necessarily consciously aware of this themselves. It is not accurate simply to reduce desistance to a series of social processes.
- *Shapland and Bottoms' (2011) theory of the early stages of desistance.* This theory focuses on the early development of desistance in 19–22-year olds. It emphasises the combination of individual agency with structural aspects of desistance (see also Best et al., 2021, for a discussion of the relationship between structure and agency).
- *Vaughan's (2007) internal conversation theory.* Desisters are understood to have internal conversations about who they want to be, weighing up gains and losses.
- *Paternoster and Bushway's (2009) theory of the 'feared self'.* Desistance is understood as a decision that is consciously taken, in the context of a life that is a project that is always in process.

As well as different theories, it can be helpful to consider different types of desisters. Dufour and Brassard (2014) refer to three categories of offenders. The first of these they describe as the 'transformed', who offend as children but then later take on the role of highly regarded citizens. They describe the second group as 'the remorseful', who offend as adults without ever thinking of themselves as offenders, and desist by returning to the personal identity they had prior to the offence. The third group are 'the rescued', who also begin offending as adults but need an external intervention—either from the criminal justice system or through finding employment—to assist in the cessation of offending.

Farrall et al. (2014) found five categories of desisters in the sample of people who had committed offences they followed in their longitudinal sample:

1 *Offenders with limited criminal careers.* These people were never fully committed to an offending identity. They would be those who drifted into crime but still maintained some commitment to the norms of wider society (see Sykes and Matza, 1957; Matza, 1964). These people can be supported to return to a non-offending lifestyle.
2 *Drug offenders who desisted.* They often went through a rehabilitation program and then moved away from the area.
3 *Street offenders who desisted.* In these cases, desistance related to marriage, having children and/or finding employment.

4 *Alcoholics who desisted.* Some alcoholics desisted because they gave up alcohol, while others continued to drink but no longer offended.
5 *Desistance through ill-health.*

These categories do not contradict those outlined by Dufour and Brassard (2014); again, there is an emphasis both on different approaches being right for different groups and on the role of the practitioner being one of providing support and direction, rather than imposing something on the client.

Closely associated with the desistance approach is the Good Lives Model, a strengths-based approach that reduces risk while building the capacity of people who have committed offences to live lives that are personally meaningful and fulfilling (Ward and Maruna, 2007; Chu, Ward and Willis, 2014). The Good Lives Model is based on an understanding that offenders are goal directed and prioritise human goods in their lives in the same way as non-offenders do. However, their offending arises from using inappropriate means to achieve these goals—possibly through a lack of capacity or opportunity to use legitimate means. The Good Lives Model takes a strengths-based response to rehabilitation, aiming to create new skills and capacities within the life-plans set by the individual (Ward and Maruna, 2007). The Good Lives Model was set out in most detail by Ward and Maruna (2007), and they state that it has seven general principles:

1 Offenders seek the same primary goods as anyone else;
2 Rehabilitation is a value-laden process;
3 Correctional interventions should promote good as well as manage and reduce risk;
4 Rehabilitation involves a new conception of the self;
5 People can only function within a community that provides support;
6 Risk is multi-faceted;
7 Treatment plans should be explicitly constructed to fit the Good Lives Model and they should be rights-based.

The Good Lives Model allows workers to work with offenders and to focus on their lives and their interests, not to have to ask them to think of others or the community in general. Workers seek to take a positive approach, taking account of the individual's priorities and life-plan. Work with people who commit offences is not required to have an explicit and direct focus on offending behaviour. Meeting non-criminogenic needs is a condition to meeting criminogenic needs, and the Good Lives Model encourages the putting of other measures in place to prevent a return to offending (Chu, Ward and Willis, 2014). However, the Good Lives Model does not provide a program that needs to be strictly adhered to. It is possible to work in sympathy with the Good Lives Model values and principles without explicitly setting out to follow its approach.

> **Box 10.2**
>
> **Multi-Systemic Therapy (MST) and the good lives model**
>
> Ward and Maruna (2007) suggest that Multi-Systemic Therapy is an example of the operationalisation of the Good Lives Model. MST's emphasis on strengths, approach goals and working on the systems that surround a young person, not just on the young person, make it entirely consistent with GLM principles. Further, MST interventions do not simply target offending behaviour but rather seek to preserve home placements and educational progress.
>
> Research into the Intensive Supervision Program (ISP), a program of Juvenile Justice NSW that is a licensed version of MST, drew on desistance approaches as part of the evaluation (Stout, Schraner and Dalby, 2016; Stout, Dalby and Schraner, 2017)). Given the difficulties in defining desistance for young people—they have not had sufficient opportunity to show that they no longer offend—the researchers defined a desister as someone who had not offended since the program, was in education or employment, had stable accommodation and was avoiding drug use and alcohol abuse. Nine of the 24 young people in the sample met those criteria, and a similar number again could credibly claim to be on a path to desistance.
>
> The research found that the ISP's particular strength was in supporting parents and caregivers—primarily mothers—to help young people achieve desistance. ISP clinicians approached their work in a spirit of co-working, seeking to support the young people and families in achieving objectives that they had set for their own lives and in overcoming obstacles. Clinicians would work with young people in changing their attitude to school, but would also work with the education authorities to ensure the offer of a viable school placement. The clinicians played the role of 'normal-smiths' in the lives of the young people and especially their families, demonstrating with words and actions that the offences committed were not what should define the young person's life.

Desistance and young people

One of the challenges of a desistance approach is in work with young people. Clearly, it is difficult to say with any confidence that a young person has permanently desisted from offending and taken on a new identity when there is still so much of their identity still to form. Desistance can be achieved through a number of pathways, including parenthood, marriage and employment. Young people have not yet reached this life stage, and the path that they take to adulthood and desistance is likely to be a zig–zag one (Weaver and McNeill, 2007b). However, work with young people is particularly well suited to be considered within a desistance framework because of the complexity of the client group. When working with young people and their families, it is not appropriate to consider simply whether a particular intervention 'works'. The impact of a criminal justice intervention can be as varied as the young people and families themselves. However, the importance of an effective intervention is clear: Serious young offenders are likely to become serious adult offenders, a trend that is particularly pronounced among young men from an Indigenous background (Brame, Mazarolle and Piquero, 2010). A criminal justice intervention might not lead immediately to a cessation of offending for a young person, but that does not necessarily mean that it has not been effective. Asking whether a particular approach has 'helped' can be more useful and appropriate. However, agency clarity is also helpful in supporting practitioners in their work with young people, some report confusion between the different approaches and suggested paradigms, including between supportive, child-centred approaches and conceptions of young people as carriers of risk (Day, 2022).

Desistance can be related to place (Flynn, 2010; Farrall et al., 2014), and this can be particularly relevant to young people; those who return to school will live their lives in different places than those who are on street corners, associating with offending peers. Desisters will consciously create routines for themselves and distance themselves from offending peers.

Desistance is a process, not an event; individuals often go through a process of a reduction of offending or a winding path of some desistance, but some intermittent offending, before permanently ceasing offending. This is particularly true for young people. Research in the UK (Macdonald et al., 2011) identified that the two factors that were associated in leading short-term offending careers into serious, long-term careers were a growing dependence on drugs and a complete disengagement from education. Young people who were successful in desistance will become involved in purposeful activities and disassociate themselves from offending friends. An approach that can achieve this will promote desistance in young people. Understanding the three main strands of youth transition—from school to work, family, career and housing—is necessary to understand the desistance process and its fragile nature (Macdonald et al., 2011). For a young person, becoming a desister is like becoming an adult: It is not a simple transition, but rather a series of complex processes (Rocque, 2014). As with adults, desistance in young people is achieved through a combination of structural factors and changes in personal approach, so that desisters take a hopeful, optimistic and future-focused attitude to their lives despite their bleak current circumstances (Macdonald et al., 2011).

The role of the practitioner

Another shift from the RNR paradigm to the desistance paradigm is in how work with people who have committed offences is conceptualised. Rather than seeing rehabilitation as something that is done *to* individuals who have committed offences, a desistance approach emphasises co-production and working together. The role of the practitioner in supporting desistance is an important focus of research into the approach. This co-production involves interaction with families and communities, and a focus on goals more broad than simply a discussion of offending behaviour and the offender. Supporting desistance requires addressing those social obstacles and lack of opportunities that might impede the desistance process (Weaver, 2014).

Desistance is not simply managed by criminal justice practitioners; as well as the co-production with the individuals themselves there is a need to work with families, community organisations, schools and employers. Family-focused work is crucial in providing support, particularly after the support provided by criminal justice practitioners has ceased (Weaver, 2014).

A high-quality relationship with a criminal justice practitioner who is supportive, optimistic and takes a holistic approach to the work is crucial in the promotion of desistance (McNeill et al., 2005). Practitioners themselves, when asked, also identify this relational aspect of the work as crucial to any concept of quality supervision (Grant and McNeill, 2014). Service users value someone they can trust and respect, and with whom they get on well. Practitioners need to move beyond services focusing solely on abstinence from offending to those that build capacity, remove barriers and support the development of good lives (Weaver, 2014).

An important aspect of this relationship between worker and client lies in the hope and optimism that the worker will show in believing that the individual is not irredeemably bad and that they can make a change in their life. Farrall et al. (2014) refer to this as a worker being a 'normal-smith', someone who does not need convincing of the good character of the individual, thus facilitating their transition away from a deviant identity. The converse of this is a 'deviant-smith', who will reinforce the deviant identity of the individual. The longitudinal research carried out by Farrall and colleagues (2014) was somewhat negative about the work of criminal justice practitioners, finding that there was almost nothing they could do in the absence of a motivated individual, and that their main positive role was to help the individual in overcoming the barriers that they had identified. This is in line with the values of a desistance approach: It is something done *with* an individual, not something done *to* an individual, so no progress can be made without the motivation of the individual, supported by the confidence of those around them. For someone who is entrenched in criminal networks to successfully change their life is a difficult process, requiring self-belief and the support and optimism of those around them (Maruna and Lebel, 2010).

However, over the course of the three research interviews with the participants in their study, the researchers found a number of ways in which probation, or broader criminal justice interventions, might work to support desistance (Farrall et al., 2014):

- Probation interventions signal to offenders that change is needed;
- Talking therapies provide support, advice and practical help. They can be drawn on at the time of the therapy or later;

- Criminal justice workers can be 'normal-smiths', emphasising the non-offending part of the offender's identity;
- The impact of probation or another intervention can emerge slowly; individuals may draw on the lessons at a later stage in their lives;
- The interventions and effect of probation can seem mundane; often, the interventions that led to change were neither radical nor ground-breaking.

These positive impacts do not occur in all cases. In fact, a criminal justice intervention can actually have a negative effect, particularly if the attitude of the workers serves to reinforce the client in their deviant, or offender, identity.

Workers use their skills—often social work skills—to mediate the potentially harsh impact of the criminal justice system on young people. The quality of the relationship and the communication between worker and client works alongside the leverage provided by the hard edge of criminal justice sanctions: Curfews and the use of custody.

The desistance approach places an emphasis upon practitioner skills and the relationship between the client and the worker. Clinicians need to be 'normal-smiths' (Farrall et al., 2014) believing in the essential goodness and non-deviance of the client with whom they are working. Young desisters needed to possess hope in their future (Macdonald et al., 2011) and the worker should support that. Maruna and Lebel (2010: 76) refer to this as a 'Pygmalion effect': People will become what others believe them to be. The worker should (Trotter and Evans, 2010; Trotter, 2014):

- Be clear about their role;
- Be reliable, fair and modelling pro-social values;
- Help the offender in solving problems he identifies;
- Encourage the offender in focusing on problems associated with offending;
- Help the offender to develop strategies to deal with issues;
- Take a holistic approach;
- Develop a therapeutic alliance by working in a collaborative, friendly and optimistic way.

Effective workers can explain and model a role that combines both support and authority. It is important that those on statutory orders meet their legal obligations and comply with the terms of the order, but a skilled practitioner will ensure that such compliance goes beyond a mere adherence to the minimum legal requirements. Compliance that leads to desistance will be longer-term, substantive and will arise from the offender's own commitment to address their offending behaviour (Robinson and McNeill, 2010) and their ability to view themselves in a more positive way (see Box 10.3). For a practitioner to support compliance, they need to work in an individualised and relational way that is responsive to the particular circumstances and context (Weaver et al., 2020).

Box 10.3

Changing the narrative and making good

The three main strands of the interpretation of desistance are usually understood to be maturational reform theory, social bonds theory and changing the individual's self-narrative from thinking that they are an offender to taking on a more positive label (McCulloch and McNeill, 2009). This narrative approach to the explanation of desistance is best exemplified in Shadd Maruna's (2001) research in the Liverpool Desistance Study, described in his book *Making Good*. Maruna interviewed 65 individuals, asking them to describe their life stories and classifying them into desisters and persisters.

Based on the responses to his interviews, Maruna argues that, for an individual to desist from crime, they need to be able to make sense of their life. A desister needs to have a positive self-narrative—a consistent way of explaining their life. For offenders desisting from crime, this coherent self-narrative needs to explain both why they committed offences in the first place and also why they have now moved away from offending. Maruna (2001: 8) describes his theory of desistance as a response to a question posed by Lofland (1969: 282) about how a life that is discontinuous and radically changing can be turned into a related and meaningful series of events.

What Maruna's research found was that the self-narratives adopted by those who desisted from crime often involved an element of self-deception. The need for them to think positively about themselves and their current lives led them to minimise the harm that they had caused and to describe their lives in ways that did not match the reality of events. This is described as a redemption script, and these scripts—although distinct for every individual—have some common characteristics. The desister considers that they are essentially a good person who has become ensnared in offending through circumstances, not their own volition. Desisters have an optimistic view of the future and a particular faith in their own ability to take control over their own destiny. They also have a desire to give something back and to contribute to society. This redemption script as a self-narrative did not require a taking of responsibility for offending actions or a facing up to what they had done. It was sometimes easier for desisters to build a positive self-narrative by ignoring, minimising or excusing their previous offending actions.

These insights into the self-narrative of desisting offenders did present two main challenges to traditional correctional practice.

> Firstly, the conventional wisdom, and the basis for much CBT work, was that offenders should face up to the harm they had caused and take responsibility for their actions. CBT approaches challenge the cognitive dissonance that allow offenders to commit offences without thought for the consequences on others. The desistance approach suggests that this cognitive dissonance might actually be helpful in leading offenders to think of themselves in a positive way and take on a pro-social identity. Secondly, desistance approaches encourage co-working alongside offenders, supporting their own efforts to desist from crime. This contrasts with an approach that sees criminal justice interventions as something to be done *by* workers *to* offenders.

The influence of the practitioner does not necessarily occur only during the time of the intervention. It is possible for a worker to have a very positive influence on the life of an individual who has committed offences, but for the positive effect to only become apparent many years later. In cases such as these, Farrall et al. (2014: 48) describe how the worker had an 'imprint' rather than an impact: Some of what they said or tried to convey was mentally retained by the offenders and then drawn on at the time when they were ready to change their lives:

> take words seriously ... 'Words' eventually 'filter through' ... time is required for changes in both the outlook and the life circumstances of ex-probationers to take place before these changes and the advice of their officer becomes 'aligned' and, as such, meaningful for the recipients of such advice.
> (Farrall and Calverley, 2006: 196)

The advice provided about how to change could predate the desire to change by many years, but it could be stored up, then drawn upon when needed. Indeed, the cessation of offending behaviour does not even need to be a primary focus of the work; practice that is carried out ethically, with a focus on personal goals and on overcoming obstacles, can indirectly, or obliquely, lead to desistance from offending behaviour. Desistance is achieved when offending behaviour is no longer relevant or appropriate in a life that has changed (Canton, 2012).

Finally, it is worth emphasising again that, although practitioner skills are crucial, promoting desistance is not simply an approach of training practitioners to implement magic solutions. It is not simply a talking therapy: There is a need to build social as well as human capital (McCulloch and McNeill, 2009). Promoting desistance is a process of co-production between the individual who has committed the offence, the worker and the community, requiring work with the community to support individuals as well as with the individuals themselves (Weaver and McNeill, 2007a, 2007b). There is also an important role for the agency. Best et al. (2021) introduce the concept of justice capital, and the idea that the criminal justice agency itself can be an important factor in whether desistance is supported or impeded. This is particularly important in Australia in light of the history of interaction between the criminal justice system and Indigenous communities (Best et al., 2021).

Practitioners might find that the relationship with them is considerably less important in promoting desistance than the individual's relationship with friends, family and other non-professional staff (McNeill, 2006).

Desistance in Australia

There has been limited research into desistance approaches in Australia, and Halsey (2006) comments that there is little evidence of a desistance model being enacted in Australia. The research that has been carried out in Australia is in line with the conclusions drawn elsewhere. Moore, McArthur and Saunders (2013) interviewed young people leaving custody and found that they said that they most valued practical help in overcoming obstacles to returning to the community. They found it difficult to return to school and to gain support to live in the community, and they valued workers who could help them with this. These young people wanted to identify the key issues for themselves and have some control, but not to feel solely responsible for their own desistance. Practitioners should take a co-working approach, focus on problems identified by the young people and support their return to education or employment. They should recognise the strong need for connections to employment, education or other networks, and should support young people in culturally responsive ways, particularly in light of the high representation of Indigenous and Pacific Islander young people in the juvenile justice system (Moore, McArthur and Saunders, 2013) (see Calverley, 2013, for a discussion of how desistance might be supported in different cultural groups).

Young men who have been through a custodial institution and are seeking to move away from offending do find great challenges in building a law-abiding life. They wish to socialise with friends, to earn a good income and to spend their lives engaging in activities that give them a sense of purpose and value, but these desires can conflict with attempts to move away from offending (Halsey, 2006). Moments where they are frustrated with the desistance process and seem to return to offending are often more related to frustration or the fragility of their circumstances as to any active desire to return to offending (Halsey, Armstrong and Wright, 2017).

Halsey and Deegan (2015) studied young men going through the prison system in South Australia. They used the concept of generativity to explain these men's desistance; it was when they started to take steps to move beyond self-absorption to start caring for others that they started to make changes in their lives. The experience of caring, or of being cared for, led them to experience hope and to start the process of turning away from offending.

Facilitating desistance and building good lives 173

This research highlights the role family can play in supporting desistance. Where the men had fathers who had been through the prison system themselves, they could take on the role of 'wounded healers', supporting their children to follow a pathway away from their offending behaviour (Halsey and Deegan, 2012). However, it was often mothers and female partners who took on the burden of providing support to achieve desistance (Halsey and Deegan, 2014). It is these women who are often the main change agents through which desistance is enacted, as they can provide hope and encouragement:

> Overwhelmingly, in picking up the pieces, women adopted the role(s) of carer (of children), home-maker, communicator (letter-writer, phone-caller, visitor), peacemaker (in relation to ongoing family disputes or troubles with ex-partner (s)) and absolver (the person who repeatedly forgives, up to a point, the transgressions of their loved one).
> (Halsey and Deegan, 2014: 17)

The women play these roles at considerable cost to themselves and their own well-being, so it is crucial that they too are provided with support. Although women play a strong role in supporting desistance in men, this partner support is not present in the same way for women. Women who have committed offences are overwhelmingly concerned about the welfare of their children, so those children need to be placed at the centre of any post-release plan (Baldry, 2010). Women need a safe space away from negative relationships, so supported housing is crucial to women's post-release provision (Baldry, 2010).

Research (Trotter, Baidawi and Evans, 2015) has shown that the therapeutic relationship, discussed above, is particularly important in the supervision of Indigenous young people. As well as the incredible over-representation of Indigenous young people in the youth justice population, there is an added complexity in the relationship because of the long history of mistrust and anger felt by Indigenous groups to the social work profession. The researchers set out five principles for the effective supervision in youth justice:

1 Culturally informed communication;
2 Valuing Indigenous knowledge;
3 The importance of the working relationship;
4 The significance of family;
5 Highlighting strengths and achievements.

An approach to support desistance in Indigenous Australians requires an understanding of the cultural and social context, and the legacy of disadvantage and marginalisation. Goldsmith and Halsey (2013) emphasise the importance of what they describe as both the background and the foreground. The background understanding of the lives of Indigenous people and their place in contemporary Australia provides the context to explain the high rates of offending in this group. The foreground understanding of individuals and families explains why it is that some young people commit offences and others do not. The authors identify key factors in supporting desistance from offending in Indigenous young people. These factors include a sense of place: Indigenous young people have an identification and a connection with the country, but it is the excitement of the city that draws them into offending. As well as understanding place, working with Indigenous young people requires an understanding of family, kinship and belonging. A connection to their Indigenous culture is an important part of desistance for Indigenous young people and adults, suggesting that narrative scripts can extend beyond individual life stories (Richards, Death and McCartan, 2020). Siblings and cousins can be associates in offending, but family can also be a key protective factor. An attraction to cars or a damaging use of alcohol can draw Indigenous young people into offending. Attempts to support desistance can be hampered by the long legacy of distrust between Indigenous groups, the police, social services and other statutory bodies. Any attempt to support desistance needs to take place in this context, and incorporate work to build trust and understanding.

Community justice and desistance in Australia

There are clear and obvious links between community justice and the promotion of desistance. One connection is the emphasis given to citizenship values and community involvement (Farrall et al., 2014). Farrall and colleagues describe a relationship between liberal citizenship values and citizenship, particularly that desisters exhibit fewer self-centred values and their wider pro-social values are associated with their move to a non-offending identity. Importantly, this needs to be a two-way relationship, with community institutions supporting the reintegration of individuals while those individuals take steps to adopt pro-social values and become involved in a positive way in the community. Farrall and colleagues (2014) draw on the capability approach of Sen (1985, 1999) and Nussbaum (2000): Desisters need to achieve something that they value or enjoy doing, but society also has to provide the opportunity for them to achieve this. An example of an approach that could be taken to promote the pro-social identity of individuals is offering higher education in prisons, enabling a change from an identity as a 'prisoner' to an identity as a 'student' (Lerman and Sadin, 2022). A respectful and caring approach to individuals after they have been released from prison can be important in reaffirming human dignity and supporting desistance (Canton, 2022).

A community approach to desistance is particularly important in work with Indigenous communities. This work requires a community, rather than an individual, focus. Ideally, Indigenous workers should be employed to work with Indigenous young people, but all workers engaged with this client group should have a working knowledge of Indigenous culture. A desistance approach links with the community justice approach in emphasising connections, community and the achievement of other goals beyond the achievement of a reduction in the headline reoffending rate.

Desistance also has in common with community justice the fact that it presents a challenge to the values and assumptions of the current criminal justice system. It focuses on society at large, rather than just criminal justice responses, and the person as a whole, rather than just their offending behaviour. Implementing policies based on desistance would require a fairly fundamental change in thinking, so that those who do commit further offences are not seen as failures but as continuing to take steps to move towards a law-abiding life (Halsey, 2006).

Further reading

Stephen Farrall's three books (Farrall and Calverley, 2006; Farrall, 2007; Farrall et al., 2014), following his longitudinal research with groups of people subject to probation orders, provide a very good overview of the development of desistance theory. McNeill (2006) provides a clear and comprehensive account of the main aspects of the theory. Halsey and Deegan's (2015) book applies desistance theory to an Australian context, and shows the difficulties that serious and persistent offenders face in achieving desistance.

Practical task

One of the challenges for practitioners in supporting a desistance approach is that it is not always possible to identify in the present what conversations, experiences or interventions might be supporting future desistance. Imagine you are working with 25-year-old Matthew (first introduced in chapter one): What are the sort of indicators that you might be looking for to assure you that your work was having a positive impact?

Reflective questions

10.1 It is suggested that desistance approaches and community justice fit well together. Do you agree with this? Are their values bases similar?
10.2 If we accept that desistance is achieved in one of four ways—spirituality, marriage, parenthood or employment—what implications does this have for community justice practice?
10.3 How could a community justice worker be persuaded that a young person was a desister, given that any time period without offending is likely to be a short one?

11 Values, ethics, human rights and children's rights

Introduction

Working in the community with people who have committed offences is a morally significant task. Practitioners are interacting with some of the most vulnerable people in society at a time when they are in crisis and, in many cases, are at risk of causing harm to others. The moral significance of the work and the need to be led by values and principles is seen in the attention given to criminal and youth justice matters in international human rights instruments and by international human rights bodies, as well as by the practice of national and state organisations to set out their values in working with people who have committed offences. This chapter considers the values and principles set in Australia for working with people who have committed offences in community justice and the statements of the relevant international human rights instruments as they relate to community justice in Australia. It draws upon the social work literature's long tradition of engaging with values debates, addressing some of what is covered in the literature with relation to values in community justice, and looking at Australian examples where scrutinising bodies have criticised Australian criminal justice agencies for failing to meet human rights standards.

A social work approach to community justice values

Although there is no requirement that community justice practitioners hold a social work qualification, and many social work programs in Australia pay little attention to working with people who have committed offences as a distinct client group, the discussion of values in the social work literature has strong relevance to the discussion of values in community justice. Across the world, there is a decreasing involvement of social work in criminal justice but the values remain worth defending (Patterson, 2012). Values and ethics need to be considered in the practice and organisational context. Ethics is not simply about abstract debate; it requires engagement with the reality of people's lives, often by practitioners who are over-burdened with work, operating in complicated systems (Bowles et al., 2006). Practitioners in community justice

DOI: 10.4324/9781003193814-12

may have chosen to work in that profession because of their commitment to social justice and human rights, but may find an apparent contradiction between their vision of the work and everyday practice. Community justice, like other areas of social work, works with a client group of people who are disempowered, and practitioners need to recognise the power dynamics in their working relationship. There needs to be an understanding of the fragmented, plural society in which they work, and how that is associated with their accountability. Community justice workers are accountable to their employers, but also to their clients, to victims and to the wider community.

The traditional models of ethical decision-making are, firstly, the deontological or duty-based approach, following Kantian categorical imperatives and, secondly, the consequentialist approach, where what matters is outcomes and individuals are held to be morally responsible for outcomes that could be reasonably foreseen. Bowles et al. (2006) suggest that a third model is appropriate for practitioners: A virtue-based model that emphasises the importance of good character. In practice, this is not just about becoming a 'good person', but about the goals of practice; acting ethically in community justice requires a clear understanding of the goals of community justice. An approach to ethics that is based on character, moral courage and behaving as an ethical, virtuous practitioner is appropriate to community justice, as the messy, complex world of practice does not easily allow for a formal ethical decision-making approach to be taken. Practitioners do not aim to achieve ethical purity; they seek to make the best decision possible in the circumstances they face. Ethical practitioners will courageously apply ethical skills and knowledge in a pluralist way, drawing on different models as appropriate (Bowles et al., 2006).

A character-based approach to ethics focuses on the character of the individual practitioner, rather than on abstract moral principles—an action is right if it is what a virtuous person would do at the time. Virtue ethics involves the development of moral character and the modelling of moral choices and actions to others. The virtues most relevant to social work are somewhat contested, with different writers listing different virtues, but Bowles et al. (2006) list 12 virtues that arise from an Australian context:

1 Open-mindedness;
2 Practical reasoning;
3 Moral courage;
4 Reflectiveness;
5 Critical reflection;
6 Empathy;
7 Integrity;
8 Commitment to social work values;
9 Discretion;
10 Tolerance;
11 Valuing diversity;
12 Good judgement/wisdom.

These virtues need to be seen within the context of what is trying to be achieved, and in community justice this brings together an ethics of care for the individual with an ethics of justice for both the individual and the wider society. The ethics of social justice, in the form of situated ethics, is particularly relevant and important in community justice in that it seeks equality in social outcomes, with solidarity towards clients and the wider community. Moral courage is critical; community justice workers will need to act ethically in difficult situations where they might feel anxious or fearful.

More recently, Dominey and Canton (2022) have taken this argument further, suggesting that it is a form of virtue ethics that focuses on caring that would be most appropriate for working in the community with those who have offended. Care ethics emphasises relationships and interdependence between individuals. A caring approach is the appropriate approach not simply because it might lead to positive outcomes but because it is the right way for people to interact with each other. It also aligns with the motivations many practitioners state as being the reason why they chose to work in the profession (Dominey and Canton, 2022).

Human rights are universal rights, and social work considers itself to be a human rights profession (Ife, 2012, 2016; Staub-Bernasconi, 2016). A rights discourse, despite its sometimes Western orientation (Sewpaul, 2016), has been successful in promoting the rights of minority groups and in taking the focus of social work away from individual relationships onto wider societal concerns. It is only the commitment of society to protecting the rights of people to lead a dignified life that allows social work to exist.

Banks (2012) describes ethical practitioners as those who are reflective and reflexive, able to locate themselves in the situation they face and to analyse ethical dilemmas with an understanding of the power dynamics. This contrasts with merely defensive practitioners, who take a technician approach and simply follow organisational requirements. Ethical behaviour requires, firstly, the moral sensitivity to be aware of how actions affect others; secondly, the moral reasoning skills to be able to make critical decisions based on moral reasoning; thirdly, the moral motivation to prioritise moral values above non-moral values and finally, the moral courage to hold to moral values under pressure.

Social work values refer to a number of beliefs about what is worthy or valuable in the social work context, including the nature of a good society and the desirable qualities or character traits of professional practitioners (Banks, 2012).

An emphasis on the diversity of particular groups can neglect the fact that social workers and community justice practitioners work with some of the poorest people in society, and that an emphasis on individual responsibility takes the focus away from values of welfare and redistribution (Green, 2008).

The power of social work comes from its ethical dimension, the essence (or *teleos*) of being a social worker is its ethical element—its promotion of social justice and respect for all people's inherent dignity (Bowles et al., 2006). Ethical social work requires self-awareness, empathy, reflection upon decision-making and the development of the ability to take into account a variety of perspectives and explain the action taken. Ethics is about action, not merely about values and judgement. This is an important element of the understanding of community justice: It is ethical work, and practitioners are not merely functionaries. The training of community justice workers should include training in ethical judgement and action. Ethics is at the heart of community justice, and Bauman's (2000) quote about social work (in Bowles et al., 2006: 220) should apply equally to community justice: 'I cannot promise a quiet night's sleep, a quiet conscience, or feeling comfortable ... The decision to be a social worker means a very rewarding, satisfying and extremely difficult life' (Bauman, 2000).

Values in the criminal justice system context

As with social work, the pursuit of criminal justice is a moral enterprise; we need to agree on the right approach to take with those who have caused harm to others. In the history of probation, particularly in the UK, probation was a humanising force in criminal justice, emphasising the need to take an individual approach to each person and to consider both the social and psychological context (Nellis, 2007). Probation showed kindness and respect, rather than simply relying on punishment. A community justice approach can take a narrow interpretation of values, with a focus on the individual interaction between worker and client, with less attention given to the wider criminal justice context. An understanding of this wider context is crucial to ethical community justice practice, and Nellis (2005) identifies three competing values discourses in the understanding of criminal justice:

1. A punitive-repressive approach expresses no belief in the potential for people to change, and simply relies on scaring those who offend into abiding by the law;
2. A surveillant-management approach focuses on assessment, management, control and reduction of risk and harm;
3. The humanistic-rehabilitative approach seeks to work with individuals through education or rehabilitation to end criminality. The humanist approach is based on the acceptance of the absolute moral worth of all human beings.

In recent times, humanistic values have become over-shadowed by a retributive discourse (Nellis, 2005). Humanistic values are now rarely discussed in debates about how to respond to offending; even rehabilitation is discussed in terms of targets and outcomes, rather than values or the quality of interactions. It is important for community justice practitioners to use language that reflects their values and promotes the humanistic approach. The language of respect, equality and decency can do that, and can convey the desired nature of the worker-client relationship. Restorative justice and human rights discourses will promote humanistic values in a criminal justice environment that can be hostile towards them. However, this language is not yet enough to connect the individual relationship with the wider debate of the nature of criminal justice (Lancaster, 2008). The criminal justice debate is heated and emotive, and merely focusing on rehabilitation and on the rights of the offender can lead to the voice being ignored by those who are concerned with victim rights or wider issues of public protection. Nellis (2005) uses the UK experience of the separation of probation training from social work training to argue that social work values have not been sufficient to contribute to wider debates on criminal justice, as they can leave practitioners sounding like they do not fully appreciate the harm that offending does to communities. Community justice might be able to achieve this, in that it references both the need for local responses and the importance of the concept of justice. Bauman (1989, in Nellis, 2005) uses the term 'adiaphorization' to discuss the separation of values concerns from regimes of management. Community justice can connect justice practices to values concerns by using a language that promotes humanistic values.

The discourse of human rights has also been discussed as a possible way to promote community justice values in a language that is widely understood and can be engaged with beyond social work and associated professions (see, for example, Nellis and Gelsthorpe, 2003; Gelsthorpe, 2007). Although this is particularly challenging in Australia, where rights are not embedded in legislation as they are in many European jurisdictions, a human rights discourse does provide some hope for promoting a rights agenda. Even the incorporation of human rights into national legislation does not guarantee the enhancement of civil liberties in that society (Nellis and Gelsthorpe, 2003). A human rights approach encourages the need for public safety to be balanced with due process and a focus on rehabilitation. Individual practitioners can be encouraged to not merely follow legal minimums, but to act ethically in their use of discretion: 'Ideally, criminal justice systems should balance the aspirations to deal justly with offenders, to contribute to crime reduction and public safety and to provide redress and reassurance for victims' (Gelsthorpe, 2007: 503).

Community justice values are not concerned just with the individual relationships between practitioners and those with whom they work; they are also related to the wider criminal justice system. Kleinig (2008) considers the wider moral context of criminal justice, particularly the dependence on the use of imprisonment, as the central part of the response to offending. Imprisonment is now so widely accepted as the central disposal in criminal justice (as demonstrated by the regular descriptions of community disposals as 'alternatives to custody') that its place is rarely questioned. However, whether it is justified in terms of rehabilitation, deterrence or incapacitation, the evidence for the effectiveness of prison is quite modest, and provides support for attempts to respond to offending in different ways. There is also a duty to ensure that those who are incarcerated are able to return to society as easily as possible, with the presumption that they have served their punishment. We know that employment, housing and family support are crucial elements of supporting desistance and protecting against recidivism, but we also have an ethical responsibility to ensure that those convicted of offences can easily return to society and that we need to remove as many barriers to their re-entry to society as we can (Kleinig, 2008).

Values statements in Australia

The moral significance of work with people who commit offences is generally acknowledged, and agencies in that field do make statements of their values base or of the guidelines that should steer their work. The Guiding Principles for Corrections in Australia were developed in 1986. These were an addition to the earlier Minimum Standards for Prisoners that had been developed in 1976, based on the United Nations Standard Minimum Rules for the Treatment of Prisoners and the Council of Europe Standard Minimum Rules (see Australian Institute of Criminology (AIC), 2012, for a presentation of the standards and a description of how they were devised). The guidelines were revised in 2012 and then in 2018, as outcome focused principles. They are presented as best practice to be achieved, in line with international standards, rather than standards to be enforced, and each Australian state and territory must develop its own standards, across five outcomes:

- Governance;
- Respect;
- Safety and security;
- Health and wellbeing;
- Rehabilitation and reintegration.

The states have set their own values for working in community corrections, although none of these statements could be described as contradictory to the national standard guidelines, and many of them link to the Guiding Principles on their website.

NSW

Corrective Services NSW (2022) makes a commitment to service on its website, identifying that recipients of its service include offenders themselves, their families as well as the wider community. Their commitment includes fairness, respect, clarity of communication, confidentiality and effectiveness in monitoring and supervision.

Queensland

Queensland expresses its vision in slightly different language, saying that it wishes to enhance the safety of Queenslanders by maximising rehabilitation and reducing recidivism (Prochaska and DiClemente, 2022). Its values are shared across the Queensland public sector and are professionalism, integrity, accountability and innovation. Queensland states that it is seeking to achieve the fair and humane treatment of people who have committed offences through effective and innovative programs and services, and a commitment to equity and cultural diversity.

South Australia

South Australia's vision is for 'a safer community by protecting the public and reducing reoffending', and its mission is to 'manage offenders in a safe, secure and humane environment and provide opportunities for rehabilitation and reintegration' (South Australia Correctional Services, 2022). It states that its values are honesty and integrity; professionalism and accountability; being socially responsible; ethical and respectful behaviours; equity, diversity and cultural inclusion; courage and tenacity; and service.

Tasmania

Tasmania's vision in community corrections is to reduce reoffending and to increase the ongoing safety of the Tasmanian community by supporting a humane and effective correctional system and providing the opportunity for personal development, rehabilitation and engagement with the community. Tasmanian Corrections works with people who have committed offences to ensure compliance and develop pro-social behaviour, and with the community to facilitate reintegration (Tasmania Department of Justice, 2022).

Western Australia

In Western Australia, the corrective services values are stated to be respecting rights and diversity, fostering service excellence and being fair and reasonable (WA Corrective Services, 2022). Its stated philosophy concerns contributing to community safety through offender management, with a focus on reoffending. Western Australia's principles include some that seem more like tasks or objectives, such as the provision of timely advice and the upholding of statutory obligations.

Values statements are associated with professional associations as well as with employing organisations, and the Probation and Community Corrections Officers Association (PACCOA) sets out principles of practice on its website (PACCOA, 2022). This is an organisation with lesser status than some professional associations—it is not a regulatory body and it plays no role in accrediting training—but its principles are still a useful indication of the priorities of probation officers in Australia. The principles emphasise confidentiality, integrity, professionalism and commitment to the dignity of others. However, there is little to set them aside from the values expected of others in the criminal justice system (such as lawyers or police officers), or to distinguish youth justice, probation and community corrections officers as a distinct professional group.

The benefits and limitations of values statements and codes of ethics

Codes of ethics can be useful in identifying core principles and values, giving a guide and a standard and a sense of priorities. They can act as a form of empowering, professional pledge, maintaining and reinforcing a professional identity.

However, there are also some risks with these codes (Bowles et al., 2006). Firstly, they might be dangerous, by giving too much priority to one factor at the expense of others. For example, a community justice practitioner might unduly prioritise client confidentiality, to the potential detriment of effective inter-agency practice. Many social and community workers have to balance their helping function with their controlling function, and weigh up their duty to the individual client with their duty to society; however, these tensions are particularly acute for community justice workers. Secondly, codes of ethics might be irrelevant or inadequate. Any statement of community justice values in Australia that does not give priority to addressing Indigenous over-representation would be out of step with the realities of society.

In most of the countries of the world, it is professional associations that develop and promote codes of ethics, including that of the Australian Association of Social Workers (AASW) (see Box 11.1), and these tend to be principle based, rather than based on relationships or character. There are many

---

Box 11.1

AASW code of ethics

The AASW Code of Ethics (Australian Association of Social Workers (AASW), 2020) makes little direct reference to criminal or community justice, but it does have a strong relevance to workers in that field. The Code starts with a strong statement, in the preamble, about the need to acknowledge and understand the implications of disadvantage experienced by Indigenous peoples for social work practice.

The Code sets out social work values as three core principles:

1 *Respect for Persons.* Every individual has inherent worth and the right to wellbeing, and the social work profession needs to respect this, while respecting the rights of others.
2 *Social Justice.* Societies need to uphold social fairness and provide maximum benefit for all members. This includes eliminating the violation of human rights, promoting community participation and promoting the protection of the natural environment.
3 *Professional Integrity.* The profession values 'honesty, trustworthiness and good character' (AASW, 2010: 10).

The Code also provides guidance on ethical decision-making and sets out the ethical responsibilities and behaviours expected of social workers in Australia, including responsibilities to clients, colleagues and the profession. The influence of human rights approaches is seen in the

> appendix listing the human rights documents relevant to social work practice in Australia.
>
> The Code is a very important document for social work-qualified community justice workers in Australia, and the responsibilities set out—particularly with their emphasis on Indigenous people—are just as relevant to community justice as they are to other areas of social work. A greater focus on the area of community justice would, perhaps, have led to more emphasis on the balance between the responsibilities to the individual client and to wider society and public protection. However, the document as it is currently presented does provide a more detailed, thoughtful and practically useful guide to ethical practice for community justice workers than any other comparable Australian document.

similarities between country codes, largely due to the influence of the International Federation of Social Workers (IFSW) (Banks, 2012). These codes protect clients, and provide guidance and protection to practitioners. They also enhance the professional status of the discipline and maintain discipline and identity. The reliance on codes has attracted criticism, including that they are too general, can locate blame for practice errors with individual workers and can undermine professional judgement and autonomy (Banks, 2012).

A social justice and human rights-led approach to social work takes away the emphasis on individual casework, giving a greater priority to the role of the individual in society. The notion of social justice does not have one clear definition, but rather is connected to ideas of fairness, justice, the common good and inclusiveness. The definition provided by the International Federation of Social Workers (in Bowles et al., 2006) suggests that social justice has five elements:

1. Challenging negative discrimination;
2. Recognising and respecting diversity of societies;
3. Delivering resources fairly and equitably, according to need;
4. Challenging unjust policies and practices;
5. Working in solidarity.

A concern with social justice links together social work and community justice values.

Human rights and criminal justice in Australia

The criminal justice system in Australia is held to high standards, both through national evaluations and via the scrutiny of international bodies. The international human rights instruments and declarations that have relevance for community justice and youth justice practice in Australia include the Universal Declaration of Human Rights (1948), the Declaration on the Rights of Indigenous People (2007), the UN Convention on the Rights of the Child (1989), the UN Standard Minimum Rules for the Treatment of Prisoners (1955), the US Standard Minimum Rules for the Administration of Juvenile Justice (Beijing Rules) (1985) and the United Nations Guidelines for the Prevention of Juvenile Delinquency (Riyadh Guidelines) (1990).

Practice in the criminal justice system is judged against international human rights instruments, and on a number of occasions investigations have identified occasions where practice in Australia has fallen short of the highest standards. The national scrutiny of criminal justice has been led by the Human Rights Law Centre (HRLC) and the Australian Human Rights Commission (AHRC).

The focus of concern of human rights groups has tended to be on young people, and on people from Indigenous backgrounds. In general, all prisoners have the right to be treated with humanity, dignity and respect, only subject to the restrictions that are inherent to a closed environment. This right is enshrined in the International Covenant on Civil and Political Rights (ICCPR), the Convention on the Rights of the Child (CRC) and the Convention against Torture and other Cruel, Inhuman or Degrading Treatment or Punishment (CAT) (Australian Human Rights Commission [AHRC], 2012).

The HRLC (2015a) set out a National Human Rights Action Plan that contained statements relevant to the administration of criminal and youth justice:

- Indigenous peoples continue to be denied proper access to interpreter services. This means that they have difficulty communicating with court and justice officials, including their own lawyer, inhibiting their access to a fair trial.
- Mandatory sentencing laws in Western Australia and the Northern Territory have a disproportionate impact on Indigenous people and contribute to the over-representation of these groups in the criminal justice system. The report highlights the over-representation in Australia, with particular reference to those two jurisdictions:

> In the Northern Territory, incarceration rates of Aboriginal and Torres Strait Islander peoples are 3.5 times the national rate of imprisonment, and Aboriginal and Torres Strait Islander peoples constitute 83% of the prison population in the Northern Territory. In Western Australia, expansion of mandatory sentencing laws has seen the number of Aboriginal and Torres Strait Islander people in prison double since 2002. Aboriginal and Torres Strait Islander juveniles are 28 times as likely to be detained as other Australian juveniles, and Aboriginal women prisoners are the fastest growing demographic amongst the prison population, with an increase in incarceration rates of 420% in the decade to 2005.
> (HRLC, 2015b: n.p.)

- Australia does not have a national policy framework for children's rights, despite its ratification of the UN Convention on the Rights of the Child (UNCRC) in 1990.
- The Australian government accepted the recommendations made by the UN Human Rights Council in 2011, but the steps taken have not yet led to success in reducing the over-representation of Indigenous people in custody or the high rates of deaths in custody from this group.

The HRLC reported that the United Nations criticised Australia for falling below international standards in the treatment of children in criminal and civil contexts (HRLC, 2015b). The criticisms include the use of strip-searching and solitary confinement, imposition of life sentences without parole and the over-representation of Indigenous people in the juvenile justice system. It recommended that the age of criminal responsibility be raised from ten to twelve and that children should be charged as minors until the age of 18 (not 17, as it is in Queensland).

Previously, in 2014, the HRLC had requested UN intervention to prohibit Queensland from introducing legal reforms that would make it more likely for juveniles to be imprisoned (HRLC, 2014). These reforms included the removing of the principle that imprisonment of juveniles be a measure of last resort, the naming and shaming of children aged 10 to 16 and the automatic transfer of 17-year-olds to adult prison. The HRLC was concerned about all aspects of these proposed reforms, but particularly the disproportionate impact that they were likely to have on Indigenous young people, who were already over-represented in the system.

The AHRC (2014b) draws the link between childhood mistreatment, experience of out-of-home care and youth offending. Children in out-of-home care are more than 15 times more likely to enter the juvenile justice system than the general population, but the coordination between the two systems is generally poor. Children fall between the gaps in the two services and receive poorly integrated and poorly connected support. The system also lets young people down in using custody for welfare needs, such as when children do not have stable accommodation or are not able to return to their homes. This is clearly in contravention of the UN Convention on the Rights of the Child, which requires incarceration to be used as a last resort and for the shortest possible period of time. The Commission also reported that when the state had parental responsibility for the child, the responsible child protection officer only attended the court hearing in one case out of 62 (AHRC, 2014b).

The AHRC (2001) recommended the increased use of diversion for young people who have committed offences, in line with Article 40 of the UNCRC, the Beijing Rules and the Riyadh Guidelines. Diversionary measures seek to reduce the stigma associated with involvement in the criminal justice process as well as tempering the most punitive approaches. The Beijing Rules state that diversionary measures should not be restricted to minor offences or first-time offenders, although in practice this is the group of people who are most often diverted. An effective diversion regime requires a range of community-based alternatives to custody to be made available. At the time of the AHRC report, there were few such alternatives available, with diversion being utilised mainly via the mechanisms of conferencing or police cautions. These can be effective measures, but it is important to follow due process to ensure that young people are treated fairly and do not face the risk of being exposed to a sanction or detrimental outcome without an opportunity for a proper hearing.

Indigenous young people are less likely to benefit from diversion—including police cautions—than other young people, and this is another contributing factor to their over-representation in the formal criminal justice system and in custody (AHRC, 2001). The Royal Commission into Aboriginal Deaths in Custody made a series of recommendations relating to increasing the use of diversionary measures for Indigenous young people, including the need to use expertise from Indigenous people in designing and delivering the programs.

Attempts to respond to earlier criticisms have also been investigated. Borowski (2011) reports an evaluation into Children's Koori Courts, where Indigenous Elders assist the presiding magistrate. It found that the practice was effective in building cultural responsiveness and also in building community and Indigenous ownership of legal administration. However, Children's Koori Courts by themselves are not able to reduce Indigenous over-representation.

Another strategy to address over-representation of Indigenous people in the justice system is the Change the Record campaign (see Box 11.2).

Box 11.2

Change the record campaign

The Change the Record Campaign (Change the Record, 2022) aims to address both the over-representation of Indigenous groups in custody and the increased levels of violence experienced by Indigenous people—particularly women and children. They aim to address both these issues by 2040, with 12 principles for reform:

1. *Invest in communities, not prisons.* Government funding should be invested into initiatives that address the underlying causes of crime;
2. *Local communities have the answers.* Directly affected people are best placed to identify local issues and provide tailored solutions, with community support. Indigenous organisations can provide culturally appropriate services;
3. *Recognise the driving factors of imprisonment.* Early intervention strategies addressed at child abuse and domestic violence will have a preventative effect on people who might otherwise become involved in the criminal justice system;

4 *Focus on safety.* Successful early intervention against domestic violence and child abuse will also increase community safety, particularly for women and children;
5 *Services, not sentences.* Criminal justice is an ineffective and inappropriate response to mental illness, drug abuse or homelessness. Better services in these areas will have more chance of success;
6 *Community policing, not policing the community.* The ways in which police interact with disadvantaged and marginalised communities can build trust, rather than exacerbate already difficult relationships;
7 *Smarter Sentencing.* A fair sentencing system will include a range of non-custodial options, allowing appropriate and tailored sentences;
8 *Eliminate unnecessary imprisonment.* Community options should be used for minor offences or fine non-payment. Prison is costly and leads to further involvement in the criminal justice system;
9 *Adopt community justice approaches.* The criminal justice system can help individuals and rebuild relationships by using therapeutic and restorative approaches, including Koori and Murri courts;
10 *Young people don't belong in prison.* Young people are still developing, and youth detention experiences can increase the likelihood of adult criminal behaviour;
11 *Rehabilitation, not just punishment.* Almost all prisoners will eventually be released, so should have access to education, programs and support services;
12 *Reintegration, not recidivism.* Not enough support is provided to allow people to lead productive lives, fulfil their potential and transition back to the community.

Source: Change the Record, 2015.

Amnesty International (2015) has reported in detail on the treatment of Indigenous children in Australian criminal justice. Its report highlights the disruptive impact that the incarceration of Indigenous children—some as young as 10 years old—has on their connections to home and to community. Again, the report highlights that the national over-representation is particularly pronounced in some states:

> The rates of Indigenous and non-Indigenous youth detention vary from one jurisdiction to another. Western Australia, Queensland and the Northern Territory have, respectively, the highest rate of over-representation of Indigenous youth in detention; the fastest growing rate of Indigenous youth detention; and the highest proportion of youth in detention who are Indigenous.
>
> (Amnesty International, 2015: n.p.)

Under International human rights obligations, it is the Australian government that bears ultimate responsibility for the treatment of Indigenous young people in all states and territories, and Amnesty International highlights a number of ways in which Australia is in breach of the UNCRC:

- The age of criminal responsibility across Australia is ten years old, despite the UNCRC setting it at 12;
- In the Northern Territory, young people in detention are only separated from adults by a fence and are taken to a visiting block at the adult prison. Article 37(c) of the CRC requires children to be separated from adults. In Darwin in 2014, all children in detention were transferred to a dilapidated former adult facility (see Box 11.3);

Box 11.3

Don Dale Youth Detention Centre

In 2016 the Australian government instituted a Royal Commission into the Protection and Detention of Children in the Northern Territory (NTRC, 2017). This followed, firstly an investigation into an alleged riot by juvenile detainees in 2014 and a 'Four Corners' documentary broadcast by the ABC in 2016. The allegations included that young people—some as young as 14 years of age were tear-gassed in their cells, shackled to chairs and later had fabric hoods placed over their heads after transfer to adult prison. They were deprived of drinking water for more than 72 hours and kept in solitary confinement without windows or cells.

The Royal Commission recommended a new focus on diversion, community engagement and family support. The Commission recommended the closure of Don Dale but four years later, in 2022, it remained open, while a new facility is being built. Some of the practices, including the use of hooding and shackling to chairs, have been discontinued, but there is an ongoing use of long periods of isolation and the physical conditions of the current building are still very poor. The youth justice system in the Northern Territory continues to have very harsh outcomes for children and young people, particularly since the introduction of tougher bail laws in 2021, which have led to children being incarcerated from as young an age as 10. As in other states and territories, these harsh outcomes particularly impact on Indigenous young people. There have been occasions when the entire population of the juvenile detention system in the Northern Territory has been Indigenous young people.

The Commission's recommendation that the age of criminal responsibility be raised to 12 has not been implemented.

- Mandatory sentencing of juveniles in Western Australia breaches the UNCRC stipulation to only use custody as a last resort;
- The then Queensland government was criticised for its treatment of children as adults and for its law requiring that the custody as last resort principle be disregarded.

The report recommends a number of ways in which the Australian government could create a brighter future for Indigenous children. These measures focus on support for communities, potentially by re-dedicating resources through justice reinvestment approaches. Initiatives in Bourke, NSW, to keep children in prisons rather than custody are presented as a positive exemplar of such an approach (see Box 11.4). It also recommends the proper resourcing of Indigenous Legal Services and the setting of targets relating to justice as part of Closing the Gap. The report emphasises the need for effective and consistent collection of data to monitor progress.

Box 11.4

Maranguka Justice Reinvestment Project, Bourke, NSW

In March 2014, through funding provided both by government and the private sector, Justice Reinvestment NSW worked with Maranguka Justice Reinvestment NSW to develop a framework for Bourke, for presentation to the state government as a demonstration that justice reinvestment can provide alternate pathways for young people, away from incarceration and offending.

The project introduced some 'circuit breakers', including three in the justice area. These were aimed at creating an incentive to participate, at engaging the wider community and at providing immediate value to the young people of Bourke. The three justice circuit breakers addressed bail and sentencing; a targeted warrant clinic and a drivers program.

Muranguka means 'caring for others' and the Muranguka Project was based on research and expertise from other Indigenous groups and projects in Australia, New Zealand and North America. It built on existing NSW policy initiatives. The project involves establishing community-led teams, comprising a variety of disciplines and government and non-government agencies. Its aim was to develop a new accountability framework for addressing Indigenous disadvantage and to develop a fiscal framework to ensure long-term sustainability of programs and services. Maranguka does not replace existing services, but rather acts as a hub, focusing on safe families; connected communities; youth and justice reinvestment; and women's and men's action.

Maranguka partnered with Just Reinvest NSW to create a justice reinvestment framework to change the government's approach. The aim was to persuade government to shift policy and services away from incarceration and invest it in meeting community needs, particularly with reference to the underlying causes of youth crime. It is delivered using a collective impact framework, focusing on solutions and taking a whole-of-community and -government approach.

The Maranguka Reinvestment Project was evaluated by auditors KPMG in 2018 (KPMG, 2018) and they found improvements in youth development, family strength and adult empowerment that could be calculated as a $3.1 million benefit to the community.

Source: Justice Reinvestment Campaign (2022).

Although these international reports have quite strong criticisms and some distinct recommendations, there is no obligation on either state or national governments to respond to them. The status of the reports from international human rights observers is most clear when state governments are not inclined to follow their recommendations. The previous state government in Queensland took a very harsh approach to young people who committed offences, which was regularly criticised internationally, nationally and within the state. Media accounts reported the Attorney-General deliberately and publicly facing down these criticisms, saying that following the Convention on the Rights of the Child would simply lead to all young people who committed offences not serving any detention time (Guest, 2013).

Community justice, values and rights

Community justice in Australia has no one, clear professional identity. There is no single employer; even in each state, those who work with young people are employed by a different agency than those who work with adults, and many non-governmental organisations are prominent employers in the field. There is no requirement for professional registration and no strong, widely accepted professional association. There is no single disciplinary background or training path. All of this means that it is difficult to generalise about the values and attitudes of those who work with people who have committed offences in the community: some see themselves as social workers or psychologists working with this client group; for others, their professional identity is closer to that of a prison officer or corrections officer.

The absence of a unifying professional identity means that the values basis for working with people who have committed offences in the community in Australia is under-theorised and under-debated. This is true both in relation to the individual engagement between workers and clients (offenders, victims or families) and in relation to wider discussions of the purpose of community interventions and their place within the system. The absence of a professional voice promoting rehabilitative or humanist values means that the other two discourses in criminal justice debates—the punitive discourse and the managerialist discourse—will dominate, without a countervailing argument being put forward about how those in the criminal justice system should be treated and how criminal justice concerns and processes should be linked to wider societal issues.

These arguments are made by some academics, politicians and journalists, but they are not prominently heard from those who work every day within the system. Social work does not have a prominent status within criminal justice in Australia, and criminal justice issues are not widely covered within social work, but globally the social work literature and the social work profession have been most prominent in discussing and debating the importance of values concerns in human services work. The social work response can sometimes be inadequate or limited, and can seem to give too much attention to the present client and to one-to-one concerns rather than to wider society, to victims or to future community and public protection. However, an incorporation of social justice and human rights concerns into these values can help to address these limitations. The increasing prominence of restorative justice provides another framework for taking a positive, value-led approach to work with offenders in the community, and emphasises the inadequacies of purely punitive or managerialist approaches. The reports of national and international groups consistently show that the over-representation and treatment of Indigenous groups within criminal justice is the greatest crisis in the system and needs to be responded to throughout society from a human rights and social justice perspective.

Further reading

As discussed, the most detailed engagement with values debates can be found in the social work literature, with Bowles et al. (2006) being the best starting point within Australia. Sarah Banks' (2012) classic text also covers the main ethical debates in a way that is directly relevant to practitioners. Rob Canton and Mike Nellis have taught, thought, spoken and written about rights and ethics in working with people who have committed offences over a number of years, and their work sets out what a values-led, community justice practice could look like.

Practical task

A challenge of working in direct practice is that the practitioner can have little control over the context in which they work. Imagine you are working with Daniel, a 12 year old boy who has been warned by the court that any further offending could led to a custodial sentence. You know that such an outcome would be detrimental both to his rights and to his interests. How can that impact on your work with this young person?

Reflective questions

11.1 The first sentence of this chapter describes working with offenders as 'a morally significant task'. What is meant by that and how would it affect practice?

11.2 It is suggested in this chapter that values and rights are now rarely discussed in debates about criminal justice. In your experience, is this true in Australia?

11.3 When international organisations criticise aspects of criminal justice or youth justice practice in Australia, how should an Australian government respond?

12 Practitioner skills

Introduction

This final chapter is based around a case study, with each section of the case scenario description followed by a discussion of a possible theoretically informed way to respond. The structure allows a discussion of practitioner skills to be directly related to realistic practice scenarios. The case described is based on a composite of a number of different individuals, with some details changed. The case described is of a young person, but the skills and approaches are just as applicable to work with adults.

Community justice work is not simply a question of learning particular skills and then applying them to the cases with which a practitioner is presented. Any form of working with people is an emotionally demanding task, and there has been recent interest in the need for emotional literacy in this work. Knight (2014) defines emotional literacy as people who have committed offences acknowledging their own emotions and the emotions of those with whom they work, and using this knowledge and awareness for therapeutic benefit. Emotionally literate practice, including in direct work with offenders, will lead to a more intuitively intelligent justice system (Knight, Phillips and Chapman, 2016). Knight (2014) carried out research into the subject with criminal justice practitioners, and emphasises five criteria of emotional literacy:

1. *Motivation*. The motivation practitioners have to carry out the work is supported by the relationships they can build with the people with whom they work, as well as supportive relationships with colleagues;
2. *Self-awareness*. This is an understanding of one's own emotions and an ability to use one's own emotional self in work with others;
3. *Self-regulation*. Practitioners need to be aware of their own emotions, but not to be dominated by them; they need to be able to keep them under control, to allow the emotions of the person with whom they are working to be most important;
4. *Empathy*. It is crucial to be able to understand the perspective of others and to 'stand in their shoes', even when they have committed the most

DOI: 10.4324/9781003193814-13

serious offences. This ability to be empathic in this way flows from the value base of workers, not their emotions:

> The research data highlights the significance of a value base of respect, positive regard and a non-judgemental approach to offenders/service users in the exercising of emotional literacy. These values inform an understanding of the potential for making judgements based solely on emotions, and the need to withhold such judgements in face-to-face work with offenders.
>
> (Knight, 2014: 192)

5 *Social competence.* This is based on the ability to build trusting relationships with individuals. These relationships exist within the context of the work, and the knowledge that emotionally significant disclosures might also affect the risk-assessment.

Work with people who have committed offences and their families will be an emotional undertaking and will require emotional literacy, rather than merely an application of skills. The role of emotional engagement in all aspects of criminal justice is also being more widely appreciated, with Rossner's (2014) work on the role of emotions in restorative justice being of particular note.

Johnny: The referral phone call

You are employed by a community organisation that works with young people who are at risk of getting involved in offending and their families. You receive a referral from Juvenile Justice saying that one of its workers is working with a 16-year-old boy, Ryan, but has also become concerned about his 14-year-old brother, Johnny, and wants to know whether you would be prepared to work with Johnny. You agree to do so, and make an appointment with him and his mother at your office. You ask your colleague in Juvenile Justice to forward further information about Johnny to you before your first appointment with him.

You have not yet met Johnny and have not been given any details about him, but it might be worth reflecting on what we do know and what we can assume:

- We know that Johnny's older brother has committed offences. This would seem to be a risk factor for him getting involved in offending.
- We know that he is 14 years old. This is a crucial age. Young people at that age would expect to be treated more harshly in court than much younger children. It is also a crucial age at school, as any breakdown in a school placement might be hard to retrieve.
- We know that if Johnny were to become involved in offending, and in the criminal justice system, at the age of 14 that could lead to serious consequences if he sets out on a path from which he would find it difficult to deviate.
- We do, however, also know of some possible protective factors. The Juvenile Justice worker is obviously committed enough to the family to

take some time to make a referral for someone who is not her primary client. She clearly sees something in Johnny to give her confidence that work with him will be worthwhile. Johnny's mother is committed and involved enough in his life to agree to take him to the meeting with you. Perhaps most importantly, Johnny himself—who is not under any sort of court order—has voluntarily agreed to come to see you, suggesting that he also has a degree of investment in his own future.

Going through this process helps us to reflect on how much we know about both the particular individual and the approach to the work that we intend to take. Our role relates directly to offending behaviour, so our focus is on factors relating to offending. If, for example, Johnny had been referred to a family therapist, she might have been more interested in the dynamics between the family members and how they relate to past events in that family.

Johnny: The referral letter

The brief letter from your colleague repeats a lot of the information that she gave you on the phone, but adds some new material. Most notably, she informs you that Johnny recently was said to be involved with a group of other young people (including her client, his brother Ryan) in breaking into a factory at night and stealing tools. He is likely to face serious criminal charges from this incident. Your colleague has agreed with Johnny and Michelle that they will engage with you on a voluntary basis, prior to any court appearance, in the hope that this will serve him well in court. She asks you not to do work with him relating to the alleged incident itself, but rather to focus on family and school issues. Johnny lives with his mother and older brother, Ryan; there are no other siblings. Johnny's father left home when he was very young and he has had no subsequent contact with the family. Michelle works afternoons and some evenings as a cleaner at the airport.

This new information adds to the picture of Johnny that you have before you meet him:

- His alleged involvement in the offence does suggest that the issues in his life are quite serious, and that the stakes are high regarding his involvement with you. This could be turned into a positive factor, as it will give you something to work with in terms of Johnny's motivation to engage.
- The fact that Johnny is still in school, albeit in a precarious placement, is protective but might need some early attention in your intervention.

It is also worthwhile, in working with individuals and families, to reflect on your own presumptions, attitudes and possible prejudices. What is your immediate reaction to this family situation? Is there a part of you that sympathises with some of the more judgemental criticisms made about lone mothers, and that blames Michelle for the behaviour of her sons and their impact on others? Or do you sympathise with her situation: On her own, working hard both to bring up her sons and earn a living for her family?

Johnny: The first meeting

Johnny arrives on time with his mother, Michelle. Michelle does most of the talking in the session, revealing that, although she had been despairing of Ryan's offending behaviour for some time, she had always thought of Johnny as her 'good boy', who would not get involved in such behaviour. However, there has been a rapid deterioration in his behaviour over the last few months, starting with problems at school and then leading to the recent police involvement. She has seen that some of the behaviour at home that she had associated with Ryan is now being repeated by Johnny—he is staying out late, associating with anti-social friends and refusing to respect her authority at home. Johnny says little during the meeting, but does acknowledge that he hates school. The police officer who arrested him told him that he was likely to be sent to a Juvenile Justice Centre, and he is clearly frightened by this prospect. You explain your role to Johnny and Michelle and say that work with you will be entirely voluntary. You suggest that your next step will be separate one-on-one meetings with each of them, and they agree to that suggestion.

The interview in this case study takes place in an office, as that is the standard approach. However, during the time of Covid-19 and associated lockdowns, this would have been a phone conversation. The flexibility might have made it easier for Johnny and Michelle to attend but the important work of relationship building is more difficult to achieve in a phone interview (Dominey et al., 2021).

There is increasing attention being given to how practitioners engage with clients, and how that might affect their future offending behaviour (see Ugwudike, Raynor and Annison [2017a] for a comprehensive account of developments in practice, evaluation and research). In the UK, one-to-one casework, or relationship-based practice, seemed to fall from favour as a more managerialist approach was taken to probation practice, but is now again being acknowledged as important (see Burnett and McNeill, 2005, for a discussion of some of this history). Some of this recent research will be discussed later in the case study, but it is important to note that these ideas are not new, they are not solely associated with desistance approaches and the 'effective practice' literature did also place an emphasis on engagement and relational approaches (Gendreau and Andrews, 1990; Bonta, 1996; Gendreau, 1996; Gornik, 2002). This was done most notably in Dowden and Andrews' (2004) concept of core correctional practice (CCP). These researchers were working within the Risk Needs Responsivity (RNR) framework and investigated which characteristics of practitioners were most associated with good outcomes in the delivery of interventions. The importance of emotional and empathy skills, and the need for practitioners to build relationships, are discussed using a variety of terminology, including responsivity, the therapeutic alliance (see Bourgon and Guiterrez, 2013) and CCP. Dowden and Andrews' (2004) meta-analysis found that the five aspects of CCP were associated with good outcomes in treatment:

1 *Effective use of authority.* Practitioners should be able to reinforce and keep individuals to the rules in a way that is clear and firm, but free from threats or other abuse of power.

2 *Modelling pro-social behaviour and providing positive reinforcement.* The idea is that engagement with practitioners will cause the service users to learn pro-social behaviours.
3 *Problem-solving.* Practitioners should be able to teach problem-solving skills. These problem-solving skills can relate to personal or emotional problems, or to interpersonal relationships.
4 *The effective use of community resources.* The practitioner should be involved in arranging the most appropriate services, based in the community where the individual lives. This work is obviously dependent on such services being available.
5 *The quality of interpersonal relationships.* Dowden and Andrews (2004: 205) consider this to be the most important of the five dimensions and explain it in this way:

> the interpersonal influence exerted by the correctional staff member is maximised under conditions characterized by open, warm and enthusiastic communication. An equally important consideration is the development of mutual respect and liking between the offender and correctional staff member.

There is, however, a direct link between the emphasis on practitioner skills and relationship-based practice, and the promotion of the desistance paradigm (see Burnett and McNeill, 2005).

Stages of change and motivational interviewing

The approach to engaging Johnny and working through the issues in his life with him will be influenced by your understanding of his motivation and his willingness to change. The most influential approach to the idea that individuals go through the process of change in identifiable stages is from Prochaska and DiClemente (1983), who identify the six stages of change. These stages were not directly written with reference to work with people who had committed offences, but they are widely accepted as relevant to that group:

1 *Pre-contemplation.* The individual is not even considering change, and is still involved in the undesirable behaviour;
2 *Contemplation.* This is characterised by ambivalence, when the individual is considering both the positive benefits of change and its possible costs;
3 *Preparation.* An individual has an intention to change in the near future;
4 *Action.* The individual is taking positive steps to bring about change in his life;
5 *Maintenance.* When progress has been made towards change, an individual will have to take steps to consolidate the change and integrate it into their life;
6 *Relapse.* This is an important part of the understanding of the stages of change. A reversion to previous behaviour should not be seen as a failure;

it is merely a return to the start of the process. An individual may need to go through the cycle of the stages of change a number of times before achieving real, lasting change.

Closely associated with the understanding of the stages of change is the process of motivational interviewing. This approach is designed to build on an individual's own strengths, motivations and goals, and to work with them in bringing positive behavioural change (Miller and Rollnick, 2002, 2004; Megele, 2015). Motivational interviewing is a collaborative approach, facilitating autonomy and accepting the experiences of the individual. Megele (2015) summarises the four basic principles of motivational interviewing:

1 *Express empathy.* Practitioners need to connect emotionally with clients, and to understand and be led by their perspective;
2 *Support self-efficacy.* The practitioner will draw on the individual's own strengths, motivations and capability;
3 *Roll with resistance.* What appears to be resistance is often just a reflection of ambivalence, when a client is at the stage of considering both the benefits and costs of change;
4 *Develop discrepancy.* The practitioner can build upon the ambivalence and focus the individual's mind on the conflict between where they are and where they want to be, and the steps they need to take to make a change.

The practitioner will need to use the skills of motivational interviewing in following these principles. A motivational interviewing approach involves the use of positive statements and open-ended questions, along with immediate reflections and longer, more detailed summaries, all demonstrating empathy, interest and understanding (Megele, 2015). Motivational interviewing is a practice that requires training and skill, and it can be difficult to implement successfully; experiences in the United States show that even training staff in the use of motivational interviewing does not consistently lead to them applying that approach (Alexander, Lowenkamp and Robinson, 2013).

Johnny: The first individual meeting

Johnny arrives to his appointment on time (his mother brought him) and greets you briefly before sitting down. You respond by thanking him for coming and for arriving on time, and then explain the context of your work with him. You say you are working with him at the request of his mother, with a view to a possible future court appearance, but that he is not on an actual court order. He is free to choose not to work with you, but the consequences of that choice might be to disappoint his mother and negatively impact a future court appearance. You say it is possible that you will be asked to report to the court on Johnny's progress and cooperation, and that you will do so honestly and will share any comments you intend to make with Johnny. You say that you expect to be able to identify a lot of positives in Johnny's life and his attitude, and that these will be reflected in any report that you present. Johnny acknowledges that he understands this. Your early attempts to engage Johnny in conversation about school and family are frustrating, as he is reluctant to share information. You acknowledge that this is a difficult time for him, and an unusual way to get to know someone.

Although Johnny is not on a court order and will not face any direct sanctions, if he does not keep appointments with you, he does meet the definition of an involuntary client. Trotter (2015) defines an involuntary client as someone who has not made a choice to receive the services being offered. As well as those involved in the criminal justice system, involuntary clients can include mothers who are visited by child protection workers and users of drugs or alcohol undergoing mandatory treatment. It is increasingly recognised that some professional relationships go beyond being involuntary to being actively hostile. Practitioners need a different set of skills to deal with the emotional stress of work that can be characterised by hatred and aggression (Ferguson et al., 2020).

It is not realistic to draw a clear line between voluntary and involuntary clients; this can best be seen as a continuum with entirely involuntary clients (such as those on a court order) at one end and entirely voluntary clients (such as a student seeking counselling) at the other. Neither Johnny nor Michelle is at either end of the continuum, but they are each at different points along it. Michelle's place on the continuum will be discussed in the next section. Johnny is towards the involuntary end, as he has not freely chosen to meet with you and is attending due to pressure to do so from his mother and, indirectly, from the court. However, he could not be described as an entirely involuntary client, as he is not actually under a court order and the motivation to work with you is due to an assumption that it will help his future, rather than a direct obligation to do so. His interview with you shows that although he clearly does not want to be present, there are small hints that he can see the benefit for himself in attending.

Trotter (2015) identifies four principles of effective practice with involuntary clients, and it is easy to see how they follow on from the principles of CCP.

Role clarification

Role clarification does not take place only at the beginning of a new relationship between a worker and a client, but this initial conversation is a crucial time for setting out expectations of the role. It is a useful time for both worker and client to set out what they expect to achieve from the working relationship. For those in statutory agencies, or in non-statutory agencies that may work with individuals on statutory orders, it is particularly important to use this early conversation to set out the dual care and control aspect of the work. This might include an explanation of the expectations placed on the worker by their employing agency.

An interesting aspect of the initial role clarification with Johnny is that, as the relationship is not on a statutory basis, there is a need for consent. A considerable amount of work in the community with people who have committed offences occurs when they are subject to a statutory order, so the client is not obliged to agree to work with the practitioner. This was not always the case: In the UK, probation officers previously had to negotiate contracts with those under their supervision and the courts had to agree on the work that was needed (see Raynor, 2014). Gaining consent for the work to be done with the client—even to the extent of setting out a formal contract with them in an initial session—can be a very effective way of commencing the relationship:

> If it is backed up with careful discussion of options, requirements and the purpose of probation, for example during the pre-sentence report process, then it can help to motivate, and it can be used as a reminder of original intentions when these waver later in the supervision period.
> (Raynor, 2014: 302)

Promoting pro-social outcomes

There are a number of steps involved in promoting pro-social outcomes, and Trotter (2015) breaks this down into four key points: The need to identify positive or pro-social comments and behaviours as they occur in interaction with clients; the need to 'reward' such comments or behaviours, usually verbally by acknowledging and praising them; the modelling of pro-social behaviour expressions and actions; and the challenging of any anti-social comments or behaviour. Most interaction between a practitioner and a service-user will take place in one-on-one interview situations, but that still provides an opportunity to model pro-social behaviour. In the above description of the first meeting with Johnny, the practitioner thanks him for making the effort to arrive on time. That is a small but significant example of the promotion of pro-social behaviour, in that it shows that the effort that Johnny and his mother made was noticed and not taken for granted. As the work and relationship between Johnny and the practitioner develop, the practitioner might find other opportunities to note more significant pro-social behaviour, such as if Johnny is able to describe a positive experience at school or efforts that he has made to break away from some anti-social friends.

Cherry (2010) also considers the concept of pro-social modelling in some detail, including the role of managers in ensuring that pro-social modelling is an organisational value as well as an individual one. This point is echoed by Birgden (2002), writing in an Australian context, who says the whole correctional culture needs to support behavioural change.

Problem-solving

Problem-solving is best understood as part of a co-working relationship: The role of the practitioner is to support the individual in solving problems, not simply to solve the problems for them. Trotter (2015) sets out a structured approach to problem-solving, which comprises the seven steps of problem survey, problem prioritisation, problem exploration, setting goals, developing a contract, developing strategies and tasks, and conducting an overview. Problem-solving is clearly related to case planning, and there is an obvious overlap between the two concepts—particularly as seen in the seven steps described. The steps can be used flexibly; the important factor is that the client defines the problem and that worker and client work together. As discussed in Chapter 10, promoting desistance in those who have committed offences is associated with supporting them in overcoming obstacles. This can sometimes involve a more proactive role from the worker than that of a co-worker. These approaches are not necessarily in conflict with each other. For example, in Johnny's case he might identify school as a problem that he wants help with solving. The worker could work with him on his attitude, his educational goals—relating those to his long-term goals and ambitions—and perhaps address conflict-resolution or anger-management. However, this approach could be complemented by some advocacy to the school or educational authorities on Johnny's behalf, to overcome obstacles to his reintegration in school that might have arisen from his previous behaviour and reputation.

The relationship between the worker and the client

The fourth principle of the importance of the relationship between worker and client also relates to the other three principles, and again links closely to the concept of core correctional practice (CCP). Trotter (2015) suggests four main aspects of building the relationship with the client: Empathy, optimism, humour and self-disclosure. Empathy involves the worker using empathy to understand the situation from the other person's point of view. In the first meeting with Johnny, the acknowledgement of how difficult he might find the situation to be is an empathic step towards understanding his perspective.

Optimism is consistent with a research-led, strengths-based approach, in that it can focus on the positives of the situation and project confidence that a particular approach will lead to good outcomes. The optimism needs to be grounded in reality. In the meeting with Johnny, the practitioner projects optimism that she will be able to identify strengths in their work with him and produce some positives in a report. However, the practitioner does not take the further step of providing cheap reassurance; she does not say that they will have a good outcome from his court appearance, as she is in no position to predict this.

When used appropriately, humour can take the tension out of a situation, can acknowledge the emotional power of a particular set of circumstances and can build a rapport between the worker and the client. Often humour is most appropriate when a relationship has been established between practitioner and client, the practitioner does not use it in the first meeting with Johnny, but may do so later on.

Self-disclosure, similarly, can help build a relationship between worker and client. There are risks if self-disclosure is not used appropriately: It might challenge the boundaries between worker and client and, in extreme cases, might place a worker at some risk. A poor or inappropriate use of self-disclosure might actually demonstrate a lack of empathy or an inappropriate focus on the worker's life, rather than the client's circumstances. For example, saying that you understand what it is like to be unemployed because it took you a few months to find your current job might be insensitive in under-stating the difference in circumstances between yourself and the client. However, when used appropriately, self-disclosure can build trust and empathy and show understanding of the situation. Self-disclosure is a somewhat neglected approach in criminal justice contexts; in work with those who have committed offences, it can be used in two main ways. It can be used to enhance a therapeutic relationship, or it can be used to focus on criminogenic need and risk (Phillips, Fowler and Westaby, 2018). Working with parents might be an instance where the worker acknowledging, without too much detail, the challenges that they have faced with their own children might build rapport with the client. As Trotter (2015) points out, there is limited research evidence on the beneficial effect of using humour or self-disclosure, so they should be used with care, and within the limits of what feels comfortable to the worker.

In Trotter and Evans' (2010, 2012) work specifically on the skills relevant to working with young people, they also emphasise the importance of a focus on high risk and the need to use cognitive behavioural techniques. These cognitive techniques are most associated with group work but can be used in individual work as well. This Australian research into practitioner engagement with young people found that practitioners were particularly strong on relationship and pro-social modelling skills, but less strong on cognitive behavioural approaches, problem-solving and role clarification. The study found few examples of challenging anti-social or pro-criminal attitudes.

The impact of practitioner skills on recidivism and compliance

As it becomes more established that practitioner skills and practitioner behaviour have a significant impact on outcomes, there is increasing interest in researching this area and establishing what aspects of practitioner work has this positive effect. In the United States, the Skills for Effective, Engagement, Development and Supervision (SEEDS) project sought to develop a skills-based practice framework to effectively engage with people who have committed offences (see Rex and Hosking, 2013). A notable approach to researching the use of practitioner skills was the Jersey Study (Raynor, Ugwudike and Vanstone, 2010, 2014; Raynor, 2013; Miles and Raynor, 2014; Weaver et al., 2020) (see Box 12.1). The Jersey Study found that where probation practice was more skilful, the rate of reconviction was reduced. This echoed previous research findings from research into the skills used by practitioners, including Trotter and Evans's (2010, 2012) work in youth justice in Australia.

Increasing attention is being paid to the idea of compliance, what it means and how it can be achieved (see, for example, Bottoms, 2001; Robinson and

Box 12.1

The Jersey Study

A group of researchers from Swansea University in Wales carried out research into the skills used by probation officers in working with service-users on the island of Jersey.

Previous research into practitioner skills had relied on self-reports from service-users and/or practitioners, but the Jersey Study took a different methodological approach of actually video-taping the interviews. The researchers had developed a checklist of practitioner skills and they watched the video recordings, measuring the skills demonstrated by the practitioners against the skills on the checklist. The skills measured were not just verbal skills; the instrument also measured the non-verbal skills, known as SOLER (Egan, 1994): Squarely facing the client; open posture; leaning forward; eye contact and relaxed. They used a team approach to ensure consistency in how the checklist was used.

The findings supported the premise that practitioner skills are correlated with lower recidivism rates: 'to sum up, our results from this study support the belief that skills matter in probation work: when practice is more skilful, reconvictions re reduced (Raynor, 2013: 11).

The research also found strong internal consistency in how practitioners used the skills; those who were skilled in practice with some clients were likely to be so across their caseload. Equally, those who did not use the required skills failed to do so in most circumstances. This study supported findings from other research about the importance of training and the correlation between being trained in skills and using them. Probation officers were more consistent in using what were defined as relational skills than in using structuring skills.

The findings from the research supported the suggestions of desistance theorists that the relationship between practitioner and service-users was important in supporting desistance:

> [Probationers] complied when compliance had a purpose. In general, probation officers were seen as truthful, reasonable, polite and 'fair', and as genuinely trying to help, although some problems were seen as too big for their help to be effective ... From both a moral and an instrumental point of view, the pursuit of fairness

> and the solution of problems were seen as preferable to a display of toughness, and the results tend to support this choice.
> (Raynor, 2013: 117)
>
> The checklist is designed to be used by both researchers and practitioners allowing further dissemination and replication of best practice.
> *Sources:* Raynor, Ugwudike and Vanstone (2010, 2014); Miles and Raynor (2014); Raynor (2013).

McNeill, 2010; Ugwudike and Raynor, 2013). It is a concept at the heart of probation practice and connects to legitimacy, the use of discretion and the very purpose of community supervision (Canton, 2007). Practitioner skills can be a key component in how someone supervised complies with the terms of the order made. Compliance, however, needs to be understood in a number of different ways. Bottoms (2001) distinguished between the short-term compliance of adhering to the demands of the order and the longer-term compliance of desistance and adherence to the criminal law. Robinson and McNeill (2010) built on that definition, and distinguished between the formal compliance of keeping to the terms of the order and the substantive compliance of active engagement with a process of change. An audit approach and a strict enforcement regime can sometimes achieve short-term, formal compliance, but longer-term compliance requires the order to be perceived as legitimate and the practitioner to take a skilled approach in supervision.

The skills required of practitioners in supporting and achieving compliance include the general engagement skills discussed throughout this chapter as well as some specific approaches. This can be considered 'specific responsivity', an individualisation of treatment (Ugwudike and Raynor, 2013). Compliance can be achieved by providing practical support, such as by offering flexible appointments or making home visits (Ugwudike, 2010, 2013). Compliance is more likely to be achieved if the authority of the practitioner is perceived to be legitimate, and this can be shown through the use of empathy and respect, rather than a rigid, authoritarian approach (Ugwudike, 2010, 2013). This is accepted by most practitioners, who value their discretion and understand the importance of substantive, not just formal, compliance (Robinson, 2013). Engagement and genuine relationships with clients can be particularly important in supporting compliance in working with young people, and also with women (Bateman, 2013; Gelsthorpe, 2013; Trotter, 2013b).

The characteristics of the individual are important in promoting compliance. It is particularly important that they accept the need for change and are accountable for their actions (Serin et al., 2013). Again following the desistance research, it is co-production of compliance that can have most success, in the recognition that individuals can take steps to achieve their own compliance (McCulloch, 2013; Bottoms, 2013). These steps can include quite drastic and sophisticated situational compliance strategies; Bottoms (2013) describes a young person phoning his Gran rather than visiting her in order to keep himself away from the anti-social friends who lived nearby and compares this to Odysseus tying himself to the ship's mast to avoid temptation from the sirens.

Although you are at the very earliest stage of your work with Johnny, a respectful approach, together with engaging empathically with his life and challenges, will build substantive compliance as your working relationship continues.

The first individual meeting with Michelle

Michelle is very open in her meeting with you. She is desperate for help, and is sad and disappointed that Ryan's behaviour, which had caused her so much distress, is now being repeated by Johnny. She says that she is trying her best to be a good mother to her children, but her job is very demanding, she works irregular hours, and she travels a long distance to and from her place of employment. As she is unable to afford after-school care for the boys, they are left to look after themselves. As they cover up for each other, she has only recently realised how much school Johnny has missed and how much he has become involved with Ryan and Ryan's older group of friends. Michelle says that she will do anything you ask, as she is so desperate to help her sons, although she says that you will find it hard to engage Ryan in any family work. She agrees with you that it would make sense for the next session to take place in her home.

Michelle is in a different place on the voluntary–involuntary continuum than Johnny. She has made a free choice to meet with you and to involve her son in the intervention, and it is her clear intention to cooperate fully with anything that will help her family. Michelle could be classified as a fully voluntary client, although obviously this does not mean that she has made a choice to be in these circumstances in her life.

There is now increasing attention given to the need to work with families, as well as with young people themselves, in addressing the offending behaviour of young people. Family factors are linked both to the commencement of offending and to reoffending rates, and there is increasing evidence that interventions with families can be effective (Trotter, 2010). The importance of family work is identified by young people themselves (Trotter, 2010). One example of an effective family intervention is Multi-Systemic Therapy (MST) which, in the form of the Intensive Supervision Program (ISP), was delivered by Juvenile Justice New South Wales and outlined in Box 3.4 in Chapter 3. This is just one approach to family work, and families are engaged with juvenile justice in both a formal structured way and as a regular aspect of work with young people. Functional family therapy and brief strategic family therapy are both used with young people in Australia.

Some of these family therapy models need a high level of training and adherence to a set program, but the collaborative family work model devised and outlined by Trotter (2013a) can be followed easily and effectively by all practitioners. It draws on the principles of problem-solving, pro-social modelling and role clarification, and requires quite extensive preparation with the family. The steps of the collaborative family work model can be remembered through the acronym RIDGES (Rules, Issues, Decide, Goals, Explore, Strategies) (Trotter, 2013a: 69ff):

- *Setting of ground rules and clarification of roles.* As always, the process of setting the rules is as useful as the rules themselves, and that discussion is an extremely helpful way of clarifying roles and expectations;
- *Problem survey, identifying the issues to change.* This can be done by asking each individual family member in turn and then identifying common concerns or themes;
- *Problem ranking, deciding which issues to work on first.* The problems dealt with first should be practical problems, with identifiable solutions, of high concern to all family members;
- *Setting of goals and determining what is to be achieved.* These goals to be achieved will flow directly from the problems identified as a priority, and should have a timeline attached;
- *Exploring the issue in more detail.* This will follow after the problems have been identified and ranked, and goals set, so a more detailed discussion can be held within this framework;
- *Setting of strategies, tasks and ways to achieve the goals.* Strategies can take place inside and outside the family work sessions and can be carried out by any of the family members or by the worker;
- *Reviewing progress.* Regular review is important, and keeping agreed, written records of the earlier stages will facilitate this review process.

The emphasis, as in the title of the model, is on collaboration, and doing this work in partnership with the family. Trotter (2015) emphasises the need for program integrity and following the stages in the order set out, as there is a logic to the process that would be disturbed by, for example, engaging in work on a particular family issue without first going through the stage of agreeing with the family about what should be considered the most important issue.

In Michelle and Johnny's case, there is a need to start at the preparation stage. At this point, it is not even clear whether a Collaborative Family Model approach is the best way to work with this family. If Ryan was prepared to be involved in family work, along with Michelle and Johnny, then it would certainly be an approach worth trying. Investigating his attitude to this work, probably in partnership with his Juvenile Justice worker, could be attempted. If it was possible to work with the three members of the family together then, once roles had been clarified and ground rules set, a collaborative approach to surveying and ranking the problems in the family could be a very productive way of stimulating rich discussion. However, if Ryan does not choose to become engaged in such a process, then the best approach might be to work collaboratively with Michelle and Johnny but not to use the full model. The Collaborative Family Model is an extremely useful model for a practitioner to have available, but it does not need to be used in every case.

Community justice and practitioner skills

An emphasis on practitioner skills not only links practice to community justice values, but also links that work back more closely to social work. Trotter (2000, 2013b) is explicit in stating that social work qualifications and training—as well as those in psychology and a counselling orientation—are associated with the use of practice skills and therefore lower recidivism. Ugwudike and Raynor (2013) locate the effective steps to supporting compliance as being towards the care end of the care–control continuum. In Australia, the link between social work and work in the criminal justice system is not a particularly strong one. Qualified social workers do work for corrections and youth justice agencies as well as for non-government agencies that work in the community. Some university programs cover criminological ideas and allow social work students to take units that relate to criminal justice (for example, Western Sydney University offers a double degree in Social Work and Community and Criminal Justice). However, no criminal justice employer requires a social work qualification, and the curriculum standards set by the AASW make only the briefest reference to work with people who have committed offences. In the UK, there is still a strong link between social work and work with people who have committed offences in Northern Ireland and Scotland, but that link has been broken in England and Wales.

The practitioner skills that are identified as necessary for effective work with people who have committed offences are strongly associated with social work. Social workers are expected to work in relationship with people, and draw on their own skills and personal resources to do so (see Megele, 2015, for a description of how social workers might engage in a variety of case study situations). Some have made this direct link between such effective practice and a social work ethos. Trotter and Evans' (2012) study found that practitioners who possessed a relevant degree (presumably social work was included in this definition) were more likely to use effective skills. Raynor and Vanstone (2015) more explicitly argue that by focusing on relationships and on practitioner skills, their research and other findings produced findings relevant to social work. There are other reasons to suggest that social work and community justice should be closely aligned, and many of these arguments are made elsewhere in this book, but the emphasis on relationships and practitioner skills is one of the strongest of these arguments. A focus on community justice requires the use of the skills outlined in this chapter, and these skills are best taught through social work training.

A community justice focus to practitioner skills also brings attention to the over-representation of Indigenous young people in the juvenile justice system.

Working with Indigenous young people and families requires an understanding of their cultural context and a respect for the expertise brought to the interaction by the young person and family. This emphasises the need for community involvement and wider understanding, beyond simply utilisation of the skills of individual engagement. As discussed in Chapter 1, the concept of justice reinvestment and the commitment of resources to community development and crime prevention, rather than punishment and incarceration, offers great promise in supporting community justice approaches. It also provides an alternative discourse to discuss criminal justice in a way that is not focused on either punishment, or administration and management. A community should be able to reduce reoffending, but also to accommodate different ideas of the 'Good Life', and community justice should help to build such a community.

Further reading

Chris Trotter's work, much of it based on research carried out in Australia, provides research-based guidance as to how to engage effectively with people who have committed offences, families and other non-voluntary clients. More recently, his research has supported the findings of the Jersey Study in establishing the link between practitioner skills and approaches and desistance outcomes.

Practical task

You have agreed that the next appointment with Michelle and Ryan will be in their home? How will you prepare for that meeting? Set out a plan for the interview.

Reflective questions

12.1 Community justice is presented as an alternative to punitive or managerialist approaches to responding to offending. How would an affiliation to each of these approaches affect the work done with an individual young person such as Johnny?
12.2 In what way could community resources be drawn on in work with Johnny?
12.3 This chapter describes an initial meeting with Johnny. What could be described as a successful outcome from work with him? What would success consist of after three months, 12 months or three years?

References

3M Electronic Monitoring (2015), Website, viewed 1 July 2022, http://solutions.3m.com.au/wps/portal/3M/en_AU/APAC_ElectronicMonitoring/Home.
ABC News (2013a), 'Government orders review of Parole Board after conceding the system failed Jill Meagher', 11 June, viewed 1 July 2022, www.abc.net.au/news/2013-06-11/government-orders-review-of-parole-board/4747254.
——— (2013b), 'Victoria to tighten parole laws in wake of Jill Meagher's murder, to be "the toughest in Australia"', 25 June, viewed 1 July 2022, www.abc.net.au/news/2013-06-25/tougher-parole-laws-in-response-to-jill-meagher27s-murder2c-t/4778982.
——— (2015), 'Killer Sean Price's violent past proves Victoria's justice system is failing, Victims of Crime Commissioner says', 28 August, viewed 1 July 2022, http://mobile.abc.net.au/news/2015-08-28/victorian-parole-system-is-catastrophically-failing-victims/6731618.
Aboriginal Disability Justice Campaign (2015), 'Aboriginal Disability Justice Campaign (ADJC)', www.pwd.org.au/what-we-do/aboriginal-disability-justice-campaign.html.
Aboriginal and Torres Strait Islander Legal Service (2022), Submission 2012: Criminal Law Amendment Bill 2012, Brisbane.
——— (2022), Homepage, viewed 1 July 2022, www.atsils.org.au/services.
ACT Government (2012), *Blueprint for Youth Justice: Improving Outcomes for Young People Over the Next 10 Years*, Canberra: ACT Government.
Adult Parole Board of Victoria (2015), *Parole Manual*, Melbourne: APBV.
Alder, C. (2003), 'Young women and the criminal justice system', paper presented to Juvenile Justice: From Lessons of the Past to a Road Map for the Future conference, Sydney, December.
Alder, C.M. (2001), 'Young women as offenders and the challenge for restorative justice', in J. Braithwaite and H. Strang (eds.), *Restorative Justice: Philosophy and Practice*, Dartmouth: Ashgate.
Alexander, M., Lowenkamp, C. and Robinson, C. (2013), 'A tale of two innovations: Motivational interviewing and core correctional practices in United States probation', in P. Ugwudike and P. Raynor (eds.), *What Works in Offender Compliance*, London: Palgrave Macmillan.
Allan, A. and Dawson, D. (2004), *Assessment of the Risk of Reoffending by Indigenous Male Violent and Sexual Offenders*, Canberra: Criminology Research Council.
Allard, T., Rayment-McHugh, S., Adams, D., Smallbone, S. and McKillop, N. (2015), 'Responding to youth sexual offending: A field-based practice model that "closes the gap" on sexual recidivism among indigenous and non-indigenous males', *Journal of Sexual Aggression*, 22(1): 82–94.

References

Allard, T., Wortley, R. and Stewart, A. (2003), 'Role conflict in community corrections', *Psychology, Crime and Law*, 9(3): 279–89.

Amnesty International (2015), *A Brighter Tomorrow for Indigenous Kids*, Sydney: Amnesty International.

Annison, H. (2022), 'The role of storylines in penal policy change', *Punishment and Society*, 0(0): 1–23.

Annison, J. (2006), 'Style over substance: A review of the evidence base for the use of learning styles in probation', *Criminology and Criminal Justice*, 6: 239–57.

Atherton, P. and Buck, G. (2021), 'Employing with conviction: The experiences of employers who actively recruit criminalised people', *Probation Journal*, 68(2): 1–20.

Attorney-General's Department SA (2022a), *Discussion Paper: Transforming Criminal Justice*, Adelaide: SA Government.

——— (2022b), Official website, viewed 1 July 2022, www.agd.sa.gov.au/.

Australian Association for Restorative Justice (AARJ) (2020), *'Winter 2020 Review of contemporary restorative practice'*, AARJ, viewed 1 July 2022, available online at https://www.aarj.org.au/.

Australian Association of Social Workers (AASW) (2020), *'Code of Ethics'*, available online at https://www.aasw.asn.au/.

——— (AASW) (2021), *Australian Social Work and Education Standards 2021*, viewed 1 July 2022, www.aasw.asn.au.

Australian Bureau of Statistics (ABS) (2022), 'Prisoners in Australia', ABS, available online at https://www.abs.gov.au/.

Australian Federal Police (2022), Official website, viewed 1 July 2022, www.afp.gov.au/policing/cybercrime/crime-prevention.

Australian Human Rights Commission (AHRC) (2001), *Human Rights Brief No. 5: Best Practice Principles for the Diversion of Juvenile Offenders*, Canberra: AHRC.

——— (2012), 'Marlon Noble will only be truly free when his name is cleared', media release, viewed 1 July 2022, www.humanrights.gov.au/news/media-releases/marlon-noble-will-only-be-truly-free-when-his-name-cleared-2012-media-release.

——— (2014a), *Equal Before the Law: Towards Disability Justice Strategies*, Canberra: AHRC.

——— (2014b), *Juvenile Justice? Ensuring the Opportunity to Thrive*, Canberra: AHRC.

Australian Institute of Criminology (AIC) (2012), *Standard Guidelines for Corrections in Australia*, Canberra: Australian Institute of Criminology.

Australian Institute of Criminology (AIC) (2020), *Youth Justice in Australia: Themes from Recent Inquiries*, Canberra: Australian Institute of Criminology.

Australian Institute of Family Studies (AIFS) (2013a), 'Diverting Indigenous offenders from the criminal justice system', Resource sheet 24, Australian Institute of Health and Welfare.

——— (2013b), *Offender Registration Legislation in Each Australian State and Territory*, Canberra: AIFS.

Australian Institute of Health and Welfare (AIHW) (2021), *Youth Justice in Australia 2019–2020*, Canberra: AIHW.

Australian Institute of Health and Welfare (AIHW) (2020), *Young People Under Youth Justice Supervision and in Child Protection 2018–2019*, Canberra: AIHW.

Australian Institute of Health and Welfare (AIHW) (2021), *Young People Returning to Sentenced Youth Justice Supervision 2019–2020*, Canberra: AIHW.

Australian Institute of Health and Welfare (AIHW) (2021), *Youth Detention Population in Australia 2021*, Canberra: AIHW.

Australian Institute of Health and Welfare (AIHW) (2012), *Indigenous Young People in the Juvenile Justice System*, Canberra: AIHW.

——— (2014), *Youth Justice*, Canberra: AIHW.
——— (2015a), *Youth Detention Population in Australia*, Canberra: AIHW.
——— (2015b), *The Health of Australia's Prisoners: 2015*, cat. No. PHE 207, Canberra: AIHW.
Australian Juvenile Justice Agency (AJJA) (2009), Juvenile Justice Agency, AJJA, viewed 1 July 2022, available online at https://www.ics.act.gov.au/__data/assets/pdf_file/0003/1342767/AJJA-Standards-2009.pdf.
Australian Law Reform Commission (ALRC) (1997), *Seen and Heard: Priority for Children in the Legal Process*, Canberra: ALRC.
Australian Migrant Resource Centre (AMRC) (2022), Official website, viewed 19 October 2022, https://amrc.org.au/.
Avery, S. (2018), *Culture is Inclusion: A Narrative of Aboriginal and Torres Strait Islander People with Disability*, Sydney: First People's Disability Network.
Baidawi, S. (2020), 'Crossover children: Examining initial criminal justice system contact among child protection-involved youth', *Australian Social Work*, 73(3): 280–95.
Baidawi, S., Mendes, P. and Snow, P. (2014), 'Setting them up to fail: System responses to dual order child protection and youth justice clients', *Alternative Law Journal*, 39(1): 31–5.
Baidawi, S., Papalia, N. and Featherston, R. (2021), 'Gender differences in the maltreatment-youth offending relationship: A scoping review', *Trauma, Violence and Abuse*, 0(0): 1–17.
Baines, M. and Alder, C. (1996), 'Are girls more difficult to work with? Youth Workers' perceptions in juvenile justice and related areas', *Crime and Delinquency*, 42: 467–85.
Baker, K. and Kelly, G. (2011), 'Risk assessment and young people', in H. Kemshall and B. Wilkinson (eds.), *Good Practice in Assessing Risk*, London: Jessica Kingsley.
Baker, K. and Wilkinson, B. (2011), 'Professional risk taking and defensible decision making', in H. Kemshall and B. Wilkinson (eds.), *Good Practice in Assessing Risk*, London: Jessica Kingsley.
Baker, L.A., Tuvblad, C. and Raine, A. (2010), 'Genetics and crime', in E. McLaughlin and T. Newburn (eds.), *The Sage Handbook of Criminological Theory*, London: Sage.
Baldry, E. (2010), 'Women in transition: From prison to …', *Current Issues in Criminal Justice*, 22(2): 253–67.
Baldry, E. and Cuneen, C. (2014), 'Imprisoned indigenous women and the shadow of colonial patriarchy', *Australian and New Zealand Journal of Criminology*, 47(2): 276–98.
Baldry, E., McCausland, R., Dowse, L., McEntyre, E. and MacGillivray, P. (2016), 'It's just a big vicious cycle that swallows them up: Indigenous people with mental and cognitive disabilities in the criminal justice system', *Indigenous Law Bulletin*, January/February, 8(22): 10–6.
Baldry, E. and Sotiri, M. (2014), 'Corrections: Social work and prisons', in S. Rice and A. Day (eds.), *Social Work in the Shadow of the Law*, Sydney: Federation Press.
Ball, K., Buckley, L. and Moore, R. (2021), *'Caseloads, workloads and staffing levels in probation services'* HM Inspectorate of Probation: Academic Insights 2021/02.
Banks, S. (2012), *Ethics and Values in Social Work* (4th ed.), London: Palgrave Macmillan.
Barclay, E., Hogg, R. and Scott, J. (2007), 'Young people and crime in rural communities', in E. Barclay, J. Donnermeyer, J. Scott and R. Hogg (eds.), *Crime in Rural Australia*, Sydney: Federation Press.
Barnett, G. and Mann, R. (2011), 'Good lives and risk assessment: Collaborative approaches to risk assessment with sex offenders', in H. Kemshall and B. Wilkinson (eds.), *Good Practice in Assessing Risk*, London: Jessica Kingsley.
Bartels, L. (2011), *Crime Prevention Programs for Culturally and Linguistically Diverse Communities in Australia*, Canberra: Australian Institute of Criminology.
Bartels, L. and Martinovic, M. (2017), 'Electronic monitoring: The experience in Australia', *European Journal of Probation*, 9(1): 80–102.

Bartels, L. and Weatherburn, D. (2020), 'Building community confidence in community corrections', *Current Issues in Criminal Justice*, 32(3): 292–308, DOI: 10.1080/10345329.2020.1801150.

Bartkowiak, I. and Jaccoud, M. (2008), 'New directions in Canadian justice: From state workers to community "representatives"', in J. Shapland (ed.), *Justice, Community and Civil Society*, Cullompton: Willan.

Bateman, T. (2013), 'Encouraging compliance, maintaining credibility or fast tracking to custody? Perspectives on enforcement in the youth justice system', in P. Ugwudike and P. Raynor (eds.), *What Works in Offender Compliance*, London: Palgrave Macmillan.

Bauman, Z. (1989), *Modernity and the Holocaust*, Cambridge: Polity Press.

——— (2000), *A Meeting with Zygmunt Bauman (Video)*, Norway: Oslo University College.

Bazemore, G. and Schiff, M. (2001), *Restorative Community Justice: Repairing Harm and Transforming Communities*, New York: Taylor & Francis Group.

Beck, U. (1992), *Risk Society: Towards a New Modernity*, London: Sage.

Becker, H. (1963), *Outsiders*, New York: The Free Press.

Belura, B., Thornton, A., Tompson, A., Manning, M., Sidebottom, A., Bowers, K. (2020), 'A systematic review of the effectiveness of the electronic monitoring of offenders', *Journal of Criminal Justice*, 68: 101686.

Bengtsson, T. (2012), 'Boredom and action: Experiences from youth confinement', *Journal of Contemporary Ethnography*, 41: 526.

Bennett-Levy, J., Wilson, S., Nelson, J., Stirling, J., Ryan, K., Rotumah, D., Budden, W. and Beale, D. (2014), 'Can CBT be effective for aboriginal Australians? Perspectives of aboriginal practitioners trained in CBT', *Australian Psychologist*, 49(1): 1–7.

Best, D., Hamilton, S., Hall, L., Bartels, L. (2021), 'Justice capital: A model for reconciling structural and agentic determinants of desistance', *Probation Journal*, 68(2): 206–23.

Bingham, T. (2010), *The Rule of Law*, London: Allen Lane.

Birgden, A. (2002), 'Therapeutic jurisprudence and "good lives": A rehabilitation framework for corrections', *Australian Psychologist*, 37(3): 180–6.

Black, M. and Smith, R.G. (2003), *Electronic Monitoring in the Criminal Justice System*, Canberra: Australian Institute of Criminology.

Blagg, H. (1997), 'A just measure of shame? Aboriginal youth and conferencing in Australia', *British Journal of Criminology*, 37: 481–501.

Blagg, H. (2008), *Crime, Aboriginality and the Decolonisation of Justice*, Sydney: Hawkins Press.

Bloom, B., Owen, B. and Covington, S. (2005), *Gender-Responsive Strategies for Women Offenders*, Washington, DC: US Department of Justice.

Bolitho, J. and Bruce, J. (2017), 'Science, art and alchemy: Best practice in facilitating restorative justice', *Contemporary Justice Review*, 20(3): 336–62. DOI: 10.1080/10282580.2017.1348896.

Bond, C. and Jeffries, S. (2012), 'Harsher sentences? Indigeneity and prison sentence length in Western Australia's higher courts', *Journal of Sociology*, 48: 266.

Bonta, J. (1996), 'Risk–needs assessment and treatment', in J. Harland (ed.), *Choosing Correctional Options That Work: Defining the Demand and Evaluating the Supply*, Thousand Oaks, CA: Sage.

Bonta, J. and Andrews, D. (2010), 'Viewing offender assessment and rehabilitation through the lens of the risk needs responsivity model', in F. McNeill, P. Raynor and C. Trotter, (eds.), *Offender Supervision: New Directions in Theory, Research and Practice*, Cullompton: Willan.

Borowski, A. (2011), 'In courtroom 7—the Children's koori court at work: Findings from an evaluation', *International Journal of Offender Therapy and Comparative Criminology*, 55(7): 1110–34.

Borowski, A. and Sheehan, R. (2013), 'Magistrates' perspectives on the criminal division of the Children's court of Victoria', *Australian Social Work*, 66(3): 375–90.

Boswell, G. (2000), *Violent Children and Adolescents: Asking the Question Why?*, Chichester: Wiley.

Bottoms, A. (2001), 'Compliance with community penalties', in A. Bottoms, L. Gelsthorpe and S. Rex (eds.), *Community Penalties: Change and Challenges*, Cullompton: Willan.

——— (2008), 'The relationship between theory and empirical observations in criminology', in R. King and E. Wincup (eds.), *Doing Research on Crime and Justice* (2nd ed.), Oxford: Oxford University Press.

——— (2013), 'Learning from Odysseus: Self-applied situational crime prevention as an aid to compliance', in P. Ugwudike and P. Raynor (eds.), *What Works in Offender Compliance*, London: Palgrave Macmillan.

Bourgon, G. and Guiterrez, L. (2013), 'The importance of building good relationships in community corrections: Evidence, theory and practice of the therapeutic alliance', in P. Ugwudike and P. Raynor (eds.), *What Works in Offender Compliance*, London: Palgrave Macmillan.

Bowlby, J. (1951), *Maternal Care and Mental Health*, New York: Schocken Books.

Bowles, W., Collinbridge, M., Curry, S. and Valentine, B. (2006), *Ethical Practice in Social Work: An Applied Approach*, Sydney: Allen & Unwin.

Bradley, K. (2010), 'Cesare lombroso', in K. Hayward, S. Maruna and J. Mooney (eds.), *Fifty Key Thinkers in Criminology*, Abingdon: Routledge.

Braithwaite, J. (1989), *Crime, Shame and Reintegration*, Cambridge: Cambridge University Press.

——— (1999), 'Restorative justice: Assessing optimistic and pessimistic accounts', in Tonry, M. (ed.), *Crime and Justice: A Review of Research*, Chicago: University of Chicago Press.

——— (2003a), 'Does restorative justice work?', in G. Johnstone (ed.), *A Restorative Justice Reader*, Cullompton: Willan.

——— (2003b), 'Principles of restorative justice', in A. von Hirsch, J. Roberts, A. Bottoms, K. Roach and M. Schiff (eds.), *Restorative Justice and Criminal Justice: Competing or Reconcilable Paradigms?*, Oxford: Hart.

Brame, R., Mazarolle, P. and Piquero, A. (2010), 'Criminal career progression among youthful offenders in Australia', *Journal of Criminal Justice*, 38: 340–7.

Brown, D. (2020). 'Community sanctions as pervasive punishment: A review essay', *International Journal for Crime, Justice and Social Democracy*, 9(2): 183–99. https://doi.org/10.5204/ijcjsd.v9i2.1208.

Brown, D. (2013), 'Justice reinvestment: The circuit breaker?', *Insight*, 8: 36–8.

Brown, D., Schwartz, M. and Boseley, L. (2012), 'The promise of justice reinvestment', *Alternative Law Journal*, 37(2): 96–102.

Brull, M. (2011), 'The sad story of Marlon Noble', *Ramp Up*, ABC Online, viewed 1 July 2022, www.abc.net.au/rampup/articles/2011/12/09/3387845.htm.

Bryant, C. and Willis, M. (2008), *Risk Factors in Indigenous Violent Victimisation*, Technical and background paper no. 30. Canberra: Australian Institute of Criminology, viewed 1 July 2022, www.aic.gov.au/publications/current%20series/tbp/21-40/tbp030.aspx.

Bull, M. (2010), *Punishment and Sentencing: Risk, Rehabilitation and Restitution*, Melbourne: Oxford University Press.

Bureau of Crime Statistics and Research (BOCSAR) (2022), Official website, viewed 1 July 2022, www.bocsar.nsw.gov.au.

Burnett, R. and McNeill, F. (2005), 'The place of the officer-offender relationship in assisting offenders to desist from crime', *Probation Journal*, 52(3): 221–42.

Calder, M. (2011), 'Organisationally dangerous practice: Political drivers, practice implications and pathways to resolution', in H. Kemshall and B. Wilkinson (eds.), *Good Practice in Assessing Risk*, London: Jessica Kingsley.

Callinan, I. (2013), *Review of the Parole System in Victoria*, Melbourne: Department of Justice and Regulation.
Calverley, A. (2013), *Cultures of Desistance: Rehabilitation, Reintegration and Ethnic Minorities*, London: Routledge.
Canton, R. (2022), 'After-care, resettlement and social inclusion: The role of probation', *Probation Journal*, 69(3): 1–18.
Canton, R. (2007), 'Compliance', in R. Canton and D. Hancock (eds.), *Dictionary of Probation and Offender Management*, Cullompton: Willan.
——— (2012), 'The point of probation: On effectiveness, human rights and the virtues of obliquity', *Criminology and Criminal Justice*, 13(5): 577–93.
Canton, R. and Dominey, J. (2018), *Probation: Working With Offenders*, London: Routledge.
Canton, R. and Yates, J. (2008), 'Applied criminology', in B. Stout, J. Yates and B. Williams (eds.), *Applied Criminology*, London: Sage.
Carlen, P. (2013), 'Against rehabilitation: For reparative justice', *Criminal Justice Matters*, 91(1): 32–3.
Carr, N. (2020), '*Recruitment, training and professional development of probation staff*', HHM Inspectorate of Probation: Academic Insights 2020/02.
Carr, N. (2021), 'States of exception? Criminal justice systems and the COVID response', *Probation Journal*, 68(4): 391–3.
Carr, N. (2022), 'Plus ca change? Women and the criminal justice system', *Probation Journal*, 69(1): 3–5.
Carter, J.S. (2015), 'Card helps curb "national emergency" of domestic violence', *Afternoons*, ABC Radio National, 19 May.
Casey, R., McNeill, F., Barkas, B., Cornish, N., Gormley, C. and Schinkel, M. (2021), 'Pervasive punishment in a pandemic', *Probation Journal*, 68(4): 1–17.
Centre for International Crime Prevention (United Nations) (1999), *Draft Declaration on Basic Principles on the Use of Restorative Justice Programmes in Criminal Matters*, New York: United Nations.
Chang, W.K. (2017), 'When my community met the other: Competing concepts of community in restorative justice', *Canadian Journal of Law & Society*, 32: 371.
Change the Record (2022), 'Raise the Age', available online at https://www.changetherecord.org.au/raisetheage.
Change the Record (2015), *Smarter Justice, Safer Communities*, viewed 1 July 2022, https://changetherecord.org.au/about.
Chapman, T. (2010), 'Revising the national outcomes and standards for criminal justice social work services in Scotland', in F. McNeill, P. Raynor and C. Trotter (eds.), *Offender Supervision: New Directions in Theory, Research and Practice*, Cullompton: Willan.
Chapman, T. and Hough, M. (1998), *Evidence Based Practice: A Guide to Effective Practice*, London: Home Office.
Cherry, S. (2010) (2nd ed.), *Transforming Behaviour: Pro-Social Modelling in Practice*, Cullompton: Willan.
Christie, N. (1977), 'Conflicts as property', *British Journal of Criminology*, 17(1): 1–15.
Chu, C.M., Ward, T. and Willis, G. (2014), 'Practising the good lives model', in I. Durnescu and F. McNeill (eds.), *Understanding Penal Practice*, London: Routledge.
Clamp, K. (2008), 'Assessing alternative forms of localised justice in post-conflict societies: Youth justice in Northern Ireland and South Africa', in D. Frenkel and C. Gerner-Beuerle (eds.), *Selected Essays on Current Legal Issues*, Athens: ATINER.
——— (2014), *Restorative Justice in Transition*, London: Routledge.

Clancey, G., Wang, S. and Lin, B. (2020), *Youth Justice in Australia: Themes from Recent Inquiries*, Trends and Issues in crime and criminal justice, Australian Institute of Criminology.

Clear, T. (2020), 'Reinventing punitive justice and the community justice system: Address to the Asian criminological society', *Asian Journal of Criminology*, 15: 185–93.

Clear, T. (2008), 'Community justice versus restorative justice: Contrasts in family of value', in D. Sullivan and L. Tifft (eds.), *Handbook of Restorative Justice*, Abingdon: Routledge.

Clear, T.R., Hamilton J.R. Jnr and Cadora, E. (2011), *Community Justice* (2nd ed.), London: Routledge.

Cohen, S. (1979), 'The punitive city: Notes on the dispersal of social control', *Contemporary Crises*, 3: 339–63.

Cohen, S. (1985), *Visions of Social Control: Crime, Punishment and Classification*, Oxford: Polity Press.

Cole, B. (2008), 'Working with ethnic diversity', in S. Green, E. Lancaster and S. Feasey (eds.), *Addressing Offending Behaviour: Context, Practice and Values*, Cullompton: Willan.

Commissioner for Law Enforcement Data Security Victoria (2013), *Law Enforcement and Social Media*, viewed 1 July 2022, www.cpdp.vic.gov.au/images/content/pdf/cleds_special_reports/CLEDS-Social-Media-and-Law-Enforcement-11-11.pdf.

Community Protection Western Australia (2015), Official website, viewed 1 July 2022, https://www.wa.gov.au/service/security/law-enforcement/access-registered-sex-offender-information.

Community Restorative Centre (2022), Official website, viewed 1 July 2022, www.crcnsw.org.aus/.

Cooner, T., Knowles, A. and Stout, B. (2015), 'Creating a mobile app to teach ethical social media practices', *Journal of Social Work Education*, 1–15, doi: 10.1080/02615479.2015.1042361.

Cornish, D.B. and Clarke, R.V.G. (eds.) (1986), *The Reasoning Criminal: Rational Choice Perspectives on Offending*, New York: Springer.

Corrections Victoria (2009), *Correctional Management Standards for Women Serving Community Correctional Orders*, Melbourne: Corrections Victoria, viewed 1 July 2022, http://assets.justice.vic.gov.au/corrections/resources/44b01ba8-a655-4768-aa88-2a399e3ca702/cms_women_cco2009.pdf.

——— (2015a), 'Koori candidates', viewed 1 July 2022, http://correctionsjobs.vic.gov.au/koori-recruitment.

——— (2015b), 'Testimonials', viewed 1 July 2022, http://correctionsjobs.vic.gov.au/community-corrections-officers/testimonials.

Corrections Victoria (2022), Website, viewed 1 July 2022, www.corrections.vic.gov.au.

Corrective Services NSW (2010), 'Case management policy', viewed 1 July 2022, www.correctiveservices.justice.nsw.gov.au/Documents/Related%20Links/open-access-information/offender-classification/3.1-CSNSW-Case-Management-Policy.pdf.

Corrective Services New South Wales (CSNSW) (2022), *'Compendium of Offender Behaviour Change Programs'*, Department of Communities and Justice, Offender Services & Programs Offender Management & Programs Division.

Council of Europe (2019). Guidelines Regarding Recruitment, Selection, Education, Training and Professional Development of Prison and Probation Staff. Available at https://rm.coe.int/guidelines-training-staff/1680943aad.

Cox, A. (2020), 'The language of incarceration', *Incarceration*, 1(1): 1–13.

Coyle, I. (2011), 'The cogency of risk assessments', *Psychiatry, Psychology and Law*, 18(2): 270–96.

Crawford, A. (2008), 'Refiguring the community and professional in policing and criminal justice: Some questions of legitimacy', in J. Shapland (ed.), *Justice, Community and Civil Society*, Cullompton: Willan.

Crawford, A. and Newburn, T. (2003), *Youth Offending and Restorative Justice*, Cullompton: Willan.

Cripps, K., Miller, L. and Saxton-Barney, J. (2010), '"Too hard to handle": Indigenous victims of violence with disabilities', *Indigenous Law Bulletin*, 7(21): 4. www.austlii.edu.au/au/journals/ILB/2010/39.html.

Cubitt, T. and Morgan, A. (2022), *Predicting High-Harm Offending Using Machine Learning: An Application to Outlaw Motorcycle gangs*, Australian Institute of Criminology.

Cullen, F., Lero Jonson, C. and Mears, D. (2017), 'Reinventing community corrections', *Crime and Justice*, 46, University of Chicago.

Cunneen, C. (1997), 'Community conferencing and the fiction of indigenous control', *Australian and New Zealand Journal of Criminology*, 30: 292–311.

—— (2002), 'Restorative justice and the politics of decolonization', in E. Weitekamp and H. Kerner (eds.), *Restorative Justice: Theoretical Foundations*, Cullompton: Willan.

—— (2004), 'What are the implications of restorative justice's use of indigenous traditions?', in H. Zehr and B. Toews (eds.), *Critical Issues in Restorative Justice*, Cullompton: Willan.

—— (2006), 'Racism, discrimination and the over-representation of indigenous people in the criminal justice system: Some conceptual and explanatory issues', *Current Issues in Criminal Justice*, 17(3): 329–46.

—— (2006), 'Restorative justice', in E. McLaughlin and J. Muncie (eds.), *The Sage Dictionary of Criminology*, London: Sage.

—— (2007), 'Reviving restorative justice traditions?', in G. Johnstone and D. Van Ness (eds.), *Handbook of Restorative Justice*, Cullompton: Willan.

—— (2008), 'Exploring the relationship between reparations, the gross violation of human rights, and restorative justice', in D. Sullivan and L. Tifft (eds.), *Handbook of Restorative Justice*, Abingdon: Routledge.

Cunneen, C., Baldry, E., Brown, D., Brown, M., Schwartz, M. and Steel, A. (2013), *Penal Culture and Hyperincarceration: The Revival of the Prison*, Farnham, Surrey: Ashgate.

Cunneen, C. and Porter, A. (2017), 'Indigenous peoples and criminal justice in Australia', in A. Deckert and R. Sarre (eds.), *The Palgrave Handbook of Australian and New Zealand Criminology, Crime and Justice*, New York: Springer International Publishing.

Cunneen, C., Russell, S. and Schwartz, M. (2021), 'Principles in diversion of aboriginal and torres strait islander young people from the criminal jurisdiction', *Current Issues in Criminal Justice*, 33(2): 170–90.

Cunneen, C. and White, R. (2006), 'Australia: Control, containment or empowerment', in J. Muncie and B. Goldson (eds.), *Comparative Youth Justice*, London: Sage.

Cunneen, C., White, R. and Richards, K. (2015), *Juvenile Justice: Youth and Crime in Australia*, Oxford: Oxford University Press.

Dadich, A., Stout, B. and Hosseinzadeh, H. (2015), 'Reacting to and managing change within juvenile justice', *Journal of Organizational Change Management*, 28(2): 315–8.

Daems, T. (2020), *Electronic Monitoring: Tagging Offenders in a Culture of Surveillance*, Cham, Switzerland: Palgrave Macmillan.

Daly, K. (2001), 'Conferencing in Australia and New Zealand: Variations, research findings and prospects', in A. Morris and G.M. Maxwell (eds.), *Restorative Justice for Juveniles, Conferencing Mediation and Circles*, Oxford: Hart.

—— (2003a), 'Mind the gap: Restorative justice in theory and practice', in A. Von Hirsch, J. Roberts and A. Bottoms (eds.), *Restorative Justice and Criminal Justice*, Oxford: Hart.

—— (2003b), 'Restorative justice: The real story', in G. Johnstone (ed.), *A Restorative Justice Reader*, Cullompton: Willan.

——— (2007), 'Feminist perspectives in criminology: A review with gen y in mind', in M. Maguire, R. Morgan and R. Reiner (eds.), *The Oxford Handbook of Criminology* (4th ed.), Oxford: Oxford University Press.

——— (2016), 'What is restorative justice? Fresh answers to a vexed question', *Victims & Offenders*, 11(1): 9–29. DOI: 10.1080/15564886.2015.1107797.

Daly, K. and Nancarrow, H. (2009), 'Restorative justice and youth violence towards parents', in J. Ptacek (ed.), *Restorative Justice and Violence Against Women*, Oxford: Oxford University Press.

Daly, K., Bouhours, B., Broadhurst, R. and Loh, N. (2013), 'Youth sex offending, recidivism and restorative justice: Comparing court and conference cases', *Australian and New Zealand Journal of Criminology*, 46(2): 241–67.

Day, A. (2022), 'It's a Hard Balance to Find': The Perspectives of Youth Justice Practitioners in England on the Place of 'Risk' in an Emerging 'Child-First' World, *Youth Justice*, 1–18.

Day, A. (2021), '*Experiences and pathways of children in care in the youth justice system*', Academic Insights, Her Majesty's Inspectorate of Probation.

Day, A., Carson, E., Boni, N. and Hobbs, G. (2014), 'The management of sex offenders in the community: From policy to practice', *Australian Journal of Social Issues*, 49(3): 249–64.

De Vries, N., Macdonald, G., Mears, J. and Nettheim, A. (2012), *One Life, Two Stories*, Sydney: Darlington Press.

Deckert, A. (2016), 'Criminologists, duct tape, and indigenous peoples: Quantifying the use of silencing research methods', *International Journal of Comparative and Applied Criminal Justice*, 40(1): 43–62.

Denning, R. and Homel, R. (2008), 'Predicting recidivism in juvenile offenders on community-based orders: The impact of risk factors and service delivery', *Journal of Offender Rehabilitation*, 46(3–4): 189–215.

Department of Correctional Services (DCS) (NSW) (2022), *New South Wales Compendium of Correctional Services*, Sydney: NSW Government.

Department for Correctional Services SA (2022), Official website, viewed 1 July 2022, www.corrections.sa.gov.au.

Department of Human Services (DHS) Victoria (2014), 'Probation: Information for young people', viewed 1 July 2022, www.dhs.vic.gov.au/home.

Department of Justice NSW (2014), 'Department of Justice Social Media Policy', viewed 1 July 2022, www.justice.nsw.gov.au/Pages/publications-research/social-media-policy.aspx.

Department of Justice Tasmania (2010), 'Breaking the cycle', discussion paper, Tasmania: Department of Justice.

——— (2011), *Breaking the Cycle: A Strategic Plan for Tasmanian Corrections*, Hobart: Department of Justice.

Department of the Attorney-General and Justice NT (2015), *Cross-Border Justice Scheme*, viewed 1 July 2022, www.nt.gov.au/justice/crossborder.

Developmental Crime Prevention Consortium (1999), *Pathways to Prevention: Developmental and Early Intervention Approaches to Crime in Australia*, Canberra: Attorney-General's Department.

Dignan, J. (2005), *Understanding Victims and Restorative Justice*, Maidenhead: Open University Press.

Dillon, M. (2015), 'GPS tracking of sex offenders begins in SA', The Advertiser, 3 March 2015, viewed 1 July 2022, https://www.adelaidenow.com.au/news/south-australia/gps-tracking-of-sex-offenders-begins-in-sa/news-story/d33813be21f972a183ec9780e3343f63.

Dollery, R. (2013), 'GPS Devices used to track 16 sex offenders', ABC News, 12 June 2013, viewed 25 August 2015, www.abc.net.au.

Dominey, J. (2007), 'Responsivity', in R. Canton and D. Hancock (eds.), *Dictionary of Probation and Offender Management*, Cullompton: Willan.

——— (2019), 'Probation supervision as a network of relationships: Aiming to be thick, not thin', *Probation Journal*, 66(3): 283–302.

Dominey, J. and Canton, R. (2022), 'Probation and the ethics of care', *Probation Journal*, 1–17.

Dominey, J., Coley, D., Devitt, K. and Lawrence, J. (2021), 'Putting a face to a name: Telephone contact as part of a blended learning approach to probation supervision', *Probation Journal*, 68(4): 394–410.

Dominey, J. and Gelsthorpe, L. (2020), 'Resettlement and the case for women', *Probation Journal*, 67(4): 393–409.

Dowden, C. and Andrews, D.A. (2004), 'The importance of staff practice in delivering effective correctional treatment: A meta-analytical review of the literature', *International Journal of Offender Therapy and Comparative Criminology*, 48(2): 203–14.

Drug and Alcohol Multicultural Education Centre (DAMEC) (2022), Official website, https://www.damec.org.au/.

Drum, K. (2013), 'America's real criminal element: Lead', *Mother Jones*, viewed 1 July 2022, www.motherjones.com/environment/2013/01/lead-crime-link-gasoline.

Duarte, O. (2013), 'Can design support community safety and crime prevention programmes in areas of socio-economic disadvantage?', *Crime Prevention and Community Safety*, 15(3): 223–39.

Duarte, O., Lulham, R. and Kaldor, L. (2011), 'Co-designing out crime', *CoDesign*, 7(3–4): 155–68.

Dudgeon, P. and Kelly, K. (2014), 'Contextual factors for research on psychological therapies for aboriginal Australians', *Australian Psychologist*, 49(1): 8–13.

Dufour, I. and Brassard, R. (2014), 'The convert, the remorseful and the rescued: Three different processes of desistance from crime', *Australian and New Zealand Journal of Criminology*, 47(3): 313–35.

Dunlevie, J. (2014), 'Northern Territory alcohol offenders to be monitored by ankle bracelet like Lindsay Lohan', ABC News, viewed 1 July 2022, https://www.abc.net.au/news/2014-11-26/alcohol-offenders-to-share-hollywood-stars-ankle-bracelet/5919460.

Dunsby, R. and Howes, L. (2019), 'The NEW adventures of the digital vigilante! Facebook users' views on online naming and shaming,' *Australian & New Zealand Journal of Criminology*, 52(1): 41–59.

Durkheim, E. (1897), *Suicide: A Study in Sociology*, New York: The Free Press.

Durnescu, I. and Stout, B. (2011), 'A European approach to probation training: An investigation into the competencies required', *Probation Journal*, 58(4): 395–405.

Egan, G. (1994), *The Skilled Helper: A Problem Management Approach to Helping*, Pacific Grove, CA: Brooks/Cole.

Eriksson, A. (2009). 'A bottom-up approach to transformative justice in Northern Ireland', *The International Journal of Transitional Justice*, 3(3): 301–20.

Etzioni, A. (1995), *The Spirit of Community*, London: Fontana.

——— (1997), *The New Golden Rule: Community and Morality in a Democratic State*, London: Profile Books.

Evans, R. (2012), 'Parenting orders: The parents attend yet the kids still offend', *Youth Justice*, 12: 118.

Executive Session on Community Corrections (2017), *'Toward an Approach to Community Corrections for the 21st Century: Consensus Document of the Executive Session on Community Corrections'*, Program in Criminal Justice Policy and Management, Harvard Kennedy School.

Eysenck, H. (1964), *Crime and Personality*, Boston: Houghton Mifflin.

Fair, H. and Walmsley, R. (2022), 'World Prison Population List 13th Edition', Institute for Crime and Justice Policy Research, available online at https://www.prisonstudies.org/.

Fang, L., Mishna, F., Zhang, V.F., Van Wert, M. and Bogo, M. (2014), 'Social media and social work education: Understanding and dealing with the new digital world', *Social Work in Health Care*, 53: 800–814.

Farrall, S. (2007), 'Desistance studies vs. cognitive behavioural therapies: Which offers most hope for the long term?', in R. Canton and D. Hancock (eds.), *Dictionary of Probation and Offender Management*, Cullompton: Willan.

Farrall, S. and Calverley, A. (2006), *Understanding Desistance from Crime*, Maidenhead: Open University Press.

Farrall, S., Hunter, B., Sharpe, G. and Calverley, A. (2014), *Criminal Careers in Transition: The Social Context of Desistance from Crime*, Oxford: Clarendon Press.

Farrow, K., Kelly, G. and Wilkinson, B. (2007), *Offenders in Focus*, Bristol: Policy Press.

Faulkner, D. and Burnett, R. (2012), *Where Next for Criminal Justice?*, Bristol: Policy Press.

Feeley, M. and Simon, J. (1992), 'The new penology: Notes on the emerging strategy of corrections and its implications', *Criminology*, 30(4): 449–74.

Ferguson, H., Disney, T., Warwick, L., Jadwiga, L., Singh Cooner, T. and Beddoe, L. (2020), 'Hostile relationships in social work practice: Anxiety, hate and conflict in long-term work with involuntary service users', *Journal of Social Work Practice*, DOI: 10.1080/02650533.2020.1834371.

Finnane, M. (1997), *Punishment in Australian Society*, Melbourne: Oxford University Press.

Fisher, C. (2013), 'Changed and changing gender and family roles and domestic violence in African refugee background communities post-settlement in Perth, Australia', *Violence Against Women*, 19(7): 833–47.

Fitzgibbon, W. (2011), *Probation and Social Work on Trial: Violent Offenders and Child Abusers*, Basingstoke: Palgrave Macmillan.

Flynn, N. (2010), *Criminal Behaviour in Context: Space, Place and Desistance from Crime*, Cullompton: Willan.

Fox, C., Albertson, K. and Wong, K. (2013), *Justice Reinvestment*, Abingdon: Routledge.

Fredriksson, T. and Galnander, R. (2020), 'Fearful futures and haunting histories in women's desistance from crime: A longitudinal study of desistance as an uncanny process', *Criminology*, 1–20.

Freiberg, A. (2003), 'Therapeutic jurisprudence in Australia: Paradigm shift or pragmatic incrementalism', in M. McMahon and D. Wexler (eds.), *Therapeutic Jurisprudence: Law in Context 20/2*, Sydney: Federation Press.

Freiberg, A. and Bartels, L. (2020), 'Penal Diversity, penality and community sanctions in Australia', *Punishment & Society*, 1–23.

G4S Electronic Monitoring Services (2015), 'Supporting governments in creating safer communities', viewed 1 July 2022, www.au.g4s.com/media/1605/g4s-electronic-monitoring-final.pdf.

Gadd, D. (2004), 'Criminal careers, desistance and subjectivity: Interpreting men's narratives of change', *Theoretical Criminology*, 8(2): 123–56.

Garland, D. (2001), *The Culture of Control: Crime and Social Order in Contemporary Society*, Oxford: Oxford University Press.

Garside, R. (2020), 'Prisons and politics', *Prison Service Journal*, September, 250: 4–12.

Gelsthorpe, L. (2007), 'Probation values and human rights', in L. Gelsthorpe and R. Morgan (eds.), *Handbook of Probation*, Cullompton: Willan.

——— (2013), 'Working with women in probation: "Will you, won't you, will you, won't you, won't you join the dance"', in P. Ugwudike and P. Raynor (eds.), *What Works in Offender Compliance*, London: Palgrave Macmillan.

Gendreau, P. (1996), 'Offender rehabilitation: What we know and what needs to be done', *Criminal Justice and Behaviour*, 23: 144–61.

Gendreau, P. and Andrews, D. (1990), 'Tertiary prevention: What the meta-analysis of the offender treatment literature tells us about "what works"', *Canadian Journal of Criminology*, 32: 173–84.

Gillett, G. and Tamatea, A.J. (2012), 'The warrior gene: Epigenetic considerations', *New Genetics and Society*, 31(1): 41–53. DOI: 10.1080/14636778.2011.597982.

Giordina, P.C., Cernkovich, S.A. and Rudolph, J.L. (2002), 'Gender, crime, and desistance: Toward a theory of cognitive transformation', *American Journal of Sociology*, 107(4): 990–1064.

Giroux, H. (2011), 'Youth in the suspect society and the politics of disposability', *Power Play: A Journal of Educational Justice*, 3(1): 3–21.

Goeghegan, R. (2012), *Future of Corrections*, London: Policy Exchange.

Goffman, A. (2014), *On the Run: Fugitive Life in an American City*, Chicago: University of Chicago Press.

Goldsmith, A. and Halsey, M. (2013), 'Cousins in crime: Mobility and place in indigenous co-offending', *British Journal of Criminology*, 53: 1157–77.

Goldson, B. (2002), *Vulnerable Inside: Children in Secure and Penal Settings*, London: Children's Society.

Goodman-Delahunty, J. and O'Brien, K. (2014), *Parental Sexual Offending: Managing Risk Through Diversion*, Canberra: Australian Institute of Criminology.

Gordon, F., Klose, H. and Storrod, M. (2021), Youth (in)justice and the COVID-19 pandemic: Rethinking incarceration through a public health lens, *Current Issues in Criminal Justice*. DOI: 10.1080/10345329.2020.1859966.

Gornik, M. (2002), 'Moving from correctional program to correctional strategy: Using proven practices to change criminal behaviour', *ICCA Journal on Community Corrections*, April: 24–33.

Government of Australia (2018), *'Guiding Principles for Corrections in Australia'*, Government of Australia through the Corrective Services Administrators Council, available online https://www.corrections.vic.gov.au/guiding-principles-for-corrections-in-australia.

Grant, S. and McNeill, F. (2014), 'What matters in practice? Understanding "quality" in the routine supervision of offenders in Scotland', *British Journal of Social Work*, 45(7): 1–18.

Green, S. (2008), 'Discrimination and the poor. Using incentives and privileges as a framework for anti-discriminatory practice', in S. Green, E. Lancaster and S. Feasey (eds.), *Addressing Offending Behaviour*, Cullompton: Willan.

Grosz, E. (1987), 'Feminist theory and the challenge to knowledge', *Women's Studies International Forum*, 10(5): 208–17.

Guest, A. (2013), 'Queensland's juvenile justice plan impinges human rights: Commissioner', *ABC News*, viewed 1 July 2022, www.abc.net.au/news/2013-07-27/juvenile-justice-plan-impinges-children27s-rights-commissioner/4847788.

Hakiaha, M. (2004), 'What is the state's role in indigenous justice processes?', in H. Zehr and B. Toews (eds.), *Critical Issues in Restorative Justice*, Cullompton: Willan.

Hall, M. (2020), 'Changes in new South Wales criminal justice since 2010', *Current Issues in Criminal Justice*. DOI: 10.1080/10345329.2020.1813388.

Halsey, M. (2006), 'Negotiating conditional release: Juvenile narratives of repeat incarceration', *Punishment and Society*, 8(2): 147–81.

Halsey, M., Armstrong, R. and Wright, S. (2017), "F*ck it!': Matza and the mood of fatalism in the desistance process', *British Journal of Criminology*, 57: 1041–60.

Halsey, M. and Deegan, S. (2012), 'Father and son: Two generations through prison', *Punishment and Society*, 14(3): 338–67.

―――― (2014), '"Picking up the pieces": Female significant others in the lives of young (ex) incarcerated males', *Criminology and Criminal Justice*, 15: 131–51.

―――― (2015), *Young Offenders: Crime, Prison and Struggles for Desistance*, Basingstoke: Palgrave Macmillan.

Halsey, M., Goldsmith, A. and Bamford, D. (2015), 'Achieving restorative justice: Assessing contrition and forgiveness in the adult conference process', *Australian and New Zealand Journal of Criminology*, 48(4): 483–97.

Hamm, M.S. (2005), 'Doing terrorism research in the dark ages: Confessions of a bottom dog', in S. Lyng (ed.), *Edgework: The Sociology of Risk*, New York: Routledge.

Harding, J. (2000), 'A community justice dimension to effective probation practice', *Howard Journal*, 39(2): 132–49.

―――― (2007), 'Community justice', in R. Canton and D. Hancock (eds.), *Dictionary of Probation and Offender Management*, Cullompton: Willan.

Hardman, A. (2010), 'The not-so-standard indigenous question: Identifying aboriginal and torres strait islander victims', *Indigenous Law Bulletin*, 7(16): 17–9.

Harker, H. and Worrall, A. (2011), 'From "community corrections" to "probation and parole" in Western Australia', *Probation Journal: The Journal of Community and Criminal Justice*, 58(4): 363–71.

Harris, N. and Maruna, S. (2008), 'Shame, sharing and restorative justice: A critical appraisal', in D. Sullivan and L. Tifft (eds.), *Handbook of Restorative Justice*, Abingdon: Routledge.

Hayes, H. and Daly, K. (2003), 'Youth justice conferencing and reoffending', *Justice Quarterly*, 20(4): 725–64.

Hayes, H. and Snow, P. (2013), *Oral Language Competence and Restorative Justice Processes: Refining Preparation and the Measurement of Conference Outcomes*, Canberra: Australian Institute of Criminology.

Hayward, K., Maruna, S. and Mooney, J. (eds.) (2009), *Fifty Key Thinkers in Criminology*, Abingdon: Routledge.

Heidensohn, F. and Gelsthorpe, L. (2007), 'Gender and crime', in M. Maguire, R. Morgan and R. Reiner (eds.), *The Oxford Handbook of Criminology* (4th ed.), Oxford: Oxford University Press.

Hirschi, T. and Hindelang, M. (1977), 'Intelligence and delinquency: A revisionist view', *American Sociological Review*, 42(4): 571–87.

Hobsbawm, E. (1995), *Age of Extremes: The Short Twentieth Century, 1914–1991*, London: Abacus.

Hollin, C. (2006a), 'Rehabilitation', in E. McLaughlin and J. Muncie (eds.), *The Sage Dictionary of Criminology* (2nd ed.), London: Sage.

―――― (2006b), 'Social learning theory', in E. McLaughlin and J. Muncie (eds.), *The Sage Dictionary of Criminology* (2nd ed.), London: Sage.

―――― (2007), 'Criminological psychology', in Maguire, M., Morgan, R. and Reiner, R. (eds.), *The Oxford Handbook of Criminology* (4th ed.), Oxford: Oxford University Press.

Hoyle, C. and Zedner, L. (2007), 'Victims, victimization and criminal justice', in M. Maguire, R. Morgan and R. Reiner (eds.), *The Oxford Handbook of Criminology*, Oxford: Oxford University Press.

Hucklesby, A. (2013), 'Insiders' views: Offenders' and staff's experiences of electronically monitored curfews', in M. Nellis, K. Beyens and D. Kaminski (eds.), *Electronically Monitored Punishment: International and Critical Perspectives*, Abingdon: Routledge.

Hughes, N. and Chitsabesan, P. (2015), *Supporting Young People with Neurodevelopmental Impairment*, London: Centre for Crime and Justice Studies.

Human Rights and Equal Opportunity Commission (HREOC) (2005), *Indigenous Young People with Cognitive Disabilities and Australian Juvenile Justice Systems: Report by Aboriginal and Torres Strait Islander Social Justice Commissioner*, Sydney: HREOC.

Human Rights Law Centre (HRLC) (2014), 'Letter to the UN Special Rapporteur on the Rights of Indigenous People', viewed 1 July 2022, https://www.hrlc.org.au/.

Human Rights Law Centre (HRLC) (2015a), *National Human Rights Action Plan*, Melbourne: HRLC.

―――― (2015b), *UN Report: A Reminder That Australia's Youth Justice Practices Are Failing to Meet International Standards*, Melbourne: HRLC.

Hunt, N. (2015), 'Instant bracelet alcotest and random drug testing likely for home detention prisoners in SA', *The Advertiser* (Adelaide), 9 August.

Hutchinson, T. and Richards, K. (2013), 'Scared straight: Boot camps for Queensland', *Alternative Law Journal*, 38(4): 229–33.

Hwang, Y., Simpson, P. and Butler, T. (2021), 'Participant experiences of a post-release electronic monitoring program for domestic violence in new South Wales, Australia', *Journal of Criminology*, 54(4): 482–500.

Ife, J. (2012), *Human Rights and Social Work: Towards Rights-Based Practice* (3rd ed.), Cambridge: Cambridge University Press.

―――― (2016), 'Human rights and social work: Beyond conservative law', *Journal Human Rights Social Work*, 1: 30–9.

Informa Australia (2013), 'Is social media the secret to improving OHS in correctional facilities?', Informa Insights, 2 March 2015, viewed 1 July 2022, https://www.informa.com.au/insight/is-social-media-the-secret-to-improving-ohs-in-correctional-facilities/.

International Centre for Prison Studies (2022), *World Prison Population List*, viewed 1 July 2022, www.apcca.org.

James, F. (2015), 'NT police investigating criminal allegations at Don Dale Youth Detention Centre amid claims teens forced to fight', *ABC News*, viewed 1 July 2022, www.abc.net.au/news/2015-09-23/darwin-youth-detention-centre-investigated-by-police/6796988.

Jarldorn, M. and Emery, S. (2022), 'Getting ID after exiting prison is harder than you might think. So we built a chatbot to help', *The Conversation*, 26 April 2022, available online https://theconversation.com/getting-id-after-exiting-prison-is-harder-than-you-might-think-so-we-built-a-chatbot-to-help-180570.

Jesuit Social Services (2013), *Thinking Outside: Alternatives to Remand for Children*, Melbourne: Jesuit Social Services.

Journey Towards Hope (Jothe) (2022), Official website, viewed 1 July 2022, https://www.vallibatchelor.com/.

Justice Reinvestment Campaign (JRC) (2022), Official website, viewed 1 July 2022, www.justreinvest.org.au.

Kandola, R. and Fullerton, J. (2004), *Managing the Mosaic*, London: Institute of Personnel and Development.

Karp, D. and Clear, T. (2000), 'Community justice: A conceptual framework', *Boundary Changes in Criminal Justice Organisations*, 2: 323–68.

―――― (eds.) (2002), *What Is Community Justice?*, Thousand Oaks, CA: Sage.

Kelly, A. (2014a), 'Managing the risks of public discourse on the new South Wales police force facebook site', *Salus Journal*, 2(1): 19–42, viewed 1 July 2022, www.salus-journal.com/wp-content/uploads/sites/29/2013/03/Kelly_Salus_Journal_Issue_2_Number_1_2014_pp_19-42.pdf.

―――― (2014b), 'Why police should be on Facebook: Lessons from the NSW Police Force', *ConnectedCops*, viewed 1 July 2022, http://connectedcops.net/why-police-should-be-on-facebook-lessons-from-the-nsw-police-forces-project-eyewatch-strategy.

Kemshall, H. (2007), 'Risk assessment and risk management', in R. Canton and D. Hancock (eds.), *Dictionary of Probation and Offender Management*, Cullompton: Willan.
——— (2008), *Understanding the Community Management of High Risk Offenders*, Maidenhead: Open University Press.
——— (2010), 'Risk rationalities in contemporary social work policy and practice', *British Journal of Social Work*, 40: 1247–62.
——— (2012), 'The sex offender public disclosure pilots in England and Scotland: Lessons for "marketing strategies" and risk communication with the public', *Criminology and Criminal Justice*, 12(5): 549–65.
——— (2014), 'Conflicting rationalities of risk: Disputing risk in social policy—Reflecting on 35 years of researching risk', *Health, Risk and Society*, 16(5): 398–416.
Kemshall, H. (2021), *Risk and Desistance: A Blended Approach to Risk Management*, Her Majesty's Inspectorate of Probation.
Kemshall, H., Dominey, J. and Hilder, S. (2012), 'Public disclosure: Sex offenders' perceptions of the pilot scheme in England. Compliance, legitimacy and living a "Good life"', *Journal of Sexual Aggression*, 18(3): 311–24.
Kemshall, H., Wilkinson, B. and Baker, K. (2013), *Working with Risk*, Cambridge: Polity Press.
Kemshall, H. and Wood, J., with Westwood, S., Stout, B., Wilkinson, B., Kelly, G. and Mackenzie, G. (2010), *Evaluation of the Child Sex Offender Review Public Disclosure Pilots*, London: Home Office.
Kenny, D.T. and Frize, M. (2010), 'Intellectual disability, aboriginal status and risk of re-offending in young offenders on community orders', *Indigenous Law Bulletin*, 7(18): 14.
Kleinig, J. (2008), *Ethics and Criminal Justice: An Introduction*, Cambridge: Cambridge University Press.
Knight, C. (2014), *Emotional Literacy in Criminal Justice*, Basingstoke: Palgrave Macmillan.
Knight, C., Phillips, J. and Chapman, T. (2016), 'Bringing the feelings back: Returning emotions to criminal justice practice', *British Journal of Community Justice*, 14(1): 45–58.
Knight, C. and Stout, B. (2009), 'Probation and offender management training: An argument for an integrated approach', *Probation Journal*, 56(3): 269–83.
Kornhauser, R. and Laster, K. (2014), 'Punitiveness in Australia: Electronic monitoring vs the prison', *Crime Law and Social Change*, 62: 445–74.
KPMG (2018), '*Maranguka Justice Reinvestment Project*', available online at https://www.justreinvest.org.au/.
Kurki, L. (2003), 'Evaluating restorative justice practices', in A. Von Hirsch, J. Roberts and A. Bottoms (eds.), *Restorative Justice and Criminal Justice*, Oxford: Hart.
Lageson, S. (2020), *Digital Punishment*, Oxford: Oxford University Press.
Laing, L., Irwin, J. and Toivenan, C. (2012), 'Across the divide: Using research to enhance collaboration between mental health and domestic violence services', *Australian Social Work*, 65(1): 120–35.
Lancaster, E. (2008), '"Values talk" in the criminal justice system', in S. Green, E. Lancaster and S. Feasey (eds.), *Addressing Offending Behaviour*, Cullompton: Willan.
Lansdell, G., Anderson, J. and King, M. (2011), '"Terror among the gum trees"—is our criminal legal framework adequate to curb the peril of bushfire arson in Australia?', *Psychiatry, Psychology and Law*, 18(3): 357–77.
Larsen, J. (2014), *Restorative Justice in the Australian Criminal Justice System*, Canberra: Australian Institute of Criminology.
Laub, J. and Sampson, R. (2003), *Shared Beginnings, Divergent Lives: Delinquent Boys to Age 70*, Cambridge, MA: Harvard University Press.

Law Council of Australia (2010a), *Policy Statement on Registration and Reporting Obligations for Child Sex Offenders*, viewed 1 July 2022, www.lawcouncil.asn.au/lawcouncil/images/LCA-PDF/a-z-docs/LCAPolicyPrinciplesonRegistrationandReportingObligationsofChildSexOffenders100610Final.pdf.

——— (2010b), *Registration and Reporting Obligations for Child Sex Offenders: Law Council Policy Principles v Current State and Territory Practice*, viewed 1 July 2022, www.lawcouncil.asn.au/lawcouncil/images/LCA-PDF/a-z-docs/LCAPolicyPrinciplesvStateandTerritoryPractice.pdf.

Law Council of Australia (2019), 'Cautious approach for sex offender register required, says Law Council', available online https://www.lawcouncil.asn.au/media/media-releases/cautious-approach-for-sex-offender-register-required-says-law-council.

Leibling, A., Elliott, C. and Arnold, A. (2001), 'Transforming the prison: Romantic optimism or appreciative realism?', *Criminology and Criminal Justice*, 1(2): 161–80.

Leibling, A., Maruna, S. and McAra, L. (2017), *The Oxford Handbook of Criminology*, Oxford: Oxford University Press.

Lennings, C.J., Kenny, D.T., Howard, J., Arcuri, A. and Mackacy, L. (2007), 'The relationship between substance abuse and delinquency in female adolescents in Australia', *Australian Academic*, 14(1): 100–110.

Lerman, A. and Sadin, M. (2022), 'Transformational learning and identity shift: Evidence from a campus behind bars', *Punishment & Society*, 1–24.

Lipton, D., Martinson, R. and Wilks, J. (1975), *The Effectiveness of Correctional Treatment: A Survey of Treatment Valuation Studies*, New York: Praeger.

Lofland, J. (1969), *Deviance and Identity*, Englewood Cliffs, NJ: Prentice Hall.

Lombroso, C. (1911), *Crime: Its Causes and Remedies*, Boston: Little, Brown.

Luke, G. and Lind, B. (2002), 'Reducing juvenile crime: Conferencing vs. court', *Crime and Justice Bulletin*, 69, viewed 1 July 2022, www.aic.gov.au/media_library/publications/crm/crm020.pdf.

Lutze, F., Johnson, W., Clear, T., Latessa, E. and Slate, R. (2012), 'The future of community justice is now: Stop dreaming and take action', *Journal of Contemporary Criminal Justice*, 28(1): 42–59.

Lynch, S. and Bartels, L. (2017), 'Transgender prisoners in Australia: An examination of the issues, law and policy', *Flinders Law Journal*, 19: 185–231.

Lyng, S. (1990), 'Edgework: A social psychological analysis of voluntary risk taking', *American Journal of Sociology*, 95(4): 851–86.

——— (2005), 'Edgework and the risk-taking experience', in S. Lyng (ed.), *Edgework: The Sociology of Risk*, New York: Routledge.

——— (2014), 'Action and edgework: Risk taking and reflexivity in late modernity', *European Journal of Social Theory*, 17: 443–60.

Macdonald, R., Webster, C., Shildrick, T. and Simpson, M. (2011), 'Paths of exclusion, inclusion and desistance: Understanding marginalised young people's criminal careers', in S. Farrall, M. Hough, S. Maruna and R. Sparks (eds.), *Escape Routes: Contemporary Perspectives on Life after Punishment*, Abingdon: Routledge.

Macgregor, S. (2008), 'Sex offender treatment programs: Effectiveness of prison and community based programs in Australia and New Zealand', *Indigenous Justice Clearinghouse*, viewed 1 July 2022, http://indigenousjustice.gov.au/briefs/brief003.pdf.

MacIntyre, A. (2007 [1981]). *After Virtue* (3rd ed.), Notre Dame, IN: University of Notre Dame Press.

Mackenzie, D.L. (2000), 'Evidence-based corrections: Identifying what works', *Crime and Delinquency*, 46(4): 457–71.

Maden, T. (2011), 'Mental health and risk', in H. Kemshall and B. Wilkinson (eds.), *Good Practice in Assessing Risk*, London: Jessica Kingsley.

Madsen, L.B. and Addison, S.A. (2013), 'A review of the evidence for the use of polygraphy in the supervision and management of community based sexual offenders: An Australian context', *Sexual Abuse in Australia and New Zealand*, 5(1): 45–51.

Magistrates Court of Tasmania (2022), Official website, viewed 1 July 2022, https://www.magistratescourt.tas.gov.au/home.

Magistrates Court of Victoria (2012), 'Family violence court programs', viewed 1 July 2022, www.magistratescourt.vic.gov.au/jurisdictions/intervention-orders/family-violence-court-programs.

Maguire, M., Morgan, R. and Reiner, R. (eds.) (2007), *The Oxford Handbook of Criminology* (4th ed.), Oxford: Oxford University Press.

Mahoney, D. (2005), *Inquiry into the Management of Offenders in Custody and in the Community*, Perth: Government of Western Australia.

Maiden, S. (2015), 'Abbott government wants GPS tracking for repeat offenders who bash their partners on COAG agenda', *Daily Telegraph*, 17 May.

Mair, G. and Burke, L. (2012), *Redemption, Rehabilitation and Risk Management*, Abingdon: Routledge.

Mair, G. and Nellis, M. (2013), '"Parallel tracks": Probation and electronic monitoring in England, Wales and Scotland', in M. Nellis, K. Beyens and D. Kaminski (eds.), *Electronically Monitored Punishment: International and Critical Perspectives*, Abingdon: Routledge.

Marchetti, E. (2009), 'Indigenous sentencing courts', viewed 1 July 2022, www.indigenousjustice.gov.au/briefs/brief005.pdf.

—— (2010), 'Indigenous sentencing courts and partner violence: Perspectives of court practitioners and elders on gender power imbalances during the sentencing hearing', *The Australian and New Zealand Journal of Criminology*, 43(2): 263–81.

—— (2011), 'How the mainstream criminal court system is still getting it wrong', *Indigenous Law Bulletin*, 7(26): 27–30.

—— (2015), 'An Australian indigenous-focussed justice response to intimate partner violence: Offenders' perceptions of the sentencing process', *British Journal of Criminology*, 55: 86–196.

Marchetti, E. and Daly, K. (2007), 'Indigenous sentencing courts: Towards a theoretical and jurisdictional model', *Sydney Law Review*, 29(3): 415–43.

Martinovic, M. (2010), *The Complexity of Punitiveness of Electronically Monitored Sanctions: The Western World Analysis*, Saarbrücken, Germany: Lambert Academic Publishing.

—— (2014), 'Abolishing electronic monitoring in Australia', *Criminal Justice Matters*, 95(1): 16–7.

Martinson, R. (1974), 'What works? Questions and answers about prison reform', *The Public Interest*, 22–54, viewed 1 July 2022, www.pbpp.pa.gov/research_statistics/Documents/Martinson-What%20Works%201974.pdf.

—— (1979), 'New findings, new views: A note of caution regarding sentence reform', *Hostra Law Review*, 7: 242–58.

Maruna, S. (2001), *Making Good: How Ex-Convicts Reform and Re-Build Their Lives*, Washington, DC: American Psychological Society.

—— (2002), 'Afterword: In the shadows of community justice', in D. Karp and T. Clear (eds.), *What Is Community Justice?*, Thousand Oaks, CA: Sage.

—— (2006), 'Desistance from crime', in E. McLaughlin and J. Muncie (eds.), *The Sage Dictionary of Crime* (2nd ed.), London: Sage.

Maruna, S. and Lebel, T. (2010), 'The desistance paradigm in correctional practice: From programs to lives', in F. McNeill, P. Raynor and C. Trotter (eds.), *Offender Supervision: New Directions in Theory, Research and Practice*, Cullompton: Willan.

Maruna, S. and Mann, R. (2019), 'Reconciling 'Desistance' and 'What Works'', HM Inspectorate of Probation: Academic Insights.

Martinovic, M. and Schluter, P. (2012), 'A researcher's experience of wearing a GPS-EM device', *Current Issues in Criminal Justice*, 23(3): 413–32.

Matza, D. (1964), *Delinquency and Drift*, Washington, DC: Transaction.

Mawby, R. and Walklate, S. (1994), *Critical Victimology*, Thousand Oaks, CA: Sage.

Mawby, R.C. and Worrall, A. (2013), *Doing Probation Work: Identity in a Criminal Justice Occupation*, London: Routledge.

Maxwell, G. (2008), 'Crossing cultural boundaries: Implementing restorative justice in international and indigenous contexts', in H.V. Miller (ed.), *Restorative Justice: From Theory to Practice. Vol. 11: Sociology of Crime, Law and Deviance*, Bingley: JAI Press.

Maxwell, G. and Hayes, H. (2007), 'Regional reviews: Section f: Pacific', in G. Johnstone and D. Van Ness (eds.), *Handbook of Restorative Justice*, Cullompton: Willan.

Maxwell, G., Morris, A. and Hayes, H. (2008), 'Conferencing and restorative justice', in D. Sullivan and L. Tifft (eds.), *Handbook of Restorative Justice*, Abingdon: Routledge.

McAra, L. and McVie, S. (2011), 'Youth justice', in S. Farrall, M. Hough, S. Maruna and R. Sparks (eds.), *Escape Routes: Contemporary Perspectives on Life after Punishment*, Abingdon: Routledge.

McCausland, R., Baldry, E. and Johnson, S.E. (2013), *People with Mental Health Disorders and Cognitive Impairment in the Criminal Justice System: Cost–benefit Analysis of Early Support and Diversion*, Sydney: Human Rights Commission.

McCold, P. (2004), 'What is the role of community in restorative justice theory and practice?', in H. Zehr and B. Toews (eds.), *Critical Issues in Restorative Justice*, Cullompton: Willan.

McCold, P. and Wachtel, T. (2002), 'Restorative justice theory validation', in E. Weitekamp and H.-J. Kerner, (eds.), *Restorative Justice: Theoretical Foundations*, Cullompton: Willan.

────── (2003), 'Community is not a place: A new look at community justice initiatives', in G. Johnstone (ed.), *A Restorative Justice Reader*, Cullompton: Willan.

McCulloch, T. (2013), 'Reanalysing the compliance dynamic: Toward a co-productive strategy and practice', in P. Ugwudike and P. Raynor (eds.), *What Works in Offender Compliance*, London: Palgrave Macmillan.

McCulloch, T. and McNeill, F. (2009), 'Desistance-focused approaches', in S. Green, E. Lancaster and S. Feasey (eds.), *Addressing Offending Behaviour*, Cullompton: Willan.

McEvoy, K. and Eriksson, A. (2008), 'Who owns justice? Community, state and the Northern Ireland tradition', in J. Shapland (ed.), *Justice, Community and Civil Society*, Cullompton: Willan.

McGaughey, F., Tulich, T. and Blagg, H. (2017), 'UN decision on MarlonNoble case: Imprisonment of an aboriginal man with intellectual disability found unfit to stand trial in Western Australia', *Alternative Law Journal*, 42(1): 67–70.

McGlade, H. and Hovane, V. (2007), 'The *Mangolamara case*: Improving Aboriginal community safety and healing', *Indigenous Law Bulletin*, 18, viewed 1 July 2022, www.austlii.edu.au.ezproxy.uws.edu.au/au/journals/ILB/2007/29.html.

McGovern, A. (2010), 'Tweeting the news: Criminal justice agencies and their use of social networking sites', paper presented at the Australian and New Zealand Critical Criminology Conference 2010, viewed 1 July 2022, http://ses.library.usyd.edu.au//bitstream/2123/7378/1/McGovern_ANZCCC2010.pdf.

McGrath, A. (2010), 'The subjective impact of contact with the criminal justice system: The role of gender and stigmatization', *Crime and Delinquency*, 60(6): 884–908.

McGuire, M. (2007), 'Cognitive-behavioural', in R. Canton and D. Hancock (eds.), *Dictionary of Probation and Offender Management*, Cullompton: Willan.

McLaughlin, E. and Newburn, T. (eds.) (2010), *Sage Handbook of Criminological Theory*, London: Sage.

McNeill, F. (2019), 'Mass supervision, misrecognition and the 'Malopticon'', *Punishment & Society*, 21(2): 207–30.

McNeill, F. (2006), 'A desistance paradigm for offender management', *Criminology and Criminal Justice*, 6: 37–60.

McNeill, F., Batchelor, S., Burnett, R. and Knox, J. (2005), *21st Century Social Work: Reducing Re-Offending: Key Practice Skills*, Edinburgh: Social Work Inspection Agency.

Meade, B. and Steiner, B. (2010), 'The total effects of boot camps that house juveniles: A systematic review of the evidence', *Journal of Criminal Justice*, 38(5): 841–53.

Megele, C. (2015), *Psychosocial and Relationship-Based Practice*, Northwich: Critical Publishing.

Mendes, P., Snow, P.C. and Baidawi, S. (2012), *Young People Transitioning from Out-of-Home Care in Victoria: Strengthening Support Services for Dual Clients of Child Protection and Youth Justice*, Melbourne: Monash University.

Merton, R. (1938), 'Science, technology and society in seventeenth century England', *Osiris*, 4(2): 360–632.

Mickleberg, P. (2010), 'Leafy suburbs home of Crime', Herald Sun, 15 February, viewed 25 August 2016, www.heraldsun.com.au.

Milavanovic, D. (2005), 'Edgework: A subjective and structural model of negotiating boundaries', in S. Lyng (ed.), *Edgework: The Sociology of Risk*, New York: Routledge.

Miles, H. and Raynor, P. (2014), *Welfare and Society: Reintegrative Justice in Practice: The Informal Management of Crime in an Island Community*, Farnham: Ashgate.

Miller, J. (1989), 'Does nothing work?', in P. Priestley and M. Vanstone (eds.), *Offenders or Citizens? Readings in Rehabilitation*, Cullompton: Willan.

Miller, W. and Rollnick, S. (2002), *Motivational Interviewing: Preparing People for Change*, New York: Guilford Press.

Miller, W. and Rollnick, S. (2004), 'Talking oneself into change: Motivational interviewing, stages of change, and therapeutic process', *Journal of Cognitive Psychotherapy: An International Quarterly*, 18(4): 299–308.

Mills, M. and Pini, B. (2014), 'Punishing kids: The rise of the "boot camp"', *International Journal of Inclusive Education*, 19(3): 270–84.

Mitchell, M. (2014), 'Juvenile justice? Ensuring the opportunity to thrive', speech delivered to 5th Annual National Juvenile Justice Summit, Melbourne, 25 March.

Moffit, T.E. (1994), 'Natural histories of delinquency', in E.G.M. Weitekamp and H.-J. Kerner (eds.), *Cross-National Longitudinal Research on Human Development and Criminal Behaviour*, Dordrecht: Kluwer.

Moore, D. and O'Connell, T. (2003), 'Family conferencing in wagga wagga: A communitarian model of justice', in G. Johnstone (ed.), *A Restorative Justice Reader*, Cullompton: Willan.

Moore, R., Gray, E., Roberts, C., Taylor, E. and Merrington, S. (2006), *Managing Persistent and Serious Offenders in the Community*, Cullompton: Willan.

Moore, T., McArthur, M. and Saunders, V. (2013), 'Young people talk about transitioning from youth detention to the community: Making good', *Australian Social Work*, 66(3): 328–43.

Morseu-Dopp, N. (2013), 'Indigenous yarning modalities: An insider's perspective on respectful engagement with torres strait islander clients', in B. Bennett, S. Green, S. Gilbert and D. Bessarab (eds.), *Our Voices: Aboriginal and Torres Strait Islander Social Work*, Melbourne: Palgrave Macmillan.

Moses, A. (2010), 'Facebook Six prison officers beat bid to sack them', *Sydney Morning Herald*, 25 March, viewed 1 July 2022, www.smh.com.au/technology/technology-news/facebook-six-prison-officers-beat-bid-to-sack-them-20100325-qy1k.html.

Moskos, P. (2011), *In Defense of Flogging*, New York: Basic Books.

Mueller-Smith, M. and Schnepel, K. (2021), 'Diversion in the criminal justice system', *Review of Economic Studies*, 88: 883–936.

Mukherjee, S. (1999), *Ethnicity and Crime*, Canberra: Australian Institute of Criminology.

Muncie, J. (1998), 'Deconstructing criminology', *Criminal Justice Matters*, 34(1): 4–5.

——— (2006), 'Responsibilisation', in E. McLaughlin and J. Muncie (eds.), *Sage Dictionary of Criminology*, London: Sage.

——— (2009), *Youth and Crime* (3rd ed.), London: Sage.

Nash, M. (2008), 'Working with dangerous offenders', in S. Green, E. Lancaster and S. Feasey (eds.), *Addressing Offending Behaviour: Context, Practice and Values*, Cullompton: Willan.

National Audit Office (NAO) (2022), *Improving Outcomes for Women in the Criminal Justice System*, London: National Audit Office.

National Inquiry into the Separation of Aboriginal and Torres Strait Islander Children and Their Families (NISATSIC) (1997), *Bringing Them Home*, Canberra: Commonwealth of Australia.

National Mental Health Commission (NMHC) (2013), *Contributing Lives, Thriving Communities: Review of Mental Health Programmes and Services*, Canberra: NMHC.

Neighbourhood Justice Centre (2022), Official website, viewed 1 July 2022, www.neighbourhoodjustice.vic.gov.au.

Nellis, M. (2001), 'The new probation training in England and Wales: Realising the potential', *Social Work Education*, 20(4): 415–32.

——— (2003), 'Probation training and the community justice curriculum', *British Journal of Social Work*, 33: 943–59.

——— (2005), 'Dim prospects: Humanistic values and the fate of community justice', in J. Winstone and F. Pakes (eds.), *Community Justice: Issues for Probation and Criminal Justice*, Cullompton: Willan.

——— (2007), 'Humanising justice: The English probation service up to 1972', in L. Gelsthorpe and R. Morgan (eds.), *Handbook of Probation*, Cullompton: Willan.

——— (2009a), 'Surveillance and confinement: Explaining and understanding the experience of electronically monitored curfews', *European Journal of Probation*, 1(1): 41–65.

——— (2009b), '24/7/365: Mobility, locatability and the satellite tracking of offenders', in K. Franko Aas, H. Oppen Gundhas and H. Mork Lomell (eds.), *Technologies of Insecurity: The Surveillance of Everyday Life*, Abingdon: Routledge.

——— (2010), 'Electronic monitoring: Towards integration into offender management', in F. McNeill, P. Raynor and C. Trotter (eds.), *Offender Supervision: New Directions in Theory, Research and Practice*, Cullompton: Willan.

——— (2013a), 'Surveillance, stigma and spatial constraint: The ethical challenges of electronic monitoring', in M. Nellis, K. Beyens and D. Kaminski (eds.), *Electronically Monitored Punishment: International and Critical Perspectives*, Abingdon: Routledge.

——— (2013b), 'Surveillance-based compliance using electronic monitoring', in P. Ugwudike and P. Raynor (eds.), *What Works in Offender Compliance*, London: Palgrave Macmillan.

Nellis, M., Beyens, K. and Kaminski, D. (2013), 'Introduction', in M. Nellis, K. Beyens and D. Kaminski (eds.), *Electronically Monitored Punishment: International and Critical Perspectives*, Abingdon: Routledge.

Nellis, M. and Gelsthorpe, L. (2003), 'Human rights and the probation values debate', in W.H. Chui and M. Nellis (eds.), *Moving Probation Forward: Evidence, Arguments and Practice*, Harlow: Pearson.

New South Wales Department of Justice (2014), 'Smarter and more secure: New offender electronic monitoring equipment introduced', media release from Brad Hazzard MP, Attorney General, Minister for Justice, viewed 1 July 2022, https://www.justice.nsw.gov.au/Documents/Media%20Releases/2014/MR_14_smarter_and_more_secure_new_offender_electronic_monitoring.pdf.

——— (2015), *ATSI Employment Strategy 2015–2017*, viewed 1 July 2022, www.justice.nsw.gov.au/Documents/Careers/atsi-employment-strategy-2015-2017.pdf.

New South Wales Parole Authority (2013), 'Parole determination: Killick, John Reginald', viewed 1 July 2022, www.paroleauthority.nsw.gov.au/Documents/PAROLE-DETERMINATION-KILLICK-JOHN-REGINALD-19-JULY-2013.pdf.

New South Wales Police Force (2012), 'Project Eyewatch', viewed 1 July 2022, www.police.nsw.gov.au/about_us/structure/operations_command/project_Eyewatch.

Newburn, T. (2012), *Criminology* (2nd ed.), Cullompton: Willan.

News.com.au (2007), 'Sofia's killer jailed for life over toilet murder', viewed 1 July 2022, www.news.com.au/national/sofias-killer-jailed-for-life-over-toilet-murder-story-e6frfkp9-1111114822414.

No Bars (2022), Official website, viewed 1 July 2022, www.nobars.org.au.

No to Violence (2015), Official website, viewed 19 October 2022, http://ntv.org.au.

No to Violence (2022), Official website, viewed 1 July 2022, http://ntv.org.au.

North Australian Aboriginal Justice Agency (2022), Official website, viewed 1 July 2022, www.naaja.org.au.

Northern Territory Department of Correctional Services (NT DCS) (2022), Official website, viewed 1 July 2022, www.correctionalservices.nt.gov.au.

Northern Territory Government (2019), *'Everyone Together: Aboriginal Affairs Strategy 2019–2029'*, Northern Territory Government.

Northern Territory Royal Commission (NTRC) (2017), *'Royal Commission into the Protection and Detention of Children in the Northern Territory'* available online at https://www.royalcommission.gov.au/child-detention/final-report.

Nussbaum, M. (2000), *Women and Human Development*, Cambridge: Cambridge University Press.

Nyoongar Patrol (2013), Official website, viewed 19 October 2022, www.nyoongaroutreach.com.au.

O'Donahue, E. (2013), 'Coalition Government introduces GPS monitoring of offenders', media release from Edward O'Donahue MLC, viewed 25 August 2016, edwardodonahue.com.au.

O'Loan, J. (2011), 'Switch to GPS tracking of sex offenders would cost less than $250,000', *Courier-Mail*, 3 June, viewed 1 July 2022, www.couriermail.com.au/news/queensland/show-support-for-safety-of-our-kids/story-e6freoof-1226068233293.

O'Mahony, D., Doak, J. and Clamp, K. (2012), 'The politics of youth justice reform in post-conflict societies: Mainstreaming restorative justice in Northern Ireland and South Africa', *Northern Ireland Legal Quarterly*, 63(2): 269–90.

O'Malley, P. (1992), 'Risk, power and crime prevention', *Economy and Society*, 21(3): 252–75.

Ooi, E., Poynton, S. and Halloran, N. (2020), 'Social impact investment and recidivism: A field experiment with high-risk parolees,' Crime and Justice Bulletin, NSW Bureau.

O'Toole, S. (2006), *The History of Australian Corrections*, Sydney: UNSW Press.

Oberfield, Z. (2014), *Becoming Bureaucrats: Socialization at the Front Lines of Government Services*, Philadelphia, PA: University of Pennsylvania Press.

Office of the Inspector of Custodial Services (OICS) (2013), *Directed Review into an Incident at Banksia Hill Detention Centre on 20 January 2013*, Perth: OICS.

Office of the Northern Territory Children's Commissioner (ONTCC) (2015), *Own Initiative Investigation Report: Services Provided by the Department of Correctional Services at the Don Dale Youth Detention Centre*, Darwin: ONTCC.

Oldfield, M. (2007), 'Risk society', in R. Canton and D. Hancock (eds.), *Dictionary of Probation and Offender Management*, Cullompton: Willan.

Palk, G., Freeman, J. and Davey, J. (2008), 'Australian forensic psychologists' perspectives on the utility of actuarial versus clinical assessment for predicting recidivism among sex offenders', in *Proceedings of the 18th Conference of the European Association of Psychology and Law*, Maastricht, Netherlands, viewed 1 July 2022, http://eprints.qut.edu.au/15102/1/15102.pdf.

Parekh, B. (2000), *Report of the Commission on the Future of Multi-Ethnic Britain*, London: Runnymede Trust, www.hrmguide.co.uk/diversity/parekh_report.htm.

Parragirls (2016), 'Parramatta female factory precinct', viewed 19 October 2022, www.parragirls.org.au.

Parragirls (2022), 'Parramatta female factory precinct', viewed 1 July 2022, www.parragirls.org.au.

Paternoster, R. and Bushway, S. (2009), 'Desistance and the feared self: Toward an identity theory of criminal desistance', *Journal of Criminal Law and Criminology*, 999(4): 1103–56.

Paterson, C. (2013), 'Commercial crime control and the development of electronically monitored punishment', in M. Nellis, K. Beyens and D. Kaminski (eds.), *Electronically Monitored Punishment: International and Critical Perspectives*, Abingdon: Routledge.

Patterson, G. (2012), *Social Work Practice in the Criminal Justice System*, Taylor & Francis Group.

Peckover, S., Broadhurst, K., White, S., Wastell, D., Hall, C. and Pithouse, A. (2011), 'The fallacy of formalisation: Practice makes process in the assessment of risks to children', in H. Kemshall and B. Wilkinson (eds.), *Good Practice in Assessing Risk*, London: Jessica Kingsley.

Petersen, S., Stephens, J., Dickey, R. and Lewis, W. (1996), 'Transsexuals within the prison system: An international survey of correctional services policies', *Behavioural Sciences and the Law*, 14: 219–29.

Phillips, D. (2007), 'Risk principle', in R. Canton and D. Hancock (eds.), *Dictionary of Probation and Offender Management*, Cullompton: Willan.

―――― (2008), 'Beyond the risk agenda', in S. Green, E. Lancaster and S. Feasey (eds.), *Addressing Offending Behaviour: Context, Practice and Values*, Cullompton: Willan.

Phillips, J., Fowler, A. and Westaby, C. (2018), 'Self-disclosure in criminal justice: What form does it take and what does it achieve?', *International Journal of Offender Therapy and Comparative Criminology*, 62(12): 3890–909.

Phillips, J., Westaby, C., Ainslie, S. and Fowler, A. (2021), '"I don't like this job in my front room": Practising probation in the COVID-19 pandemic', *Probation Journal*, 68(4): 1–18.

Phoenix, J. and Kelly, L. (2013), '"You have to do it for yourself": Responsibilisation in youth justice and young people's situated knowledge of youth justice practice', *British Journal of Criminology*, 53: 419–37.

References

Poynton, S. (2013), *Rates of Recidivism Among Offenders Referred to Forum Sentencing*, Sydney: NSW Bureau of Crime Statistics and Research.

Poynton, S. and Menendez, P. (2015), 'The impact of the NSW Intensive Supervision Program on recidivism', *Crime and Justice Bulletin*, Sydney: NSW Bureau of Crime Statistics and Research.

Pratt, J. and Eriksson, A. (2013), *Contrasts in Punishment: An Explanation of Anglophone Excess and Nordic Exceptionalism*, Oxford: Routledge.

Price, S., Prenzler, T., McKillop, N. and Rayment-McHugh, S. (2022), 'The evolution of youth justice conferencing in Queensland, 1990–2021', *Current Issues in Criminal Justice*, 34(1): 77–94.

Probation and Community Corrections Officers Association (PACCOA) (2022), Official website, viewed 1 July 2022, www.paccoa.com.au/home.

Prochaska, J. and DiClemente, C. (1983), 'Stages and processes of self-change of smoking: Toward an integrative model of change', *Journal of Consulting and Clinical Psychology*, 51: 390–5.

Putt, J. (ed.) (2010), *Community Policing in Australia*, Canberra: AIC, viewed 1 July 2022, www.aic.gov.au/media_library/publications/rpp/111/rpp111.pdf.

Queensland Corrective Services (2007), 'The management of convicted sex offenders in Queensland', viewed 1 July 2022, www.correctiveservices.qld.gov.au/About_Us/The_Department/Probation_and_Parole/Managing_sex_offenders_in_the_community/MgtSexOffenders.pdf.

——— (2015a), 'Electronic monitoring', viewed 1 July 2022, www.correctiveservices.qld.gov.au/About_Us/The_Department/Probation_and_Parole/Electronic_Monitoring/index.shtml.

——— (2022), 'Our vision', viewed 1 July 2022, www.correctiveservices.qld.gov.au.

Queensland Government (2013), *Evidence Informing the Youth Boot Camp Program Models*, Brisbane: Department of Justice and Attorney-General.

Queensland Police (2022), 'Multicultural Awareness Online Learning Product (MOLP)', viewed 1 July 2022, www.police.qld.gov.au/programs/community/CulturalAdvisory/mcltrlAwrnsOnlnLrnngProut.htm.

Ragonese, E., Rees, A., Ives, J. and Dray, T. (2014), *The Routledge Guide to Working in Criminal Justice: Employability Skills and Careers in the Criminal Justice Sector*, London: Routledge.

Ravulo, J. (2015), 'Pacific youth offending within an Australian context', *Youth Justice*, 16(1): 34–48.

Rawls, J. (1971). *A Theory of Justice*, Cambridge, MA: Belknap Press.

Raynor, P. (2019), *'Supervision Skills for Probation Practitioners'*, Academic Insights 2019/05, Manchester: Her Majesty's Inspectorate of Probation.

Raynor, P. (2018), 'From 'nothing works' to 'post-truth': The rise and fall of evidence in British probation', *European Journal of Probation*, 10(1): 59–75.

Raynor, P. (2007), 'Community penalties: Probation, "what works", and offender management', in M. Maguire, R. Morgan and R. Reiner (eds.), *The Oxford Handbook of Criminology* (4th ed.), Oxford: Oxford University Press.

——— (2013), 'Compliance through discussion: The Jersey experience', in P. Ugwudike and P. Raynor (eds.), *What Works in Offender Compliance*, London: Palgrave Macmillan.

——— (2014), 'Consent to probation in England and Wales: How it was abolished and why it matters', *European Journal of Probation*, 6(3): 296–307.

Raynor, P. and Vanstone, M. (2015), 'Moving away from social work and half way back again: New research on skills in probation', *British Journal of Social Work*. DOI: 10.1093/bjsw/bcv008.

Raynor, P., Ugwudike, P. and Vanstone, M. (2010), 'Skills and strategies in probation supervision: The Jersey Study', in F. McNeill, P. Raynor and C. Trotter (eds.), *Offender Supervision: New Directions in Theory, Research and Practice*, Cullompton: Willan.

—— (2014), 'The impact of skills in probation work: A reconviction study', *Criminology and Criminal Justice*, 14(2): 235–49.

Redman, D.T. (2011), 'Government agencies — Memorandum of Understanding on dangerous offenders', statement by Minister for Corrective Services Mr D.T. Redman (Blackwood–Stirling), viewed 1 July 2022, www.parliament.wa.gov.au/Hansard%5Chansard.nsf/0/02397a0311cbfc404825795700415fda/$FILE/A38%20S1%2020111124%20p9828f-9829a.pdf.

Reinfrank, A. (2015), 'Canberra jail inmates' cell selfie on Facebook draws fire from ACT Liberals', *ABC News*, 11 May, viewed 1 July 2022, www.abc.net.au/news/2015-05-11/canberra-jail-inmates-cell-selfie-on-facebook-draws-fire/6459976.

Renzema, M. (2013), 'Evaluative research on electronic monitoring', in M. Nellis, K. Beyens and D. Kaminski (eds.), *Electronically Monitored Punishment: International and Critical Perspectives*, Abingdon: Routledge.

Rex, S. and Hosking, N. (2013), 'A collaborative approach to developing probation practice: Skills for effective engagement, development and supervision', *Probation Journal*, 60(3): 332–8.

Richards, K. (2010), *Police-Referred Restorative Justice for Juveniles in Australia*, Canberra: Australian Institute of Criminology.

—— (2011), *Trends in Juvenile Detention in Australia*, Canberra: Australian Institute of Criminology.

—— (2014a), 'Locating the community in restorative justice for young people in Australia', *British Journal of Community Justice*, 14(2): 1–16.

—— (2014b), 'Blurred lines: Reconsidering the concept of "diversion" in youth justice systems in Australia', *Youth Justice*, 14(2): 122–39.

Richards, K., Death, J. and McCartan, K. (2020), 'Toward Redemption: Aboriginal and/or torres strait islander men's narratives of desistance from sexual offending', *Victims & Offenders*, 15(6): 810–33.

Riches, V., Permenter, T., Wiese, M. and Stancliffe, R.J. (2006), 'Intellectual disability and mental illness in the NSW criminal justice system', *International Journal of Law Psychiatry*, September–October, 29(5): 386–96.

Ringland, C., Weatherburn, D. and Poynton, S. (2015), *Can Child Protection Data Improve the Prediction of Re-Offending in Young Persons?*, Sydney: NSW Bureau of Crime Statistics and Research.

Robinson, A. (2011), 'Risk and intimate partner violence', in H. Kemshall and B. Wilkinson (eds.), *Good Practice in Assessing Risk*, London: Jessica Kingsley.

Robinson, G. (2007), 'Rehabilitation', in R. Canton and D. Hancock (eds.), *Dictionary of Probation and Offender Management*, Cullompton: Willan.

Robinson, G. (2013), 'What counts? Community sanctions and the construction of compliance', in P. Ugwudike and P. Raynor (eds.), *What Works in Offender Compliance*, London: Palgrave Macmillan.

Robinson, G. (2018b), 'Transforming probation services in the Magistrates' courts', *Probation Journal*, 65(3): 316–34.

Robinson, G. (2019), 'Delivering McJustice? The probation factory at the Magistrates' court', *Criminology and Criminal Justice*, 19(5): 605–21.

Robinson, G., Burke, L. and Millings, M. (2016), 'Criminal justice identities in transition: The case of devolved probation services in England and Wales', *British Journal of Criminology*, 56: 161–78.

Robinson, G. and Crow, I. (2009), *Offender Rehabilitation: Theory, Research and Practice*, London: Sage.

Robinson, G. and McNeill, F. (2010), 'The dynamics of compliance with offender supervision', in F. McNeill, P. Raynor and C. Trotter (eds.), *Offender Supervision: New Directions in Theory, Research and Practice*, Cullompton: Willan.

Robinson, G., Priede, C., Farrall, S., Shapland, J. and McNeill, F. (2013), 'Doing "strengths-based" research: Appreciative inquiry in a probation setting', *Criminology and Criminal Justice*, 13(1): 3–20.

——— (2014), 'Understanding "quality" in probation practice: Frontline perspectives in England and Wales', *Criminology and Criminal Justice*, 14(2): 123–42.

Roche, D. (2003), *Accountability in Restorative Justice*, Oxford: Oxford University Press.

Rock, P. (2007), 'Sociological theories of crime', in M. Maguire, R. Morgan and R. Reiner (eds.), *The Oxford Handbook of Criminology* (4th ed.), Oxford: Oxford University Press.

Rocque, M. (2014), 'The lost concept: The (re)emerging link between maturation and desistance from crime', *Criminology and Criminal Justice*, 15(3): 1–21.

Ross, R. and Fabiano, E. (1985), *Time to Think: A Cognitive Model of Delinquency Prevention and Offender Rehabilitation*, Johnson City, TN: Institute of Social Sciences and Arts.

Rossner, M. (2014), *Just Emotions: Rituals of Restorative Justice*, Oxford: Oxford University Press.

Rossner, M., Tait, D. and McCurdy, M. (2021). 'Justice reimagined: Challenges and opportunities with implementing virtual courts', *Current Issues in Criminal Justice*. https://doi.org/10.1080/10345329.2020.1859968.

Rotman, E. (1986), 'Do criminal offenders have a constitutional right to rehabilitation?', *Journal of Criminal Law and Criminology*, 77(4): 1023–68.

Rowe, S., Baldry, E. and Earles, W. (2015), 'Decolonising social work research: Learning from critical indigenous approaches', *Australian Social Work*, 68(3): 296–308.

Royal Commission into Institutionalised Responses to Child Sexual Abuse (RCIRCSA) (2014), *Child Sexual Abuse at the Parramatta Training School for Girls*, Sydney: RCIRCSA.

Rutter, N. and Barr, U. (2021), 'Being a 'good woman': Stigma, relationships and desistance', *Probation Journal*, 1–20.

Sampson, R. and Laub, J. (1993), *Crime in the Making: Pathways and Turning Points Through Life*, Cambridge, MA: Harvard University Press.

Sandel, M. (2009), *Justice: What's the Right Thing to Do?*, Harmondsworth: Penguin.

Sanders, M., Jones, L. and Briggs, E. (2021), 'A what works centre for probation: Challenges and possibilities', *Probation Journal*, 69(1): 107–14.

Sawrikar, P. and Katz, I. (2008), *Enhancing Family and Relationship Service Accessibility and Delivery to Culturally and Linguistically Diverse Families in Australia*, Canberra: Australian Institute of Family Studies.

Schinkel, M. and Lives Sentenced Participants (2021), 'Persistent short-term imprisonment: Belonging as a lens to understand its shifting meanings over the life course', *Incarceration*, 2(1): 1–20.

Schwartz, M. (2010), 'Building communities, not prisons: Justice reinvestment and indigenous over-imprisonment', *Australian Indigenous Law Review*, 14(1): 2–17.

Schwartz, M., Russell, S., Baldry, E., Brown, D., Cunneen, C. and Stubbs, J. (2020), *Obstacles to Effective Support of People Released from Prison: Wisdom from the Field*, Rethinking Community Sanctions Project, UNSW, 2020.

Sen, A. (1985), *Commodities and Capabilities*, Amsterdam: North Holland.

—— (1999), *Development as a Freedom*, New York: Knopf.
—— (2009), *The Idea of Justice*, Cambridge, MA: Harvard University Press.
—— (1993), 'Capability and well-being', *The Quality of Life*, 30: 270–93.
—— (2005), 'Human rights and capabilities', *Journal of Human Development*, Basingstoke, England, 6(2): 151–66. DOI: 10.1080/14649880500120491.
Senior, P. and Nellis, M. (2013), 'Reflections on 10 years of the *British Journal of Community Justice*', *British Journal of Community Justice*, 10(3): 41–55.
Sentencing Advisory Council Victoria (2014), *Timeline for Sentencing in Victoria*, Melbourne: SACV.
—— (2015), *A Quick Guide to Sentencing*, Melbourne: SACV.
Serin, R., Lloyd, C., Hanby, L. and Shturman, M. (2013), 'What and who might enhance offender compliance: Situating responsibilities', in P. Ugwudike and P. Raynor (eds.), *What Works in Offender Compliance*, London: Palgrave Macmillan.
Sewak, S., Bouchahine, M., Liong, K., Pan, J., Serret, C., Saldarriaga, A., Farrukh, E. (2019), *Youth Restorative Justice: Lessons from Australia: A Report for HAQ Centre for Child Rights*, Macquarie University.
Sewpaul, V. (2016), 'The West and the rest divide: Human rights, culture and social work', *Journal of Human Rights Social Work*, 1: 30–9.
Shapland, J. (2008), 'Contested ideas of community and justice', in J. Shapland (ed.), *Justice, Community and Civil Society*, Cullompton: Willan.
Shapland, J. and Bottoms, A. (2011), 'Reflections on social values, offending and desistance among young adult recidivists', *Punishment and Society*, 13(3): 256–82.
Sharpe, G. (2012), *Offending Girls: Young Women and Youth Justice*, London: Routledge.
Sheldon, W. (1940), *Varieties of Human Physique*, New York: Harper and Row.
Sherman, L. and Neyroud, P. (2012), *Offender Desistance Policing and the Sword of Damocles*, Stevenage: Civitas.
Sindicich, N., Mills, K., Barrett, E., Indig, B., Sunjic, S., Sannibale, S., Rosenfeld, J. and Najavits, L. (2010), 'Offenders as victims: Post-traumatic stress disorder and substance use disorder among male prisoners', *Journal of Forensic Psychiatry and Psychology*, 25(1): 44–60.
Sjoberg, G. (2005), 'Intellectual risk taking, organisations, and academic freedom and tenure', in S. Lyng (ed.), *Edgework: The Sociology of Risk*, New York: Routledge.
Smart, C. (1976), *Women, Crime and Criminology: A Feminist Critique*, London: Routledge and Kegan Paul.
Smith, C.W. (2005), 'Financial edgework: Trading in market currents', in S. Lyng (ed.), *Edgework: The Sociology of Risk*, New York: Routledge.
Smith, N. and Weatherburn, D. (2012a), *Youth Justice Conferences Versus Children's Court: A Comparison of Re-Offending*, Sydney: NSW Bureau of Crime and Research (BOCSAR).
—— (2012b), 'Youth justice conferences versus Children's court: A comparison of re-offending', *Contemporary Issues in Crime and Justice*, 160: 1–23.
Smith, R. (2006), 'Actuarialism and early intervention in contemporary youth justice', in B. Goldson and J. Muncie (eds.), *Youth Crime and Justice*, London: Sage.
—— (2010), 'Children's rights and youth justice: 20 years of no progress', *Child Care in Practice*, 16(1): 3–17.
—— (2011), *Doing Justice to Young People: Youth Crime and Social Justice*, Cullompton: Willan.
Smith, R. and Gibbs, A. (2013), 'Extending the electronic net in Australia and New Zealand: Developments in electronic monitoring down under', in M. Nellis, K. Beyens and D. Kaminski (eds.), *Electronically Monitored Punishment: International and Critical Perspectives*, Abingdon: Routledge.

Solonec, T. (2012), '"Tough on crime": Discrimination by another name—the legacy of mandatory sentencing in Western Australia', *Indigenous Law Bulletin*, 8(18): 7–11.

——— (2015), 'UN condemnation of our Indigenous rights: "Shameful"', NITV, 11 November, viewed 1 July 2022, www.sbs.com.au/nitv/article/2015/11/10/un-condemnation-our-indigenous-rights-shameful.

South Australia Correctional Services (SACS) (2022), 'Mission, vision, and values', viewed 1 July 2022, www.corrections.sa.gov.au/home/mission-vision-values.

Spiranovic, C. (2012), *The Static-99 and Static-99-R Norms Project: Developing Norms Based on Western Australian Sex Offenders*, Perth: University of Western Australia, viewed 1 July 2022, www.law.uwa.edu.au/__data/assets/pdf_file/0007/2253328/FinalReportForRelease141212_Static99Norms_141212.pdf.

Spivakovsky, C. (2013), 'Positioning the offender in a restorative framework: Potential dialogues and forced conversations', in D. Cornwall, J. Blad and M. Wright (eds.), *Civilising Criminal Justice*, Hampshire: Waterside Press.

Standing Council on Law and Justice (2013), *National Framework of Rights and Services for Victims of Crime*, Canberra: Attorney-General's Department.

Staub-Bernasconi, S. (2016), 'Social work and human rights: Linking two traditions of human rights in social work', *Journal Human Rights Social Work*, 1: 40–9.

Stempkowski, M. and Grafl, C. (2021), 'Probationary services in a pandemic: Results from an empirical study in Austria', *Probation Journal*, 68(4): 444–57.

Stewart, J., Hedwards, B., Richards, K., Willis, M. and Higgins, D. (2014), *Indigenous Youth Justice Program Evaluation*, Canberra: Australian Institute of Criminology.

Stout, B. (2016), 'Four Corners: Why did the two previous investigations have no impact on changing this abuse?', *The Conversation*, available online at https://theconversation.com/four-corners-why-did-the-two-previous-investigations-have-no-impact-on-changing-this-abuse-63042.

Stout, B. (2010), *Equality and Diversity in Policing*, London: Learning Matters.

——— (2014), 'Justice across borders: Sentence transfer in Europe and Australia', *Eurovista*, 3(2): 3–12.

Stout, B. and Clamp, K. (2015), 'Applied criminology and criminal justice', in J. Wright (ed.), *International Encyclopaedia of the Social and Behavioural Sciences*, vol. 1, New York: Elsevier.

Stout, B., Dalby, H., Schraner, I. (2017), 'Measuring the impact of juvenile justice interventions: What works, What helps and What matters?', *Youth Justice*, 17(3): 196–212.

Stout, B., Kemshall, H. and Wood, J. (2011), 'Building stakeholder support for a sex offender public disclosure scheme: Learning from the English pilots', *The Howard Journal of Crime and Justice*, 50(4): 406–18.

Stout, B., Schraner, I. and Dalby, H. (2016), *Research into the JJ NSW Intensive Supervision Programme*, Sydney: Juvenile Justice New South Wales.

Strang, H. (2002), *Repair or Revenge: Victims and Restorative Justice*, Oxford: Clarendon Press.

——— (2003), 'Justice for victims of young offenders: The centrality of emotional harm and restoration', in G. Johnstone (ed.), *A Restorative Justice Reader*, Cullompton: Willan.

——— (2004), 'Is restorative justice imposing its agenda on victims?', in H. Zehr and B. Toews (eds.), *Critical Issues in Restorative Justice*, Cullompton: Willan.

Studerus, K.J. (1997), *Home Detention in New South Wales*, Sydney: Department of Corrective Services, viewed 1 July 2022, http://csa.intersearch.com.au/csajspui/bitstream/10627/160/3/39339049895441.pdf.

Sturm, A., Robbers, S., Henskens, R., de Vogel, V. (2021), '"Yes, I can hear you now..." online working with probationers in the Netherlands: New opportunities for the working Alliance', *Probation Journal*, 68(4): 411–25.

Sykes, G.M. and Matza, D. (1957), 'Techniques of neutralization: A theory of delinquency', *American Sociological Review*, 22: 664–70.

Sutherland, E.H. (1933), *Principles of Criminology*, Philadelphia: Lippincott.

Szego, J. (2005), 'Matters of conviction', *The Age*, 18 April, p. 9.

Tasmania Department of Justice (2022), Official website, viewed 1 July 2022, www.justice.tas.gov.au.

Tauri, J. (2014), 'An indigenous commentary on the globalisation of restorative justice', *British Journal of Community Justice*, 14(2): 16–26.

Taylor Webb, P. and Gulson, K.N. (2013), *Policy, Geophilosophy and Education*, Rotterdam: Sense.

Thibodeau, P. and Boroditsky, L. (2011), 'Metaphors we think with: The role of metaphor in reasoning', *PLoS ONE*, 6(2): e16782.

Tidmarsh, M. (2021), 'Professional legitimacy, identity, and practice: Towards a sociology of professionalism in probation', *The British Journal of Criminology*, 62(1): 165–83.

Titterton, M. (2011), 'Positive risk taking with people at risk of harm', in H. Kemshall and B. Wilkinson (eds.), *Good Practice in Assessing Risk*, London: Jessica Kingsley.

Travers, M. (2012), *The Sentencing of Children*, Washington, DC: New Academia.

Trotter, C. (2000), 'Social work education, pro-social orientation and effective probation practice', *Probation Journal*, 47: 256–61.

——— (2006), *Working With Involuntary Clients: A Guide to Practice*, Sydney: Allen & Unwin.

——— (2010), 'Working with families in criminal justice', in F. McNeill, P. Raynor and C. Trotter (eds.), *Offender Supervision: New Directions in Theory, Research and Practice*, Cullompton: Willan.

——— (2013a), *Collaborative Family Work: A Practical Guide to Working with Families in the Human Services*, Sydney: Allen & Unwin.

——— (2013b), 'Effective supervision of young offenders', in P. Ugwudike and P. Raynor (eds.), *What Works in Offender Compliance*, London: Palgrave Macmillan.

——— (2014), 'Effective supervision in youth justice: A comparison of data sources', in I. Durnescu and F. McNeill (eds.), *Understanding Penal Practice*, London: Routledge.

——— (2015), *Working With Involuntary Clients: A Guide to Practice*, Sydney: Allen & Unwin.

Trotter, C., Baidawi, S. and Evans, P. (2015), 'Good practice in community-based supervision of aboriginal young offenders', *Australian Social Work*, 68(1): 5–18.

Trotter, C. and Evans, P. (2010), 'Supervision skills in juvenile justice', in F. McNeill, P. Raynor and C. Trotter (eds.), *Offender Supervision: New Directions in Theory, Research and Practice*, Cullompton: Willan.

——— (2012), 'Analysis of supervision skills in juvenile justice', *Australian and New Zealand Journal of Criminology*, 45(2): 255–73.

Trotter, C., McIvor, G. and Sheehan, R. (2012), 'The effectiveness of support and rehabilitation services for women offenders', *Australian Social Work*, 65(1): 6–20.

Turkle, S. (2011), *Alone Together*, Philadelphia, PA: Basic Books.

Turner, S. with Trotter, C. (2010), *Literature Review on Case Management With Women Offenders*, Melbourne: Corrections Victoria, viewed 1 July 2022, www.corrections.vic.gov.au/utility/publications+manuals+and+statistics/literature+review+on+case+management+with+women+offenders.

238 References

Ugwudike, P. (2010), 'Compliance with community penalties: The importance of interactional dynamics', in F. McNeill, P. Raynor and C. Trotter (eds.), *Offender Supervision: New Directions in Theory, Research and Practice*, Cullompton: Willan.

——— (2013), 'Compliance with community orders: Front-line perspectives and evidence-based practices', in P. Ugwudike and P. Raynor (eds.), *What Works in Offender Compliance*, London: Palgrave Macmillan.

Ugwudike, P. and Raynor, P. (2013), 'Conclusion: What works in offender compliance', in P. Ugwudike and P. Raynor (eds.), *What Works in Offender Compliance*, London: Palgrave Macmillan.

Ugwudike, P., Raynor, P. and Annison, J. (eds.) (2017a), *Evidence-Based Skills in Criminal Justice*, Bristol University Press.

Ugwudike, P., Raynor, P. and Annison, J. (2017b), 'Introduction: Effective practice skills: New directions in research', in Ugwudike, P., Raynor, P. and Annison, J. (eds.), *Evidence-Based Skills in Criminal Justice*, Bristol University Press.

Vanhaelemeesch, D. and Vander Beken, T. (2014), 'Between convict and ward: The experiences of people living with offenders subject to electronic monitoring', *Crime Law and Social Change*, 62: 389–415.

Van Zyl Smit, D. and Appleton, C. (2019), *Life Imprisonment: A Global Human Rights Analysis*, Harvard University Press.

Vaughan, B. (2007), 'The internal narrative of desistance', *British Journal of Criminology*, 47(3): 390–404.

Victoria Department of Justice and Regulation (2012), *Cultural Diversity Plan, 2012–2016*, Melbourne: Victorian Government, viewed 1 July 2022, https://assets.justice.vic.gov.au/justice/resources/1b848ace-cb82-4b0a-b9a6-a5ba26bb7acf/cultural+diversity+plan.pdf.

——— (2015), *Corrections Victoria Strategic Plan 2015–2018: Delivering Effective Correctional Services for a Safe Community*, viewed 1 July 2022, http://assets.justice.vic.gov.au/corrections/resources/3c384747-09fb-4540-a437-c345b4e63bcc/cv_strategic_plan_f32015.pdf.

——— (2022a), Official website, viewed 1 July 2022, www.justice.vic.gov.au.

Victoria Police (2022), 'Family Violence – there is no excuse', available online at https://www.police.vic.gov.au/family-violence-there-no-excuse.

Von Hirsch, A. (1976), *Doing Justice: The Choice of Punishments*, New York: Hill and Wang.

WA Department of Corrective Services (2014), *Parliament of NSW Joint Select Committee Inquiry into Sentencing Child Sexual Assault Offenders Submission from the Department of Corrective Services February 2014*, Perth: WA Department of Corrective Services.

——— (2022a), Official website, viewed 1 July 2022, www.correctiveservices.wa.gov.au/.

——— (2022b), *Boronia Pre-release Centre for Women*, viewed 1 July 2022, www.correctiveservices.wa.gov.au/_files/prisons/prison-locations/boronia-philosophy.pdf.

Walgrave, L. (2002), 'From community to dominion: In search of social values for restorative justice', in E. Weitekamp and H. Kerner (eds.), *Restorative Justice: Theoretical Foundations*, Cullompton: Willan.

Walklate, S. (2007), *Understanding Criminology: Current Theoretical Debates* (3rd ed.), Maidenhead: McGraw-Hill and Open University Press.

——— (2010), 'Criminology and feminism', in M. Herzog-Evans (ed.), *Transnational Criminology Manual*, Nijmegen: Wolf Publishing.

Wan, W., Moore, E. and Moffatt, S. (2013), *The Impact of the NSW Young Offenders Act 1997 on Likelihood of Custodial Order*, Sydney: NSW Bureau of Crime and Statistics.

Ward, T. and Maruna, S. (2007), *Rehabilitation*, London: Routledge.

Warner, K. and Bartels, L. (2015), 'Juvenile sex offending: Its prevalence and the criminal justice response', *University of New South Wales Law Journal*, 38(1): 48–75.

Weatherburn, D. (2014), *Arresting Incarceration: Pathways Out of Indigenous Imprisonment*, Sydney: Aboriginal Studies Press.

Weatherburn, D., McGrath, A. and Bartels, L. (2012), 'Three dogmas of juvenile justice', *University of New South Wales Law Journal*, 35(3): 779–809.

Weaver, B. (2014), 'Co-producing desistance', in I. Durnescu and F. McNeill (eds.), *Understanding Penal Practice*, London: Routledge.

Weaver, B. and McNeill, F. (2007a), 'Desistance', in R. Canton and D. Hancock (eds.), *Dictionary of Probation and Offender Management*, Cullompton: Willan.

——— (2007b), *Giving Up Crime: Directions for Policy*, Glasgow: Scottish Centre for Crime and Justice Research (SCCJR).

Weaver, B., Piacentini, L., Moodie, K. and Barry, M. (2020), 'Exploring and explaining non-compliance with community supervision', *British Journal of Criminology*, 61(2): 434–55.

Weitekamp, E. (2003), 'The history of restorative justice', in G. Johnstone (ed.), *A Restorative Justice Reader*, Cullompton: Willan.

Western Australia Corrective Services (2022), Official website, viewed 19 October 2022, https://www.wa.gov.au/organisation/department-of-justice/corrective-services.

Western Australia Police (2011), 'Strike Force Vulcan', media release, viewed 1 July 2022, www.police.wa.gov.au/LinkClick.aspx?fileticket=zOI8zDraxPM=&tabid=1488.

Westmarland, L. (2006), 'Classicism', in M. Maguire, R. Morgan and R. Reiner (eds.), *The Oxford Handbook of Criminology* (4th ed.), Oxford: Oxford University Press.

Westwood, J. (ed.) (2014), *Social Media in Social Work Education*, Northwich: Critical Publishing.

White, R. and Perrone, S. (2010), *Crime, Criminality and Criminal Justice*, Melbourne: Oxford University Press.

White, R. and Graham, H. (2010), *Working With Offenders: A Guide to Concepts and Practices*, Cullompton: Willan.

White, R., Haines, F. and Asquith, N. (2012), *Crime and Criminology*, Melbourne: Oxford University Press.

Whittaker, A. (2020), 'Despite 432 Indigenous deaths in custody since 1991, no one has ever been convicted: Racist silence and complicity are to blame', The Conversation, available online at https://theconversation.com/despite-432-indigenous-deaths-in-custody-since-1991-no-one-has-ever-been-convicted-racist-silence-and-complicity-are-to-blame-139873.

Whitting, L., Day, A. and Powell, M. (2014), 'The impact of community notification on the management of sex offenders in the community: An Australian perspective', *Australian and New Zealand Journal of Criminology*, 47(2): 240–58.

Wilczynski, A., Wallace, A., Nicholson, B. and Rintoul, D. (2004), *Evaluation of the Northern Territory Agreement*, Canberra: Urbis Keys Young.

Wild, K. and Gregory, K. (2015), 'Teenage detainees hooded, gassed in Northern Territory adult prison', viewed 1 July 2022, www.abc.net.au/news/2015-09-17/juveniles-hooded-in-nt-by-corrections-staff/6785344.

Williams, B. (2003), 'Editorial: The meanings of community justice', *British Journal of Community Justice*, 1(1): 1–4.

——— (2005), *Victims of Crime and Community Justice*, London: Jessica Kingsley.

Willis, L. and Osborne, T. (2014), 'Fistfight video said to be from Canberra prison prompts investigation', *ABC News*, 3 August, viewed 1 July 2022, www.abc.net.au/news/2014-08-03/amc-canberra-prison-fight-video-prompts-investigation/5644230.

Winstone, J. and Pakes, F. (2005), 'Community justice: The smell of fresh bread', in J. Winstone and F. Pakes (eds.), *Community Justice: Issues for Probation and Criminal Justice*, Cullompton: Willan.

Wood, J. (2011), 'Public health approaches to risk assessment and risk management', in H. Kemshall and B. Wilkinson (eds.), *Good Practice in Assessing Risk*, London: Jessica Kingsley.

Wood, J., Kemshall, H., Westwood, S., Fenton, A. and Logue, C. (2010), *Investigating Disclosures Made by Sexual Offenders: Preliminary Study for the Evaluation of Mandatory Polygraph Testing*, London: Ministry of Justice.

Worrall, A. (2000), 'What works at one arm point? A study in the transportation of a penal concept', *Probation Journal*, 47(4): 243–9.

Worrall, A. and Mawby, R. (2013), 'Probation worker responses to turbulent conditions: Constructing identity in a tainted occupation', *Australian and New Zealand Journal of Criminology*, 46(1): 101–18.

——— (2014), 'Probation worker cultures and relationships with offenders', *Probation Journal: The Journal of Community and Criminal Justice*, 61(4): 346–57.

Wroe, D. (2015), 'Most Australians happy with government watching social media to stop terror: Poll', *Sydney Morning Herald*, 2 July, viewed 1 July 2022, www.smh.com.au/federal-politics/political-news/most-australians-happy-with-government-watching-social-media-to-stop-terror-poll-20150701-gi2uf9.html.

Young, J. (1988), 'Radical criminology in Britain: The emergence of a competing paradigm', *British Journal of Criminology*, 28(2): 159–83.

——— (1999), *The Exclusive Society*, London: Sage.

Young, R. (2002), 'Testing the limits of restorative justice: The case of corporate victims', in C. Hoyle and R. Young (eds.), *New Visions of Crime Victims*, Portland, OR: Hart.

——— (2012), 'Just cops doing "shameful" business? Police-led restorative justice and the lessons of research', in G. Johnstone (ed.), *A Restorative Justice Reader*, Cullompton: Willan.

Zehr, H. (1990), *Changing Lenses*, Scottdale, PA: Herald Press.

Legislation

Alcoholics and Drug-Dependent Person Act 1974 (Vic)
Bail Act 1977 (Vic)
Bail Act 1980 (Qld)
Bail Act 1982 (NT)
Bail Act 1982 (WA)
Bail Act 1985 (SA)
Bail Act 1992 (ACT)
Bail Act 1994 (Tas)
Bail Act 2013 (NSW)
Bail Amendment Act 2018 (Vic)
Bail Legislation Amendment Bill 2016 (WA)
Children's Court Act 1992 (Qld)
Children's Courts Rules 2016 (Qld)

References 241

Charter of Human Rights and Responsibilities Act 2006 (Vic)
Children (Community Service Orders) Act 1987 (NSW)
Children (Criminal Proceedings) Act 1987 (NSW)
Children (Detention Centres) Act 1987 (NSW)
Children (Interstate Transfer of Offenders) Act 1988 (NSW)
Children and Young People Act 2008 (ACT)
Children and Young Persons Act 2005 (Vic)
Children, Young Persons and Their Families Act 1997 (Tas)
Children, Youth and Families Act 2005 (Vic)
Community Protection (Offender Reporting) Act 2004 (WA)
Correctional Services Act 1982 (SA)
Courts Legislation (Neighbourhood Justice Centre) Act 2006 (Vic)
Crimes Act 1958 (Vic)
Crimes (Administration of Sentences) Act 1999 (NSW)
Crimes (Administration of Sentences) Regulation, 2014 (NSW)
Crimes (High Risk Offenders) Act 2006 (NSW)
Crimes (Restorative Justice) Act 2004 (ACT)
Crimes (Sentence Administration) Act 2005 (ACT)
Crimes (Sentencing) Act 2005 (ACT)
Criminal Code Act 1899 (Qld)
Criminal Law (High Risk Offenders) Act 2015 (SA)
Criminal Law (Rehabilitation of Offenders) Act 1986 (Qld)
Criminal Law (Sentencing) Act 2017 (SA)
Dangerous Prisoners (Sexual Offenders) Act 2003 (Qld)
Dangerous Sexual Offenders Act 2006 (WA)
Family and Community Services Act 1972 (SA)
Human Rights Act 2004 (ACT)
Inspector of Custodial Services Act 2003 (WA)
Penalties and Sentences Act 1981 (Vic)
Police Offences Act 1935 (Tas)
Sentence Administration Act 2003 (WA)
Sentencing Act 1991 (Vic)
Sentencing Act 1995 (NT)
Sentencing Act 1997 (Tas)
Sentencing Act 1995 (WA)
Sentencing Act 1997 (Tas)
Sentencing Act 1991 (Vic)
Serious Sex Offenders (Detention and Supervision) Act 2009 (Vic)
Severe Substance Dependence Treatment Act, 2010 (Vic)
Social Welfare (Amendment) Act 1975 (Vic)
Young Offenders Act 1993 (SA)
Young Offenders Act 1994 (WA)
Young Offenders Act 1997 (NSW)
Young Offenders (Interstate Transfer) Amendment Act 1990 (Qld)
Young Offenders Regulations 1995
Young Persons, and Their Families (Oranga Tamariki) Legislation Act 2017
Youth Court Act 1993 (SA)
Youth Justice Act 2005 (NT)

Youth Justice Regulations 2006 (NT)
Youth Justice Act 1992 (Qld)
Youth Justice Act 1997 (Tas)
Youth Justice Regulation 2016 (Qld)

Instruments

Convention on the Rights of the Child (CRC)
Convention Against Torture and Other Cruel, Inhuman or Degrading Treatment or Punishment
Declaration on the Rights of Indigenous People
International Covenant on Civil and Political Rights (ICCPR)
United Nations Convention on the Rights of the Child
United Nations Declaration of Basic Principles of Justice for Victims of Crime and Abuse of Power
United Nations Declaration on the Rights of Indigenous Peoples, 2007
United Nations Guidelines for the Prevention of Juvenile Delinquency (Riyadh Guidelines)
United Nations Standard Minimum Rules for the Treatment of Prisoners
Universal Declaration of Human Rights
UN Standard Minimum Rules for the Administration of Juvenile Justice (Beijing Rules)

Index

3M 151

Aboriginal and Torres Strait Islander (Koori) Graduate scheme 143
Aboriginal and Torres Strait Islander Legal Service 35
Aboriginal and Torres Strait Islander people 114; employment program 142; family relationships 114; NJC 39; in Northern Territory 185; spiritual relationship 114
Aboriginality 99
Aboriginal Liaison Officers 36
Aboriginal people: Royal Commission into Aboriginal Deaths in Custody (RCIADIC) 36
Aboriginal Services Unit 36
Aboriginal young people 29
Abuse Prevention Intervention Program 36
academic criminology 73
accountability 24, 46, 76, 82, 87, 91, 127, 135, 177, 181, 182, 190
action, motivational interviewing 198
Additional Support Unit (ASU) 128
adiaphorization 180
administrative criminology 73
Adult Parole Board 106–107
adult offenders 27–42; Australian Capital Territory (ACT) 30; community corrections orders 39; community justice 40–41; Community Service Orders (CSOs) 32; New South Wales (NSW) 31–32; non-statutory services 32–33; Northern Territory 33–34; overview 27–30; Queensland 34–35; South Australia 35–36; Tasmanian 37; Victoria 37–38; Western Australia 40
African refugee communities 118
age-graded theory of social control 163

age invariance theory 163
agency-level change 22–24
age of criminal responsibility 45, 49, 51, 52, 53, 186, 189
alcoholics 165
Alcoholics and Drug-Dependent Person Act 1974 37
Alcohol Mandatory Treatment Tribunal 34
alternatives to custody 17–19, 48, 57, 59, 61, 187
Amnesty International 188
anomie (normlessness) 68–69
anti-custodialism 18
applied criminology 63, 73, 78; *see also* criminological theory
Appreciative Inquiry (AI) approach 133–134
Aquinas 9
Aristotle 9
arsonists 105, 109
Australasian Juvenile Justice Administrators (AJJA) 50
Australia as penal colony 27
Australian Association of Social Workers (AASW) 48, 183; codes of ethics 183–184; curriculum standards of 48, 208; in South Australia, eligibility for 183
Australian Bureau of Statistics (ABS) 28
Australian Capital Territory (ACT) 30; adult offenders 30; Community Corrections in 30; diversity 118; juvenile justice/youth justice 51; legislation in 51; police-run scheme 84; restorative justice 84–86; technology 149
Australian community justice 3, 147
Australian Federal Police (AFP) 155
Australian Human Rights Commission (AHRC) 48, 125, 185, 186
Australian Institute of Criminology 76

244 Index

Australian Institute of Family Studies 102
Australian Institute of Health and Welfare (AIHW) 55, 61
Australian Law Reform Commission (ALRC) 50
Australian prison regime 28
Australian regime 27
authority: approach to 13; effective use of 197; legitimate use of 133; of practitioner 205

Bail Act 1980 52
Bail Act 1982 52, 153
Bail Act 1985 53
Bail Act 1992 51
Beijing Rules 48, 57
biological theories of offending 63–65
Black Lives Matter movement 114
BOCSAR Applied Criminology Conference 68
bonding capital 12
boot camps in Queensland 58
bridging capital 12
Bringing Them Home report 44
British Multi-Agency Public Protection Arrangements (MAPPA) 104
broken windows theory 13
Bureau of Crime Statistics and Research (BOCSAR) 76, 86–87

Canada 20, 82, 93, 102
Canberra Police and Citizens Youth Club (PCYC) 118
Canberra Reintegrative Shaming Experiments (RISE) 84–85
capital 132; justice 172; punishment 27; *see also* emotional capital; financial capital; organisational capital
care ethics 178
Change the Record Campaign 187–188
character-based approach 177
Charter of Human Rights and Responsibilities Act 2006 48
Chicago School 69
childhood experiences and offending 67
childhood traumas 72
Children, Young Persons and their Families Act (1997) (Tas) 53, 241
Children, Youth and Families Act 2005 89
Children (Interstate Transfer of Offenders) Act 1988 51
Children and Young People Act 2008 51
Children's Court Act 1992 52
Children's Courts 50

Children's Courts Rules 2016 52
Children's Koori Courts 187
Circle Court 30, 34
circle sentencing 15, 20, 30, 92
citizens' panels 82
codes of ethics 182–184
cognitive behavioural therapy (CBT) 35, 65, 66–67
cognitive theories 68
collaboration 14, 24, 49, 110, 207
Collaborative Family Model 60, 207–208
Collingwood Neighbourhood Justice Centre (NJC) 39
Combined Custody and Treatment Order 39
commit crime 72
communal diversity 113; *see also* diversion; diversity
communitarianism 6, 8, 12, 82
communities: building 5, 14, 22; in Canada 20; of care 8; of choice 6; concept of 20; described 6–9; disintegrated 6; divided 6; meaning for Australian context 9; in Northern Ireland 20; as nostalgic indulgence 6; proprietary 6; in South African transition 20; virtual 6
community accountability conferences 87
Community Based Orders 28, 34, 39, 40
community-based rehabilitation 126
community boards 82
community correction(s) 15, 30; consensus 25–26; Fortress Probation 16; history of 28; human service profession 24–25; vision 16, 182; workers/staff 2, 24, 123
Community Correction Order (CCO) 39
Community Corrections Centres 35
Community Corrections Officers 35, 40, 144
Community Court 33–34
community courts 14–15
Community Custody Order 34
community justice 5–26; agency-level change 22–24; alternatives to custody 17–19; American approach 19; Canadian conception of 20; characteristics 18; corrections and 15–16; courts and 14–15; in Covid lockdown 137–138; in criminal justice 10–11, 14; defined 11; desistance and 174–175; distinctive nature of 13–14; diversity and 128–129; in England and Wales 1, 17, 19; evaluation of 22; evidence-based practice and 78–79; high volume and quality of 2; impact on Indigenous peoples 22; Indigenous communities and 20; interpretations of 19–20;

juvenile justice/youth justice and 56–61; language of 1; macro-level change 21–22; micro-level change 24–25; model for Australia 21; models for future of 16–17; neighbourhoods 11–12; in Northern Ireland 1; organisation and management 131–135, 137–142, 144–146; overview 1–4, 5; policing and 14; practitioners 136; principles of 16, 17, 19; quality in 133–134; regime 31; restorative justice and 94–95; risk-assessment/risk-management 109–112; social justice and 12; social media and 154–156; social work approach to 176–179; in South Africa 1; in universities 2; values 176–179, 180; victims approaches 19; work as form of edgework 138–140; workers 132; working in Australia 11, 141–142; in working with adults in Australia 40–41
Community Justice Centres 41
community policing 5, 10, 14, 188
Community Protection (Offender Reporting) Act 2004 104, 109
community resources, effective use of 198
Community Restorative Centre 32
community sanctions 29, 30
community sentences 28, 35, 37, 153, 158
Community Service Orders (CSO) 31, 32, 35, 37
Community Service Program 35
Community Sex Offender Notifications Scheme 103; *see also* Sarah's Law
Community Sex Offender Scheme 111
community supervision orders 57
compassion fatigue 139
Compulsory Drug Treatment Correctional Centre 32, 119
contemplation 198
control theories 69
Convention on the Rights of the Child (CRC) 185
core correctional practice (CCP) 197, 200, 202
correctional centre 32
Correctional Centre Conferencing for Indigenous people 34
Correctional Services Act 1982 152
Corrections Programs Unit 30
Corrective Services 30; NSW 181; NSW Department of 125; Queensland 142; Sex and Violent Offender Therapeutic Programs by 102; in Western Australia 144, 182
cost–benefit analysis 126

Court Integrated Services Program (CISP) 38
Courts Legislation (Neighbourhood Justice Centre) Act 2006 89
Covid-19 lockdowns 137–138
Crime and Disorder Act 1998 44
crime hot-spots 12–13
crime prevention 98
Crimes (Administration of Sentences) Act 1999 32
Crimes (Restorative Justice) Act 2004 51, 85
Crimes (Sentence Administration) Act 2005 51
Crimes (Sentencing) Act 2005 51
Crimes (High Risk Offenders) Act 2006 102
Crimes (Administration of Sentences) Regulations 2014 32
Criminal Code Act 1899 52
criminalisation and victimisation 71
criminal justice: agencies 14; careers 137; community justice in 10–11; humanistic values in 18; over-representation of Indigenous people in 2; practitioner 168; values in 179–180
Criminal Law (Rehabilitation of Offenders) Act 1986 52
Criminal Law (Sentencing) Act 1988 53
Criminal Law (High Risk Offenders) Act 2015 103
criminological research 2
criminological theory 69, 73; *see also* applied criminology
criminology: academic 73; administrative 73; applied 63, 73, 78; cognitive behavioural therapy 66; degrees 2; eugenics/social engineering and 63; feminist interest in 71–72; material outside 71; radical 69
Cross-Border Justice Scheme 30
culturally and linguistically diverse (CALD) communities 117–118
custody 30, 46; *see also* Australian Capital Territory (ACT)

dangerousness 109–112; *see also* organisational dangerousness
dangerous offenders 97, 101, 102–103, 105, 106–108, 136, 150
Dangerous Prisoners (Sexual Offenders) Act 2003 103, 150
Dangerous Sexual Offenders Act 2006 99, 104, 153
Declaration on the Rights of Indigenous People 185
defensive practitioners 178
deferred sentence orders 30

246 *Index*

democratic principles 16
Department of Health and Human Services (DHHS) 88
Department of Public Prosecutions (DPP) 115
Department of the Attorney-General and Justice NT 30
desistance 160–175; in Australia 172–174; community justice and 174–175; defined 160; different approach 162–165; Good Lives Model 166; life events and 162; Multi-Systemic Therapy (MST) 166; narrative approach 170–171; overview 160; phenomenology of 163; practitioner role 167–172; promotion 160–162; psycho-social theory of 164; theory of the early stages of 164; through ill-health 165; young people and 166–167
Detainee Behaviour Implementation Framework (DBIF) 47
detention in custody 56
detention of young people 47, 55–56
develop discrepancy 199
differential association 69
disability 125–128; discrimination 125–126, 127; diversity 113; intellectual 126–128; mental health and 125–128; non-Indigenous people 126; psychiatric 34; violence and abuse 127
Disability Justice Strategy 127
disintegrated community 6
disorganisation models 13
diversion: Beijing Rules 48, 57; for Indigenous young people 55, 92; measures 55, 186; for mental health treatment 41; restorative justice as 85; schemes 29, 50, 87, 120
diversity 113–130; Australian Capital Territory (ACT) 118; communal 113; community justice and 128–129; culturally and linguistically diverse communities 117–118; disability 113, 125–128; engagement in states and territories 118; Indigenous people 114–117; mental health 125–128; Northern Territory 120; NSW 119; overview 113; perspectival 113; Queensland 120; subcultural 113; Tasmania 120–121; Victoria 121; Western Australia 121; women 121–125
divided community 6
Domestic Abuse Maintenance Program 125
Domestic Abuse Program 125

Don Dale Youth Detention Centre 189
drug and alcohol: abuse 117, 121; problems 32–33, 119; testing 32, 35
Drug and Alcohol Multicultural Educational Centre (DAMEC) 119
Drug Court 32, 36, 38, 50, 89
drug offenders 164
Drug Treatment Order 37, 38
dual taxonomy theory 163

Early Intervention Youth Boot Camp (EIYBC) 58
edgework 138–140
effective practice 72–73, 75–77
effective use: of authority 197; of community resources 198
egalitarian principles 16
electronic monitoring (EM) 35, 147; 3M 151; effectiveness 156; G4S 151; as punishment 147, 153–156; Queensland 150; as surveillance 147, 153–156; technology 153–156; in Western Australia 153; *see also* Global Positioning System (GPS) tracking
electronic tag 153
emotional capital 132
emotional engagement 132, 195
emotional literacy 194
emotional work 131; *see also specific types*
empathy 194–195, 199; *see also* express empathy
Ending Offending program 35
England and Wales: National Probation Service (NPS) in 137
Enhanced Community Corrections Project 35
equality 9, 16, 26, 74, 127, 178, 179; *see also* inequality
ethical decision-making 177
ethical practitioners 177, 178
ethics 178–179; care 178; of social justice 178; values and 176; virtue 177–178
evidence-based practice 78–79
Exceptional Delivery Model (EDM) 137
express empathy 199

Facebook 155; *see also* community justice; social media
Facebook Six 155
Family and Community Services Act 1972 53
Family Group Conferences 92
Family Responsibility Agreements 87
Family Responsibility Orders 52
family therapy 206
family violence 23, 89, 121

female offender 64
feminist criminology 71
financial capital 132
first individual meeting 199–200, 206–208
first meeting 197–198
flogging 27, 29
Fortress Probation 16
Forum Sentencing 86
France 20, 141

G4S technology 151
gender and crime 70–72
genes 64
genetics and crime 64
Global Financial Crisis (GFC) 74
Global Positioning System (GPS) tracking 147–149, 153; *see also* electronic monitoring (EM)
good behaviour bonds 57
good behaviour orders 30
Good Lives Model 8, 79, 108, 110, 111, 165, 166
Griffiths remand 57
Griffith Youth Forensic Service 109

'Hands Across Hobart' program 120
HAQ Centre for Child Rights 95
Harvard Kennedy School 25–26
healing circles 82
higher education funding environment 2
home detention 50, 150, 152; ACT 149; for adults 35; electronic monitoring 150, 152; imprisonment by way of 32; NSW 149–150; as a sentencing option 37; stringent monitoring 115; for young people 35
Home Detention Orders (HDOs) 32, 34
human capital 171
humanistic values 179
human rights 82, 178, 184–192
Human Rights Act 2004 48, 51
Human Rights Law Centre (HRLC) 185–186
humour, use of *see* practitioner skills

imprisonment 32, 41, 83
inclusion 16, 68, 86, 103, 109, 182
Indigenous Australians 9, 64
Indigenous Canadian communities 20
Indigenous communities 5, 20
Indigenous cultures 82–83
Indigenous deaths 114
Indigenous Diversion Program (IDP) 40

Indigenous peoples: in Canada 20; community justice impact on 22; community sanctions and 29; in criminal justice system 23; custodial sanctions and 29; justice reinvestment (JR) 8; Justice Reinvestment Campaign (JRC) for 8; Nyoongar Patrol 40; as offenders 129; over-representation in criminal justice system 2; over-representation of 29; re-incarceration rate 29; Royal Commission into Aboriginal Deaths in Custody 89; sentencing court 30; stolen generations 44; wilderness programs 57
Indigenous Sentencing Lists 35
inequality 78; *see also* equality
informal social control models 13
intellectual disability 126; *see also* disability
intelligence and offending 65
intensive correction in the community (ICO) 32
Intensive Correction Order (ICO) 30, 39, 150
Intensive Drug and Alcohol Program (IDATP) 119
Intensive Drug and Alcohol Treatment Program (ITATP) 125
Intensive Supervision Program (ISP) 59–60, 166, 206
Inter-Agency Public Protection Committee (IPPC) 104
Inter-Agency Public Protection Strategy (IPPS) 104
internal conversation theory 164
International Covenant on Civil and Political Rights (ICCPR) 185
International Covenant on the Elimination of all Forms of Racial Discrimination 1969 29
International Federation of Social Workers (IFSW) 184
involuntary client 200

Jersey Study 204–205
Jesuit Social Services 57
Journey Towards Hope (JoTHe) Dance Project 121
justice: capital 172; described 9–10; legitimacy 10; philosophical approaches to 9
Justice Mediation Program 88
justice reinvestment (JR) 6, 7–8; Amnesty International 116; Indigenous people 8; Justice Reinvestment Campaign (JRC) 8;

Maranguka Justice Reinvestment Project 190–191; re-dedicating resources 190; strategy 36
Justice Reinvestment Campaign (JRC) 8
Juvenile Justice Departments 50
Juvenile Justice Teams (JJTs) 90
juvenile justice/youth justice 43–62; Australian Capital Territory (ACT) 51; Beijing Rules 48; boot camps in Queensland 58; community justice and 56–61; detention of young people 55–56; *doli incapax* principle 44, 45; legislation and policy 49–51; New Public Management (NPM) approach 46–48; New South Wales (NSW) 51–52; Northern Territory 52; overview 43; Queensland in 52–53; rights-based approach to 48–49; risk-assessment and management 108–109; South Australia in 53; Tasmania 53; Victoria 53–54; welfare model 43–45; Western Australia 54–55; workers and community 2; young people and 56–61
juvenile sex offences 109

Koori Courts 38, 89–90
Koori Graduate Recruitment and Development Scheme (KGRADS) 143

labelling theory 69–70
late-modern communities 6
Law Council of Australia 103
learning organisation 135
learning theories 67–68
legitimacy 10
liberal feminism 71
life events and desistance 162
lifers 145

macro-level change 21–22
maintenance, motivational interviewing 198
management of dangerous offenders on parole 106–108
management of dangerous sex offenders 104–106
managerialism 134–135
mandatory sentencing 54, 116, 185, 190
Maranguka Justice Reinvestment Project 190–191
maturational reform theory 161, 170
Megan's Law 103
mental health 125–128; disability and 125–128; diversion for 41; diversity 125–128; treatment in Tasmanian 41

Mental Health Court Liaison Service 38
Mental Health Review Tribunal 34
Mentally Impaired Accused Review Board 115
micro-level change 24–25
modelling pro-social behaviour 198
modern sentencing regime 30
moral courage 178
moral/non-moral values 178
motivational interviewing 198–199
motivation practitioners 194
Multicultural Futsal project 118
Multicultural Quick Reference Guides 120
Multi-Systemic Therapy (MST) 59–60, 166, 206

narrative approaches 161
National Inquiry into the Separation of Aboriginal and Torres Strait Islander Children and their Families (NISATSIC) 44
National Mental Health Commission 126
National Probation Service (NPS) 137
Neighbourhood Justice Centre in Collingwood (NJC) 38, 39
neighbourhoods 11–12, 15
neutral, universal approach 22
New Public Management (NPM) approach 46–48, 131
New South Wales (NSW) 31–32; adult offenders 31–32; Bureau of Crime Statistics and Research in 76, 86; Community Justice Centres in 34; community service orders in 32; *Crimes (High Risk Offenders) Act 2006* in 102; diversity 119; forms of imprisonment 32; Intensive Supervision Program (ISP) in 59; juvenile justice/youth justice 51–52; No Bars service 33; non-statutory services in 32; organisation and management 142; restorative justice 86–87; technology 149–150; values 181; Wagga Wagga in 83, 86–87; Youth Drug Court in 50; Youth Justice Conference 50
New Zealand model 87
Ngaanyatjarra Pitjantjatjara Yankunytjatjara (NPY) 30
Ngambra Circle Sentencing Court 30
No Bars service 33
Noble, Marlon 115
non-criminogenic needs 165
non-government organisations (NGOs) 50, 131

non-prison-based sex offender 76
non-verbal skills 204
norm affirmation 16
North Australian Aboriginal Justice Agency (NAAJA) 34
Northern Ireland 1, 2, 6, 20, 82, 208
Northern Territory 33–34; diversity 120; juvenile justice/youth justice 52; organisation and management 142; restorative justice 87; technology 150; Youth Justice Court 52
Northern Territory Community Justice Centre 34
NSW Department of Communities and Justice (NSW DCJ) 142
NSW Department of Justice's social media policy (DoJ NSW) 154
Nunga Court models 34
Nyoongar Patrol 40

offence-focused programs 35–36
Offender Management Plan (OMP) 110
offender managers 145
offenders with limited criminal careers 164
offending behaviour 2–3
online communities 6
Open Society Foundation 7
optimism 64, 91, 168, 202
organisational boundaries 13
organisational capital 132
organisational culture 24, 135, 137
organisational dangerousness 134–135
organisational socialisation 132–133
organisational stress 137
organisation and management 131–146; community justice 131–135, 137–142, 144–146; managerialism 134–135; Northern Territory 142; NSW 142; overview 131; performance monitoring 135; Queensland 142; South Australia 143; stress 136–137; Tasmania 143; typologies of probation workers 145; Victoria 143–144; Western Australia 144
'Out of the Dark' program 124, 125

Pacific Islanders 9
Pakani Arangka 36
pardons 28
parole, dangerous offenders on 106–108
Parramatta Female Factory and Girls' Home 122
partnerships 15, 39, 57, 59, 79, 89, 110–111, 119, 120, 121, 123, 124, 127, 148, 157

pecuniary emotional work 131
Penalties and Sentences Act 1981 37
periodic detention 30, 37, 50
personality traits 64, 65
Personal Ownership, Identity and Self-Empowerment (POISE) 125
perspectival diversity 113
phenomenology of desistance 163
philanthropic emotional work 131
place, defined 16
Police and Court Alcohol and Diversion Program 30
policing 5, 10, 14, 188
polygraph testing 100
Port Augusta Prison 36
postmodern feminism 71
practitioners 136–140; bias 98; cognitive behavioural theory 66, 70; criminological knowledge 72; criminology 73; defensive 178; emotional work 131; ethical 177, 178; flexible 134; professional 178; risk-assessment and risk-management 97, 98–100; risk-assessment/risk-management 98–100; role of 167–172; skilled 108, 111, 114, 169; social work 155; social work qualification 176; sociological theories 70; understandings of gender 72
practitioner skills 194–209; community justice and 208–209; first individual meeting 199–200, 206–208; first meeting 197–198; impact on recidivism and compliance 203–206; motivational interviewing 198–199; overview 194–195; problem-solving 201–202; promoting pro-social outcomes 201; referral letter 196; referral phone call 195–196; role clarification 200–201; stages of change 198–199; worker and client relationship 202–203
pre-contemplation 198
preparation 198
prescriptive emotional work 131
presentational emotional work 131
prevention of future crime 82
prison-building scheme 28
prisons and prisoners: authorities 125; building scheme 28; debates 21; female 28; high-security 29; Indigenous 28, 34; lack of effectiveness of 28; low-security women's 40; open 27; population 21, 23, 31, 33–34; private and public sector 28; rate in Australia 28; services to 32; transgender 125

Index

Probation and Community Corrections Officers Association (PACCOA) 182
Probation and Parole Unit 30
probation on trial 107–108
probation orders 35, 37, 57, 175
probation workers, typologies of 145
problem-solving 15, 198, 201–202
professional integrity 183
professionalism 20
professional practitioners 178
program integrity 22–24
promoting pro-social outcomes 201
proprietary communities 6
pro-social practice 133
providing positive reinforcement 198
psychiatric disability 34
psychoanalytical theories 65
psychological theories of offending 65–68, 72
psycho-social theory of desistance and reform 164
public safety 16
punishment 27

quality of interpersonal relationships 198
Queensland 34–35; boot camps in 58; Corrective Services 142; *Dangerous Prisoners (Sexual Offenders) Act 2003* in 103; diversity 120; electronic monitoring (EM) 150; in juvenile justice/youth justice 52–53; organisation and management 142; restorative justice 87–88; technology 150; values 181

radical criminology 69
radical feminism 71
radical theories 70
rational choice theory 67, 69, 163
recidivism 14, 30, 53, 55, 58, 75–76, 89, 94, 98, 102, 109, 128, 180, 181, 188, 203–206
referral letter 196
referral phone call 195–196
reformatron 74
regime: Australian 27; Australian prison 28; community justice 31; modern sentencing 30; principles of effective practice 76–77; youth justice 45
rehabilitation 72–74; Children's Court 54; community-based 126; effective practice and 72–73; goals of 46, 98; of offenders 77; program or community service 30, 35, 38–39; restorative justice 86; strengths-based 8, 111

reintegrative shaming 81, 87
relapse 198–199
remorseful offenders 164
remote bureaucracy 19
Repay SA 33, 35
rescued offenders 164
respect for persons 183
responsivity 75–77
restorative justice 5, 8, 80–96; Australian Capital Territory 84–86; community justice and 94–95; in contemporary Australia 84; defined 80–82; myths of 83–84; needs of Indigenous groups 91–93; Northern Territory 87; NSW 86–87; operative practices 82; origins of 82–84; overview 80; in promoting rehabilitation 86; Queensland 87–88; South Australia 88; Tasmania 88; victims of crime 90–91; Victoria 89–90; Western Australia 90
risk-assessment/risk-management 97–112; community justice and 109–112; dangerousness and 109–112; of dangerous offenders 102–103; of dangerous sex offenders 104–106; juvenile justice/youth justice 108–109; metaphors for 101; overview 97; practitioner 98–100; risk society 97–98; of sex offenders 102–103; Victoria 106–108; Western Australia 104–106
Risk Needs Responsivity (RNR) model 77, 160–161, 167, 197
risk-oriented thinking 97
risk society 97–98
role clarification 200–201
roll with resistance 199
routine activities theory 69
Royal Commission into Aboriginal Deaths in Custody (RCIADIC) 36, 41, 89
Royal Commission into Institutionalised Responses to Child Sexual Abuse (RCIRCSA) 102, 122
Royal Commission into Juvenile Detention in the Northern Territory 61

safety of workers 139
Sarah's Law 103–104; *see also* Community Sex Offender Notifications Scheme
secondary trauma 139
second careerists 145
self-awareness 194
self-regulation 194
Sentenced Youth Boot Camp (SYBC) 58

Sentence Management Unit 143
Sentencing Act 1991 37
Sentencing Advisory Council Victoria 37
Sentencing Alternatives Committee 37
Serious Sex Offenders (Detention and Supervision) Act 2009 106
sex offenders: community sex offender notifications scheme 103–104; dangerous 104–106; electronic monitoring 35; high-profile child 148; high-risk 138; international material 100; management of 97, 100, 104–106, 111; non-prison-based 76; recidivism 109; risk-assessment and management of 102–103; risk-oriented security structures 97
skilled practitioner 108, 111, 114, 169
skills: non-verbal 204; *see also* practitioner skills
Skills for Effective, Engagement, Development and Supervision project (SEEDS) 203
social bonds theory 161, 170
social capital 12
social competence 195
socialist feminists 71
social justice and criminal justice 12, 183
social learning theory 66, 68
social media 154–156
social media and community justice 154–155
Social Welfare (Amendment) Act 1975 37
social workers 2
social work qualification 141
social work values 178
sociological theories of offending 68–70
South Australia 35–36, 53; *Criminal Law (High Risk Offenders) Act 2015* in 103; organisation and management 143; restorative justice 88; technology 150–152; values 182
South Australia Department for Correctional Services (SA DCS) 143
South Australia Juvenile Justice (SAJJ) 88
South Australian Department of Corrections 35
South Australian Office of Crime Statistics and Research (OCSAR) 76
specialist court lists 37, 38
specialist courts 15, 33, 37, 38
stages of change 198–199
Static-99 assessment 99–100
stewardship 16
street offenders 164

street woman 72
strengths-based rehabilitation 8, 111
stress 136–137
Strike Force Vulcan 109
structural competency 22–24
subcultural diversity 113
subcultural theory 70
supervised treatment order (STO) 128
support self-efficacy 199

Tasmanian Aboriginal Corporation (TAC) 57
Tasmania/Tasmanian 53; adult offenders 37; community sentences in 37; court structure 37; diversity 120–121; juvenile justice/youth justice 53; mental health treatment in 41; organisation and management 143; restorative justice 88; technology 152; values 182
technology 147–159; Australian Capital Territory (ACT) 149; community justice and 156–159; electronic monitoring 153–156; GPS tracking 147, 148, 149; Northern Territory 150; NSW 149–150; overview 147–148; Queensland 150; South Australia 150–152; Tasmania 152; use in community justice in Australia 148; Victoria 152; Western Australia 153
theories of offending 63–79; biological 63–65; gender 70–72; overview 63; psychological 65–68; sociological 68–70
theory of cognitive transformation 163–164
theory of the early stages of desistance 164
theory of the 'feared self' 164
Ticket of Leave scheme 28
transformed offenders 164
transgender prisoners 125; *see also* prisons and prisoners
transitional justice 5
transportation 27–28
traumas: childhood 72; secondary 139; vicarious 139
Twitter 155; *see also* community justice; social media

UN Convention on the Rights of the Child (UNCRC) 48, 185, 186, 189
UN Declaration on the Rights of Indigenous Peoples 2007 29
United Nations Declaration of Basic Principles of Justice for Victims of Crime and Abuse of Power 91

United Nations Draft Declaration on the Rights of Indigenous people 93
United Nations Guidelines for the Prevention of Juvenile Delinquency 185
United Nations Standard Minimum Rules 181
United States Skills for Effective, Engagement, Development and Supervision project (SEEDS) 203
Universal Declaration of Human Rights 185
UN Standard Minimum Rules for the Treatment of Prisoners 185
US Department of Defense 149
US Standard Minimum Rules for the Administration of Juvenile Justice 185

values 16; benefits and limitations of 182–184; community justice 176–179, 180; in criminal justice system 179–180; ethics and 176; humanistic 179; moral/non-moral 178; NSW 181; Queensland 181; social work 178; South Australia 182; statements in Australia 181; Tasmania 182; Western Australia 182
veil of ignorance 9
vicarious trauma 139
victims and communities 15
victims of crime 19, 23, 90–91, 106
Victoria 37–38; community corrections order in 152, 158; diversity 121; home detention 152; juvenile justice/youth justice 53–54; legislation in 37; organisation and management 143–144; restorative justice 89–90; risk-assessment/risk-management 106–108; technology 152
Victoria Department of Justice and Regulation 118
Victorian Department of Justice and Community Safety (DJCS) 143
Vietnamese Transitions Project 119
violent crime 64
virtual communities 6
virtue-based model 177
virtue ethics 177–178
voluntary clients 200

Wagga Wagga model 83, 86–87
warrior gene 64
welfare model 43–45
Western Australia 40; Aboriginal Plan 114; Banksia Hill Juvenile Justice Centre in 47; Boronia pre-release Centre for Women 40; Boronia Pre-Release Centre in 125; Community Protection website in 105; diversity 121; Drugs Court 40; electronic monitoring (EM) in 153; Family Violence Court 40; GPS surveillance 153; Indigenous Diversion Program 40; Inter-Agency Public Protection Committee (IPPC) 104; Journey Towards Hope (JoTHe) Dance Project 121; juvenile justice/youth justice 54–55; Nyoongar Patrol 40; organisation and management 144; restorative justice 90; risk-assessment/risk-management 104–106; technology 153; values 182
Western Sydney University (WSU) 60
'What Works' model 75–77, 160–161
wilderness programs 57
women in criminal justice system 121–125; background of abuse 121; case management approach 123; drug and alcohol abuse 121; gender-specific approaches 121; Intensive Drug and Alcohol Treatment Program (ITATP) 125; mental illness 121; mothering at distance 125; 'Out of the Dark' program 124, 125; Parramatta Female Factory and Girls' Home 122; Personal Ownership, Identity and Self-Empowerment (POISE) 125
worker and client relationship 202–203
workers *see* practitioners

Young Offenders Act 1993 53
Young Offenders Act 1994 90
Young Offenders Act 1997 51, 87
Young Offenders (Interstate Transfer) Act Amendment Act 1990 52
Youth Court Act 1993 53
Youth Court Administration Act 2016 53
Youth Justice Act 1992 52
Youth Justice Act 1997 88
Youth Justice Act 2005 87
Youth Justice Act 2006 52
Youth Justice Administration Regulations 2016 53
Youth Justice Amendment Bill 2021 87
Youth Justice Legislation Amendment Bill 52
youth justice regime 45
Youth Justice Regulation 2016 52

zone of transition 69